The Usurper King

By the same author

Anne Boleyn
The Making of Henry VIII

The Usurper King

Henry of Bolingbroke 1366–99

by

MARIE LOUISE BRUCE

The Rubicon Press

The Rubicon Press
57 Cornwall Gardens
London SW7 4BE

First published 1986
Revised 1998

British Library Cataloguing on Publication Data

A catalogue record of this book is available from the British Library.

ISBN 0-948695-62-5

Designed and typeset by The Rubicon Press
Printed and bound in Great Britain by Biddles of Guildford
and King's Lynn

CONTENTS

List of Illustrations   vi
Foreword   vii

I	The Royal Cousins	1
II	Princes and Playmates	14
III	Betrayal	27
IV	Vengeance and Murders	41
V	The Five Lords March	54
VI	'To Depose the King'	70
VII	Richard Fights Back	82
VIII	Knights of Love and War	94
IX	The Pilgrim	104
X	The Mask of the King	115
XI	The Over-mighty Subject	127
XII	Richard's Revenge	137
XIII	The King in Glory	152
XIV	Battle to the Death	164
XV	Banished	171
XVI	The Return	182
XVII	The Usurper	194
XVIII	Death of a King	210

Bibliography   226
Notes and Sources   232
Index   243

LIST OF ILLUSTRATIONS

Cover illustration: The vacant throne claimed by Henry of Bolingbroke in a tall black hat. *By courtesy of the British Library Board.*

King Richard II. *By courtesy of the Dean and Chapter of Westminster.*

Duel. The Military Roll of Arms. *By courtesy of the British Library Board.*

Thomas Arundel preaches in Henry of Bolingbroke's cause. *By courtesy of the British Library Board.*

Henry and Richard meet at Flint Castle. *By courtesy of the British Library Board.*

Henry of Bolingbroke delivers Richard to the citizens of London. *By courtesy of the British Library Board.*

The vacant throne claimed by Henry of Bolingbroke in a tall black hat. *By courtesy of the British Library Board.*

Richard's funeral. *By courtesy of the British Library Board.*

Henry IV's effigy at Canterbury Cathedral. *By kind permission of the Dean and Chapter of Canterbury.*

FOREWORD

A sense of guilt burdened Henry IV throughout his reign, making him unique among usurpers. What drove a man with such an uncomfortably sensitive conscience to usurp the throne? Secondly, how, with such a very small force at his command, some three hundred men only, did he succeed in invading England?

The answers are surprising. Henry of Bolingbroke won the Crown at least as much by accident as design. Richard II's treatment of Henry was greatly to blame, but Richard was only acting in self-defence. Henry had become a subject so over-mighty that he posed a terrible threat. As the sixteenth century chronicler Edward Hall relates, the king looked on Henry as 'him whose life will be my death and whose death the preservation of my life'. By that time Henry could with justice say the same of Richard.

The deadly rivalry between the two princes was compounded by Richard's subjects, who by now looked on their king as a tyrant and Henry of Bolingbroke as their saviour.

Exploring the years before Henry came to the throne, I discovered a very different man from the figure I was familiar with - the sad, middle-aged monarch in Shakespeare's *King Henry IV*, or the bald stout effigy in Canterbury Cathedral with hands that appear clenched, until one realises that they were smashed by Cromwell's troops. An attractive prince, vital and popular, the foremost jouster of the age and the idol of the English commons. In the words of Froissart, 'bien aime de tous, gracieux, doux et traittable'. Patron of poets and lover of learning, a handsome and elegant courtier who liked to stride through the painted palace halls in robes of black and gold, embroidered with his favourite motto: 'Soveyne vous de Moy', remember me.

This book attempts to do as he asked, to remember Henry of Bolingbroke as he was.

A book involves many people apart from the author. I should like to thank the following for their kindness. First and foremost, my husband, George Bruce, for his work on the manuscript and his faith in it. Mr. Alan Barrett for many elegant passages of translation from medieval Latin. The president and fellows of Magdalen College, Oxford for allowing me to see the late K.B. McFarlane's transcripts of Henry of Derby's accounts. Monton Publishers, The Hague, for permission to quote from Louisa Duls's *Richard II in the Early Chronicles*. General Trythall, Colonel Kirby and Colonel D.G. Washtell of the Royal Army Educational Corps for showing me round the ruins of Eltham Palace and entertaining me royally. Miss Ursula Wyndham for her scholarly index, and correction of many errors in titles. Mrs. Barbara Cheeseman for much more than typing.

And Anthea Page and Juanita Homan of The Rubicon Press for bringing the book to life.

I THE ROYAL COUSINS

'Cousinage, dangereux voisinage.'

In the summer of 1399 Henry of Bolingbroke, duke of Lancaster, seized the throne of England from his cousin King Richard II, seemingly an act of unforgivable treachery. Nevertheless the violent events in the last year of the fourteenth century had no sudden cause; the eruption had been preparing for a long time, with secret pressure building up beneath the smooth surface of things ever since the births of the two cousins some thirty-three years earlier.

From the beginning of their lives Richard's and Henry's paths ran close. They were first cousins, born into that affectionate family created by King Edward III - perhaps in reaction to the terrible cruelties and betrayals he himself had witnessed in his own family in his childhood - and they were as close in age as in their relationship. The boys were born within a year of each other: Richard in January 1367 in the abbey of St. Andrew in Bordeaux, then the capital of the English duchy of Aquitaine; and Henry nine months earlier in April 1366 in Bolingbroke Castle, Lincolnshire. Hence his soubriquet Henry of Bolingbroke, the name by which he is known to us in Shakespeare's *Richard II.*

Family tragedy affected the childhood of both the young princes. At the time of their birth neither was very near to the throne. The heir was Richard's tall blond father, Edward the Black Prince, (misleadingly called so from the colour of his armour), aged no more than thirty-six and in every sense powerful. Four days after Richard's christening his father had ridden off to a new war in Spain, leaving his infant son behind in a palace of colourful splendour. It was adorned with the symbols of myth and heraldry, one room hung all in black, patterned with ostrich feathers, another in red, patterned with eagles and griffins, while in a third hangings with swans with women's heads decorated the walls. The Black Prince was in the prime of life, at the height of his military success and popularity.

In 1367 there was as yet no sign at all of the terrible misfortune that was so soon to overtake this potentate, referred to by contemporaries as the 'hope of England' and the 'flower of all the chivalry of the world'. Richard was not his eldest son. In the then seemingly unlikely event of any ill

1

befalling the Black Prince, waiting next in line to the throne was four-year-old Edward of Angoulême. But four more years and the appalling diseases of the age were drastically to alter Richard's prospects. On returning to France from Spain in 1368 the Black Prince fell victim to 'a great and grievous sickness' that turned him into a poor invalid who, on 19 September 1370 during the siege of Limoges, had to be carried into battle lying weakly in his armour in a carriage drawn by horses. He continued to ail and by the end of that year was forced to recognise that he no longer had the energy to administer and defend the duchy. In an emotional ceremony in January 1371 he handed over the lieutenancy of Acquitaine to his younger brother, John of Gaunt, duke of Lancaster, and embarked for England with his little family - all that is, except for one. Adversity chose this moment to strike the fallen prince yet again.

On the eve of their departure his elder son and heir, Edward of Angoulême, suddenly died at the age of seven, probably of the plague. By now it was clear also that the prince himself was doomed to an early death. Although his own physicians suggested with desperate optimism that his native air might cure him, to his enemy, the French King Charles V, medical experts reported differently. The prince had a dropsy, they declared, from which he could not recover.

It was a sad home-coming. No physicians were needed to tell the English people the truth about their hero. On arrival in Plymouth the prince rested in a priory for several weeks before he at last found the strength to travel in a litter as far as London. Peasants who left their work on the open fields to watch the procession jolt slowly past up the pot-holed roads could have judged that it was only a matter of time before four-year-old Richard became heir to the throne in his father's place.

As it happened, the Black Prince was to linger on for another six years. During this time he was carried in his litter to openings of parliament and to the court at Windsor, Richmond or Westminster, and once he even left England. By a mighty effort of will he forced himself to accompany his father in the flagship *Grace de Dieu* on an abortive naval expedition that set sail for France but was compelled by unseasonable, stormy weather to return home without ever having reached French shores. Throughout the expedition he suffered greatly and he was never to leave his native country again.

Richard's early childhood, spent largely in the Black Prince's manor of Kennington, across the Thames from London, and in his castle at Berkhamstead could not but be darkened by his parents' tragedy. For while still in the prime of life the Black Prince, a man of action with no recorded mental interests, was forced to lie prone for most of his days, unable to join in the favourite leisure pursuits of his kind, hawking, hunting and tourneying. In public he put a brave face on his illness, struggling desperately to fulfil his expected role as the king's chief counsellor, holding audiences as he reclined on a magnificent bed covered in blue silk and patterned with roses to match a favourite gown, maintaining an appearance of cheerfulness. But in his tragically frustrating circumstances it is hard to believe that this debonair attitude continued in private. The ill-tempered refusal on his deathbed to forgive Sir Richard Stury some offence seems more likely to have represented the invalid's more usual state of mind.

The Black Prince's aura of sadness and disappointment would also have surrounded Richard's mother, Princess Joan, 'the Fair Maid of Kent', who by the age of fourteen had already been wife to one man and scandalously involved with another. When she was thirty-three, a year after the death of her first husband, the prince had married her, against his parents' wishes, for love. Such a woman, reckoned by Froissart to be 'la plus belle de tout la roiaulme d'Engleterre et la plus amoureuse', the fairest in all the realm of England and the lustiest, was not suited to the life almost of a widow that she lived now. So in his father's manor and castle Richard grew up in an atmosphere of blighted youth, unaccustomed defeat, frustration and mortal illness. The atmosphere can have been scarcely healthier when he stayed at court.

The child frequently visited his grandfather's favourite palaces of Windsor, Sheen, and Westminster, but here too there was a feeling of decay. For the jovial, extrovert king whose French wars had enriched every household in England and more than doubled his father's empire in France was failing. Although not old by modern standards - he was no more than fifty-eight on the Black Prince's return from France - his mental faculties were weakening, the penalty, it was said, of over-indulgence with his mistress, Alice Perrers. The court was decadent. So completely did Alice dominate him that he even allowed her to wear his dead queen's jewels and to sit on the marble bench, the royal seat, during hearings of the king's court at Westminster Hall.

Alice emerges from the chronicles as a kind, high spirited, though perhaps rather greedy girl, Edward III's 'Lady of the Sun', the guise in which she presided over a tournament held at Smithfield in 1375. But to Edward's subjects she was the hated symbol of their beloved king's fall from grace and the decline of England's power abroad. They alleged that she also hastened his progress to senility through witchcraft 'with the aid of a certain friar and waxen images, incantations, potions and Moses rings of memory and oblivion'. For while he played with Alice the triumphant empire which, with the aid of the Black Prince and the bowmen of England, he had so triumphantly carved out of France till it stretched from the Loire to the Pyrenees, dwindled away almost to nothing until it was no larger than a coastal strip between Bordeaux and Bayonne. The true cause of this disaster - improved French military tactics and a rising tide of nationalism across the Channel - was never fully appreciated by Edward's subjects, who blamed the loss of lands in France on a corrupt government and a sinking king. By the time Richard first came to his grandfather's court, the glory had departed from the reign of Edward III.

And to make the boy's environment still more dangerous to his emerging character, he now knew himself to be uniquely precious, the heir to the throne in all but name, the repository of the hopes of his father and grandfather as well as of the ordinary people of England. At the age of five the pretty child with his golden-auburn curls was brought down to the ship *Grace de Dieu* before his father and Edward III departed for France. On board this vessel he was formally appointed regent. Naturally introspective, his sense of other people's feelings around him remained faint. He was virtually an only child. His two half-brothers and two half-sisters, the children of Joan's early first marriage to Thomas Holland, were already grown up, while any playmates of his own age would have been coached by ambitious parents to treat respectfully the royal child who held the key to their future good fortune, office at court and the bribes that always accompanied it. Even Richard's tutors, old comrades in arms of the Black Prince, the ageing Gascon, Sir Guichard d'Angle, and the well-read, magnificently dressed Sir Simon Burley, seem rarely to have crossed him, for his temper was to remain capricious and uncontrolled well into adult years. To these unfortunate influences one more was yet to be added, an all important one.

The Black Prince's death at last, on 8 June 1376, when Richard was only nine, left him to be primarily ruled through the rest of his childhood by his mother, Princess Joan, to whom he became devoted. At a time when Froissart could say of his countrymen, 'The English will never love and honour their king unless he be victorious and a lover of war against their neighbours', a woman's hand was not the most auspicious to guide a future king of England.

Adored by his subjects as a child because of his facial resemblance to his father, Richard was to grow up to be a very different sort of man, rarely taking part in the dangerous sport of jousting and, worse, inclined towards a peaceful policy in France. A contrast indeed to the prince, who even in death chose a warlike pose, stipulating in his will that there should be laid on his tomb: 'an image of gilt brass in memorial of us, fully armed in plate of war with our quartered arms and half the face exposed, with our leopard helm set beneath the head of the image'. The Black Prince had been every Englishman's hero; they were to find his son extremely disappointing.

Death also disrupted Henry of Lancaster's early childhood, but it was his mother, not his father, that he was destined to lose. In September 1369, when he was only three, the 'fair and bright' Blanche, duchess of Lancaster, died of the plague at the age of about twenty-two, leaving behind the feeling that a light had gone out. Its afterglow still lingers today in the *Book of the Duchess* by Geoffrey Chaucer, who at the time of her death was a squire in the royal household.

> I sawgh hyr dance so comlily
> Carole and synge so swetely
> Laughe and pleye so womanly
> And loke so debonairly
> So goodly speke and so frendly
> That certes y trowe that evermor
> Nas seyn so blysful a tresor

Blanche was buried in St. Paul's Cathedral, precursor to Wren's masterpiece, in an alabaster tomb surmounted by a painted marble effigy, and for some time the family was sadly split apart. The three children of the marriage, Henry and his sisters, Philippa and Elizabeth, who were respectively about six and two years older than Henry, went to live with their mother's aunt, Lady Wake, in Bourne Castle, on the edge of the fens, some thirty miles from Bolingbroke Castle. Their father, John of Gaunt, duke of Lancaster, who had returned to England to find Blanche already dead, was far too busy to look after them. He had set sail again for Aquitaine to help his elder brother the Black Prince fight the French.

In Chaucer's poem Gaunt appears as the 'man in blak', inconsolable for the death of his wife. But he was not to remain so for long. In contrast to Richard's already mortally ill father, Henry's father remained vividly alive. Far from being brought up in an atmosphere of invalidism and faded glory, Richard's cousin spent his childhood in a climate of optimism, ambition and change. Edward III's third surviving son possessed energy as vast as his estates which, as well as the palatinate of Lancaster, embraced castles, lordships and manors all over England and Wales, making him the king's richest subject, even richer than his two brothers the Black Prince and Edmund Langley, earl of Cambridge. He was also, like so many of the Plantagenets, a great lover of women.

When Henry was five his father was married again, to the Spanish Princess Constance, the seventeen-year-old elder daughter of Pedro the Cruel. After being defeated in battle by his illegitimate half-brother, Henry of Trastamare, Pedro had been treacherously stabbed to death by him, and Trastamare was now King of Castile and Leon in Pedro's place. Constance had sought refuge in Aquitaine. History has recorded only a few details of this Spanish princess; it appears that she was pious, pretty and good, and she longed to set foot once more on her native land.

Through her father she could claim to be rightful monarch of the two kingdoms, and through Gaunt she hoped to recover her heritage and her home. Had he not led in battle one of the three divisions of the Black Prince's army at Nájera, slaughtering so many of Henry of Trastamare's men-at-arms and horses that the nearby river ran red with their blood? When one is tempted to criticise Gaunt's later treatment of his duchess it is as well to recall that the marriage had been primarily one of convenience for her as well as for him. For the ambitious duke, this seemingly rather dull girl opened up a magnificent prospect: the chance to wear a crown himself, because the husband of the queen of Castile and Leon would be crowned beside her in the cathedral of Burgos.

Married in Bordeaux in September 1371, the thirty-one-year-old duke and his young bride landed in England in November and rode to London for a triumphant reception, whose excitement is captured in the *Anonimalle Chronicle*. They were welcomed before the gates by the Black Prince in his invalid's litter and escorted in royal style down the wide avenue of Cheap, crowded with 'men and women and young girls come to see the beauty of the lady'. A princess from a land so distant that few Londoners would ever see it, unless they were merchants, soldiers or pilgrims to the shrine of St. James of Compostela, Constance possessed a great romantic appeal, and the political implications of the marriage were attractive too.

Should the duke of Lancaster reign over the two Spanish kingdoms England would have an ally instead of an enemy beyond the Pyrenees and be able to cry halt to piratical raids. No longer would the Castilian galleys in alliance with France burn and sack English coastal villages at will. (The possibility that Gaunt might seek to realize his royal ambition with the help of the contents of their fat purses did not seem to have yet occurred to the rich citizens of London.)

The excitement aroused by the duke's wedding among the burgesses, journeymen and apprentices, and their wives would have been reflected in the household of Gaunt's children. They were no longer now to live with their great aunt, but to take up residence with their new step-mother at Hertford Castle, on the River Lea. For them the period of mourning was over and it was time to rejoice, for henceforth the way of life of Henry, Philippa and Elizabeth was to become much grander, as befitted the children of a potential king.

There were presents of gold fillets for the girls' hair, and a silver hanap, a large double-handled cup, for five-year-old Henry's cup-board, a start to the gleaming collection of pots that shed distinction on every great lord's hall where he would entertain his guests and preside at mealtimes over his household. From now on Gaunt's accounts show that their apartments cost the princely sum of £200 a year, not the mere £66 13s. 4d. of old; and so that the children's appearance might match their new status, vast quantities of pearls were issued to their attendants and embroidered on the collars and sleeves of the brilliantly coloured, fur-trimmed *cotehardies* and gowns that kept them warm in winter. For it was as a king that Gaunt henceforth expected to be treated. Arrogant, flamboyant and boastful, he was the true product of an age when a man's greatness was measured by the wealth he could display, the jewels on his doublet, the glitter of his horse's harness and the number of retainers, trumpeters and other minstrels who rode before and behind him as he journeyed through the countryside, where the peasants' hovels clustered about the manors, castles and abbeys of their lords. Gaunt wasted no time in proclaiming his new, additionally exalted rank. He behaved for all the world as though he were already a reigning monarch and it was he, and not Henry of Trastamare, who sat in the royal palace in Toledo, and his father, the ageing King Edward III, entered into the exciting fiction.

In January 1372 the duke had his title as King of Castile and Leon recognized by Edward III's council, then hastened to quarter the royal Spanish arms with his own. So Henry his son grew up surrounded by Spanish castles and lions jostling English leopards and French fleurs de lis on cloth of estate and heraldic banner, on tapestry and silver and gold plate. He heard his father addressed as Monseigneur d'Espagne, saw him sign himself 'Nos el rey', we the king, and insist in his London palace, the Savoy, on the observance of full royal etiquette, although in Gaunt's country castles customs were more relaxed. As a little boy Henry grew familiar with the sight of the crown which King Edward III had prematurely presented to Constance - a diadem ablaze with emeralds, pearls and balasses of pale rose or orange, placed in the keeping of one of the 'damoiselles' who looked after the family.

And from it he may have learned to share his father's view that kingdoms were not only alluring, but also attainable, a view that was to be substantiated by a future which saw crowns encircle the heads of no less than three of Gaunt's children.

To reign over the two Spanish kingdoms in fact as well as in theory was the great duke's ambition throughout Henry's childhood and to this end he was constantly scheming to raise finance and muster armies, but for many years to no avail, partly because he was constantly needed in England. With King Edward III and the Black Prince both enfeebled, he inherited their role; he was the power behind the throne and the leader of the English armies. Confident in his ability and wholly without modesty, he took in his stride the resulting problems and responsibilities.

In this respect too, Henry's experience could not have been more different from his first cousin's. Throughout the years when illness forced Richard's father to remain almost immobile, Henry's father was endlessly active, mustering archers and men-at-arms, departing for and returning from wars, quarrelling with political opponents, fighting the king's battles with parliament. He had been on board the *Grace de Dieu* with the Black Prince and the king when it was forced by bad weather to return to England in the summer of 1372; and afterwards, when the Black Prince had returned home, exhausted, he had set to work to recruit a new army. Within months he would be back in France.

This departure brought new change and excitement into his children's lives. By mid-July 1373 Henry and his sisters, with their Spanish stepmother, had moved from Hertford to Tutbury Castle, on the river Dove in Staffordshire. But their father had sailed for Calais with a grandiose ambition: to win a victory against the French so complete that it would restore to its former size the sadly shrunken duchy of Aquitaine. Afterwards he planned to march on and over the Pyrenees to oust *il batardo*, the bastard, as Henry of Trastamare was derisively designated, from the Spanish throne. Unfortunately for him he had reckoned without the newly acquired military wisdom of the French; they had learned to avoid pitched battles where they were too often mown down by the skill of English archery; and to accept English armies on their soil in the knowledge that sooner or later they would go away, since they were never numerous enough to make a permanent occupation of the country. By Christmas time the duke had achieved neither of his main objects. His expedition had turned into an inglorious *chivauchée*, as such great marches through enemy territory were then termed, from Calais to Bordeaux.

Burning crops and villages, looting and living off the land, but laying siege to no big towns, his army swarmed across the French countryside, losing as usual far too many men through illness, especially the sickness of the bowels caused through heavy drinking of French wines. When their losses were known in England the expedition was generally regarded as an expensive failure, making Gaunt so unpopular that on his return from France even he found it advisable to retire from public life for about a year. So Henry saw more than usual of his father in 1374. But by the following spring the duke of Lancaster was back in the political arena again, attempting to negotiate a treaty with France, and in the summer of 1376 he took up the cudgels for Edward III's royal prerogative, attempting to defend it against attacks by the Good Parliament.

Except for those months in 1374, during Henry's childhood his father was rarely far from the centre of events. And wherever he was to be found turbulent emotions were generated. This, more than his failure in France, was to make him unpopular with the Londoners. The chief bone of contention, as to how far the rights of the Crown as opposed to the rights of parliament extended, was to become a crucial issue, arousing passion in the reigns of both succeeding monarchs, and in 1376 and 1377 it created hostility between London and the duke. This in turn provided a breeding ground for quarrels between Richard and Henry as little boys.

At this date parliament's powers in many important ways were still undefined, the king calling it to assemble where and when he wished, usually whenever he was in need of more revenue. While the Lords had long been consulted by the king, the Commons had been in existence for less than fifty years. Then composed of shire knights and rich burgesses, men well above the rank of ordinary men, but still considerably below that of the Lords, they met humbly in the Chapter House of Westminster Abbey. In the past they had generally agreed with the Lords, but on this occasion they inconveniently found their own voice. They expressed it through a speaker, Peter de la Mare (reputed to be the first speaker of the House of Commons). Through him and with the help of some of the Lords, they attacked the court. They insisted on certain conditions being met before they would grant the king the requested taxes: Edward must consent to have his council reformed and allow his chamberlain, Lord Latimer, to be impeached; Richard Lyon, the merchant on whom Edward depended for massive loans should be imprisoned for corruption, and Edward's mistress, Alice Perrers, must be banished from the court.

Although this appeared to him a gross and unjust interference in the royal prerogative Edward was too desperately in need of money to disagree. And even Gaunt, heard to complain indignantly and typically that 'low hedge knights' were behaving as though they were 'kings and princes of the earth', dared do nothing to thwart them while parliament sat. Not until it had dissolved and the hedge knights were out of harm's way in their manors, did he act. Then with the help of a great council, which possessed some of the same powers as parliament, he found means to have their measures annulled. To Edward's delight Alice Perrers, his 'Lady of the Sun', rode back in triumph to Westminster Palace, his counsellors were reinstated, Richard Lyon was released from prison, and the speaker of the Commons, Peter de la Mare, placed behind bars in his stead.

The citizens of London were furiously indignant. Tired of seeing their tax money wasted, as they thought, by a profligate court and corrupt officials, they had approved of the stand taken by the Good Parliament, and Gaunt's high-handed reversal of its achievements created in them a murderous hatred. By now many of the respectable commons all over England hated the duke for another reason too: his loose sexual morals.

The emotional turbulence Gaunt created was not confined solely to his public life, but entered his private life too. Inside the high battlemented walls of Tutbury Castle the little Prince Henry virtually lived with two stepmothers. Although in the summer of 1372 Constance had given him a daughter, named Catherine of Lancaster, and next in line after her mother to the throne of Castile, Gaunt's heart already belonged to Katherine Swynford, his children's governess, a woman who was nearer his own age and who had been appointed to her responsible position by Gaunt's first duchess, Blanche herself.

But what scandalised peasants and gentlefolk alike was not so much the relationship itself - many great men had mistresses - but the blatant way the duke advertised it. He could have kept his mistress discreetly hidden in his retinue of retainers, but instead he rode openly through towns with the woman beside him, his hand resting lovingly on her horse's bridle, even when Constance was in his party. What made this worse in people's eyes was Katherine's comparatively inferior status. She was widow of one of Gaunt's own knights, Sir Hugh Swynford, and daughter of another knight, Sir Payne Roet of Hainault (who had married one of the ladies in the suite of Edward III's queen) and in no way a grand enough match for a duke in the fourteenth century.

It was not long before the affair had its logical consequences. Katherine Swynford was healthily fertile; throughout Henry's childhood she was giving birth to Gaunt's babies, three little half-brothers and a half-sister, known by the convenient soubriquet Beaufort, after one of Gaunt's French estates, to distinguish them from his legitimate family. John Beaufort (ancestor of King Henry VII) was almost certainly born before Gaunt took ship once again for France with his army in July 1373; after that there was to be a gap of several years before Henry, Thomas and Joan Beaufort were born. And unusually in this period of high infant mortality all these babies survived to grow up.

Strangely enough, though this all seemed scandalous to the duke's detractors, from the point of view of young Henry of Lancaster it appears to have made for a happy family life. He was probably fond of Katherine Swynford since she was to join his own wife's household in later years. And the evidence suggests that he liked her children also. John Beaufort was to betray Richard II for Henry's sake, and Thomas Swynford, son of Katherine's dead husband, Sir Hugh, was to become the companion of Henry's youthful adventures in France and Prussia, before performing in

1400 the sinister service that ensured the safety of the Lancastrian royal dynasty.

Unlike Richard's, the household Henry lived in swarmed with children. As well as Thomas Swynford, Henry and his two sisters and the Beaufort babies, Constance's daughter, Catherine, and a son, John, who died in infancy, there were two Blanches, Blanche Swynford and another illegitimate daughter of the duke's, conceived before his first marriage, who lived with them from time to time. For a boy of Henry's all-round abilities Katherine and her brood made for a lively, stimulating environment.

It was a household seemingly untainted by bitterness, partly because Katherine was a woman of character, intelligence and extraordinary tact. Froissart summed her up as 'une dame qui scavoit moult de toutes honneurs', a lady well versed in all things honourable. Cleverly she made the odd *ménage-à-trois* acceptable to the young duchess, for had Constance objected strongly the ceaseless proximity of the two women would have become unbearable to all concerned. The accounts show Gaunt's mistress performing little services for his wife Constance. It was Katherine who announced the birth of Constance's baby daughter to the king while Katherine's sister, Philippa Chaucer, wife of the poet, was one of Constance's 'damoiselles', or ladies-in-waiting, who regularly attended on her. Henry acquired a male governor, Thomas de Burton, at the age of eight, but Katherine Swynford continued in charge of Philippa and Elizabeth of Lancaster until 1383, when they were virtually grown up. To judge from these indications Constance seems to have accepted her lord's adultery meekly and unquestioningly, an estimate of her attitude which is reinforced by the *Anonimalle Chronicle*. When in 1381 political expediency drove Gaunt to apologise publicly to her for his adultery in one of those scenes of self-humiliation beloved of the age, Constance insisted on prostrating herself before her husband and begging *his* pardon for *her* faults.

The unlikely harmony in this family proceeded, one must suspect, not only from Katherine's gifts of personality but also from the exceptional character of its lord and master. In his country castle Henry's father presented a very different facet of himself from the one seen and hated by the Londoners. Pure kindness shines through his personal accounts. What other great lord would have been considerate enough to tell his tenants and bondsmen to perform their service of carrying wood to Tutbury Castle in summer, to save them the discomfort of doing so in winter? Or would have sent a cheering pipe of wine to his damoiselle Aimée of Melbourne every Christmas? Or arranged for Elyot, the 'wise woman' of Leicester, to travel 'in a charette or on horseback' whichever seemed most 'for her ease' when she came to act as midwife to Constance in June 1372?

Gaunt's accounts shed a revealing light on the household Henry grew up in. It was far more friendly and informal than the stiff royal etiquette at the Savoy would lead us to believe. Many of the key positions were held by women, 'damoiselles' with enchanting names, like Mabile Marreys, Alice Tynneslow, Aimée of Melbourne and Alyne Gerberg, and these ladies performed services for the whole family. Aimée of Melbourne and Alyne Gerberg had charge of the coffers of family jewels, while Alyne looked after Philippa of Lancaster as well as Constance, with the specially important task of dressing the new duchess's hair, plaiting it in the complicated styles of the day, then adorning it with jewelled cylinders, gold coifs and coronets studded with gems. Clearly, all these women and children were dominated by the duke's immensely strong and warm personality, and none more so than Henry.

To this unusually impressive man the most important of all his children was inevitably his eldest legitimate son and heir; constant reference to and provision for him in the accounts makes that apparent. It was a feeling that led to an especially close relationship between them. As a grown man Henry would seek his father's advice right up until the time of Gaunt's death. In him natural filial love being accentuated by the fact that Gaunt was his sole parent in a household of half-brothers and half-sisters who still possessed a mother as well as a father. So the chief influence on Henry as a child was bound to be predominantly masculine, and unlike Richard he would grow up revelling in all the violent physical pursuits of the age.

Thus, since they were products of almost opposite environments, by the time Richard was aged nine, and Henry ten, the first cousins had already become very different, incompatible personalities. But then, as now, adults were bad at detecting incompatibility in children so young. If the ranks and ages were similar they were expected to enjoy each other's company, and it was at this stage of their lives that they were brought together to live under the same roof in the process of marking Richard's sudden new importance.

For on 8 June 1376, the Black Prince had finally died and Richard had been formally declared heir to the throne by the archbishop of Canterbury. On 20 November Edward III had invested him with the ring and the gold verge and created him Prince of Wales, and as such he was expected to live in a grander style than hitherto. Among other fresh splendours he was given a brightly painted state barge with twelve oarsmen in striped livery of red and white, the royal colours, to row him along the Thames between the riverside palaces. His household was greatly increased and he was granted his own retinue composed of high-born little boys.

Among the new arrivals riding excitedly into Kennington Palace in the summer weather were two young nobles. The elder was a lad of about fourteen, Robert de Vere, earl of Oxford; the younger, who was henceforth to be dignified by one of his father's titles as earl of Derby, was ten-year-old Henry of Lancaster. With the boy king for several crucial months, Robert and Henry were to form an ill matched threesome, a threesome that held in it the seeds of jealousy and a destructive hatred that was to affect the future lives of each one of them when they grew up.

II   PRINCES AND PLAYMATES

'... wardrobe expenses of the lord Henry
of Lancaster being in the retinue of the
lord prince ... £20.' *Accounts of William de
Burghbrigge, receiver general to John of Gaunt*

May 1377 has the first record of the ill-fated cousins, Richard and Henry, living together under the same roof. The item from Gaunt's accounts, translated from the original Latin, reads:

> To Hugh Waterton, knight of the lord duke, by the hand of William Oke, concerning the wardrobe expenses of the lord Henry of Lancaster being in the retinue of the lord prince. 10 May 51st year (of Edward III's reign) £20.

The introduction of Henry into the prince's retinue was almost certainly part of a scheme of Edward III's to secure his young successor's future. For the king, prematurely aged and almost senile as he was, still had lucid moments and according to Froissart had worried about Richard in recent months, no doubt recalling the problems of government in his own youth, when at the age of fourteen he had been placed on the throne by the rebellion that forced his father King Edward II to abdicate. To make his situation even more painful, the rebellion had been led by Edward III's own mother Queen Isabella, the 'she-wolf of France', and her lover Roger Mortimer. These two had then dominated him in his minority until he found the strength and cunning to throw off their yoke. That Richard too would face a long minority, his royal grandfather could not but be aware, for that winter he had been gravely ill, so much so that at one point his physicians had refused to treat him for fear of being blamed for his death. He had been unable to eat, and had improved only very slowly on a monotonous diet of thin broth and bread soaked in goat's milk. He was still not wholly recovered.

Upon a medieval monarch depended all aspects of government, and to take some of this weight from his shoulders he needed, more than anything else, ministers he could trust. Edward himself had found these inside his own family. He had been fortunate enough to rear five exceptional sons. As Hardyng's chronicle tells us,

> There was no king Christen had such sonnes fiue,
> Of lyklynesse and persones that tyme on lyue.
> So hye and large they were of all stature,
> The leste of them was of persone able
> To haue foughten with any creature
> Singler batayle in actes marcyable;

He had relied on the services of three of these tall, strong sons in succession, first the Black Prince, who had commanded his armies in France, then Lionel, duke of Clarence, who before his sudden death in 1386 had been the king's lieutenant in Ireland, and finally John of Gaunt, who had replaced his ailing elder brother as lieutenant in Aquitaine, mustered and led armies and represented the king's interests when they were challenged by parliament. (Of the other two brothers, the kindly, easy-going Edmund of Langley lacked the necessary Plantagenet efficiency and fire to be of great use to the king, while Thomas of Woodstock had been far too young.) Judging from this experience it would be an excellent arrangement if Edward's system of family support could continue into the next generation, so that Gaunt's son, Henry, became a trusted minister of Edward's successor, King Richard.

Until then, the Plantagenets had certainly not been renowned for loving families. Queen Isabella was probably at least partly responsible for her husband King Edward II's eventual murder, and King Henry II's children had rebelled both against their father and each other. But the family that King Edward III and his good and popular Queen Philippa had created was warmly affectionate. The original family of twelve children had been tragically decimated by early deaths, and the survivors clung together. Through Froissart's chronicle in 1362 we catch a glimpse of them all descending on the manor of Berkhamstead, gathering there to bid a fond farewell to the Black Prince when he left with the Princess of Wales to take up his duties in Aquitaine. The love between Gaunt and the Black Prince was a by-word, and while Thomas of Woodstock, the most aggressive and difficult personality of the five, was to quarrel sometimes with his brothers, he was also quick to defend them if they were attacked. In the light of his relationship with his own children it was reasonable for Edward to expect the generation that came after him to work together also.

By the spring of 1377 he had recovered enough from his winter illness to set his mark on the coming together of his two grandsons. At Windsor

Castle on 23 April he bestowed on them the insignia of the Order of the Garter, the order of chivalry that he himself had created, rebuilding in its honour a large part of the castle. The delicately beautiful College of Saint George still survives, as well as the tower, named La Rose, with walls and ceilings originally decorated in white, red, vermilion, blue and gold. And from these remnants of King Edward's age we can gain some idea at least of how this ancient fortress appeared to the boy princes on the threshold of their tempestuous lives on that St. George's Day over six hundred years ago.

The king first knighted the two little auburn-haired boys in the presence of ten other young nobles and gentlemen, among them Robert de Vere, all dressed in robes of scarlet. Ten young nobles and gentlemen remained behind while in St. George's chapel - precursor of the one we can see today, built by King Edward IV - Richard and Henry received the further accolade of admission to the Order of the Garter. Each then, significantly, swore a sacred oath that he would not bear arms against his companion unless in the war of his liege lord, or in his own just quarrel. Each was invested with a hood and surcoat of white wool lined with blue and the blue garter embroidered in gold with the motto 'Hony soit qui mal y pense'; Richard took the stall in the chapel of his father, the Black Prince, and Henry that of the renowned Captal de Buch.

We can visualise the frail King Edward III smiling benevolently on this scene in which his two promising grandsons starred and congratulating himself on a wise and far-sighted move. Educated in the tradition of chivalry the young princes, Richard aged ten and Henry about eleven, were of the right age to enjoy the exciting privilege of entry into an exclusive order with a membership confined to a small number of men held to be 'the bravest in the land'. As they gazed at the chapel walls decorated with the coats of arms of such heroes of the Hundred Years' War as Sir John Candos and Sir James Audley, both perhaps dreaming of the daring feats of arms they themselves would perform in the years ahead, the king probably hoped that their creation together as Knights of the Garter at this early age would forge an unbreakable link between them.

For the old king the youthful princes would have made a touching and comforting sight, standing close together, their Plantagenet hair shining, Richard's almost golden, Henry's nearer red. They were a symbol of a future that had been taken care of, a weight off his mind. And as finally they left the chapel, proudly trailing blue mantles embroidered with tiny garters and lined with scarlet, he may have looked ahead to years when their relationship would grow closer.

Significantly, it was to be Edward's last important public appearance, the feasting and jousting that followed the ceremony proved too much for

16

his frail health. He retired to his great embroidered bed in the palace of Sheen on the River Thames, never to rise from it again. Growing steadily and visibly weaker, he lay there while his mistress lived up to her name, the Lady of the Sun, chasing away the priests ominously gathering like black clouds, and trying desperately to cheer her dying lover with talk of hunting, hawking and fowling, his favourite pastimes. Day after day she refused to allow anyone to tell him he was dying, until on 20 June 1377 he suffered a stroke and lay still. Only then did she give up the fight and leave him, taking the rings off his fingers as she went, Walsingham tells us censoriously, to give place at last to a priest at the bedside for the few hours of life that remained to him. On 21 June 1377 Edward III's life ended and Prince Richard's was about to begin as king. He was crowned at the age of ten on 16 July.

From the start, the chroniclers relate portents of disaster. Many of these were inspired by hindsight, but some were not. Throughout the coronation ceremonies ten-year-old Richard appeared pathetically frail, even allowing for his tender years. The stories illustrating this weakness come to us from chronicle after chronicle. We see him 'beautiful as Absalom' in the traditional procession from the Tower of London to Westminster Palace on 15 July; he is dressed all in white to symbolise innocence and surrounded by similarly clad lords and gentlemen, making a pure white centre to a cavalcade otherwise composed of contrasting colours, brilliant liveries and gowns of the craft gilds, civic dignitaries, German mercenaries, citizens of Gascony and the baronial retinues. From the Tower, through the City, out of the Aldgate, and past the goldsmiths' shops glittering in the Strand, Richard rides a great horse, but although a child in the fourteen century learnt to ride not long after he could walk, we note that Richard's mount has to be led by a knight. And further testimony shows him to be no more robust.

The following day it was customary for the monarch to walk shoeless on the striped carpet that stretched the short distance from palace to abbey in a procession of cross, symbolic swords, sceptre, mace and chanting monks. But instead of walking Richard was carried in a litter on the shoulders of four knights, the chronicles tell us, while on either side of them, four more knights, of the Cinque Ports, raised above him on long silver staves the purple canopy adorned with silver bells.

The ceremony of the coronation that followed proved nearly too much for him. After the crowning the king was supposed to remove his regalia, don a magnificent mantle, walk back down the aisle and out of the abbey to Westminster Hall for the banquet, but so exhausted did Richard appear that his tutor, Sir Simon Burley, disregarding all precedent and ritual, picked up the tired little boy who happened to be king in his arms and carried him into the hall, losing on the way one of the jewelled red slippers of the regalia.

Given all we now know about Richard, it seems likely that his exhaustion on this occasion was due not just to physical reasons or the strain of being so long the centre of attention, but also to something deeper, that even at that early age the unction was to him a deeply mystical experience. As he lay on the cloth-of-gold cushions and felt his head and body anointed with the oil through the unlaced gaps in his clothing he felt flow from the archbishop of Canterbury's fingers the Grace of God, changing and making him more than man, a *persona mixta*. For many years afterwards, he was to refer to the signs of the cross they made on his body, on his head, in the palms of his hands, on his breast, between his shoulders and on his arms as 'those characters impressed upon our soul by the sacramental unction', an indication that he felt he had been marked unalterably and for ever by God. Of course, such thoughts could not have been entirely the child's own, but there were those about him who might have encouraged such an interpretation.

Three of his close advisers were ardent believers in the exaltation of the monarchy, first Nicholas Littlington, reputedly Edward III's natural son and abbot of Westminster, whose office it was to explain the coronation to the king; then Richard's tutor, the devoted Sir Simon Burley, whose library included a French translation of a manual for princes, preaching royal absolutism, *De Regimine Principum*, by Egidio Colonna. Last but far from least, there was John of Gaunt, who as high steward of England had been party with Littlington to some very significant alterations in the coronation order itself.

After the king's promise to maintain the laws made 'with the assent of his magnates on demand of the people', the new rubrics added the words 'iuste et racionabiliter', 'justly and reasonably', thus setting the king's judgement above the law. And they altered the order of the ceremony too. Previously the people's assent to the king had preceded the king's oath that he would perform the duties of a sovereign, thus making the people's choice seem paramount in the creation of a king. Now by putting the king's oath before the assent Gaunt made the king seem so by right.

Nor were such advisers likely to have left the little king in doubt about the meaning of these changes, which while they increased the rights at the same time added to the burden of kingship. It was a heavy weight for a ten-year-old boy to feel settling on his shoulders. And, solitary already for much of his life, he now felt a great distance being placed between him and other people. Crowded though they were now about him on stands especially built for the coronation in Westminster Abbey, living, breathing, murmuring to each other in their elaborately folded hats and richly embroidered robes, Richard was no longer of them. The touch of the oil on his flesh set him apart. He felt far closer now to the royal dead, entombed nearby in the holy aura of Edward the Confessor's shrine, for here Richard knew he too would one day lie.

The little king's exhaustion probably indicated a maturity of mind and intelligence that compensated for a weak physique, but that is not how his performance would have struck his stalwart first cousin Henry who also had been given a role to play in the ceremonies; that had been arranged by his devoted father, who as high steward of England, clad in a blue-and-white parti-coloured robe, had presided over the court of claims that allotted the coronation offices. An illuminated document shows him in this process, a venerable figure for a man of only thirty-seven, gold verge in hand and seated on a gilded chair. After high mass in the abbey, and later standing to the right of Richard's chair of estate throughout the succeeding banquet in Westminster Hall, Henry had borne gleaming aloft the sword, Curtana, 'naked and without a point ... emblem of the execution of justice without rancour'.

Henry had performed this demanding task unflinchingly under the stern eye of his father, who with Henry Percy, as seneschal and marshal, rode up and down between the tables of banqueters keeping order.

Standing close as he was to his seated cousin, Henry would have observed the young king's moments of weakness as he tried to eat. So lacking in strength was he that the earl of March had to support the crown as he dined, and according to Adam of Usk, he 'vomited' or perhaps, allowing for exaggeration, choked on the rich food. Even today, when it is no longer so necessary for survival, physical strength is in the eyes of the average eleven-year-old boy one of the most admirable qualities. Henry's royal cousin appeared to be without it. Which was all of a piece with Richard's lack of interest in the joust later as a grown man. The difference in interests and physical stamina between the cousins could not but lead to a basic lack of sympathy between them.

After the coronation a continual council governed the kingdom and Richard continued to live under the supervision of his mother, Princess Joan, and of Simon Burley, his tutor; while Guichard d'Angle, who had grown too old for the task, retired with a title, earl of Huntingdon. The king lived mainly at Kennington where, at least until the end of the year, Henry earl of Derby seems to have stayed with him, sharing the royal pastimes and lessons from Simon Burley. Intellectually, Richard was no less able than his cousin, but in their play - the favourite boys' games of the day being wrestling, or duelling with toy swords - Henry's superior strength would have told in a companionship that is likely to have been stormy. For besides the contrast in physique, there were two other ready-made subjects of dispute.

The first of these concerned fifteen-year-old Robert de Vere, earl of Oxford and hereditary great chamberlain, who also continued to live at court, although his official duties were performed for him by his uncle, Aubrey de Vere. Robert was five years Richard's senior, old for his age, already a young man of fashion, elegant, reckless and sophisticated, and from the beginning loved by the little king. He was to become known as 'the king's kinsman' although the acid-tongued Walsingham was to hint at a more than brotherly relationship. Robert's influence on Richard was soon to grow very strong and Henry's presence too could have made it an awkward threesome.

We catch a glimpse of the three boys together in December. Ushered by obsequious monks in their black gowns, they are bringing offerings to the Benedictine Abbey of St. Albans (where Thomas Walsingham was already dictating his gossipy and often libellous chronicles). We know of their visit, for their names are contained in the *Liber Benefactorum*, an elaborately illuminated manuscript listing the name of every benefactor of the abbey.

The situation between the cousins was further complicated by the second ready-made subject for dispute, the behaviour of John of Gaunt. Throughout the summer and autumn of this first year of Richard's reign it was popularly though unjustly believed that Gaunt was disloyal to the crown. The belief had been strengthened as a result of an incident that occurred before Richard's coronation. In February the duke had again outraged the English commons by challenging another of their institutions, this time the Church, in the persons of Simon Sudbury, archbishop of Canterbury, and William Courtenay, bishop of London. These prelates had summoned John Wyclif to appear before them in St. Paul's Cathedral to answer a charge of heresy.

He had stated that it was not the duty of men to obey sinful priests and suggested that the entire venerable hierarchy of the Church was unnecessary and corrupt. The duke of Lancaster was normally no friend of heretics, but he found Wyclif's views a useful political weapon at this time, and decided to protect him from the punishment that would otherwise be his. Although not yet death - the terrible statute 'De Haeretico Comburendo', decreeing the burning of heretics, would not be passed in England until 1401 - punishment for proven heretics was still damaging and unpleasant. Wyclif risked imprisonment, excommunication and the destruction of his writings. Or he might be forced to recant after performing the humiliating penance of walking through some public place with a faggot on his shoulder.

On 19 February, the day appointed for the examination, the prelates were waiting in the Lady chapel when Wyclif entered, flanked on one side by the great duke of Lancaster, and on the other by Henry Percy, earl marshal of England, bearing his baton of office which he used to clear a way through the angry crowd. Faced with the earl marshal's presence and hearing from outside in the churchyard the clink and clatter of the large armed and mounted retinue that Gaunt had brought with him as a threat, there was little even the outspoken William Courtenay could do. After an angry exchange of words between him and the duke, in which Gaunt brutally threatened to drag the bishop out of his see by his hair, the alleged heretic and his august companions simply turned and walked out. The prelates and the Londoners were left to stare helplessly after them as they rode away over the cobbles; but Gaunt paid a price for his victory: although his tactics had triumphantly succeeded in their objective of freeing Wyclif from punishment, his own popularity suffered irrecoverably.

By next morning the news had reached every merchant, journeyman and apprentice in the city that their bishop had been insulted. For the citizens, so easily excitable at this date that they could have modelled for Shakespeare's mob in *Julius Caesar*, this was the last straw. On top of Gaunt's other sins, it was too much to be borne, and they rioted.

From the doors of St. Paul's Cathedral and Westminster Palace they tore shields of the duke's arms and hung them upside-down - the sign of a convicted traitor who had disgraced the name of knight, for no crime was too bad to impute to their enemy. So inflamed were they that they murdered a priest who spoke against the imprisoned de la Mare, dragged from his horse a knight wearing Gaunt's badge, probably the collar of the linked letter S worn round the shoulders, and frightened other Lancastrian retainers into hiding similar badges in their voluminous sleeves. That accomplished, the rabble decided to turn their wrath on the duke's collaborator. They broke down the doors of Lord Percy's house in Aldersgate Ward, stabbing the tapestries with lances, even searching the latrines for him; then they rushed to the Savoy to look for Gaunt. Luckily, both lords were dining at this perilous time with Sir John Ypres, a rich Flemish wool merchant, whose house was conveniently situated on the river, the duke's barge moored nearby; but even so, pursuit got near enough to be alarming. Stowe tells us, Gaunt 'leapt so hastily from his oysters that he hurt both his legges against the fourme', and within minutes the barge was pulling away from the bank. It is not surprising to learn that his sixteen watermen 'never stinted rowing' until they had reached the royal manor of Kennington on the other side of the Thames. In the presence of Richard, Prince of Wales, they knew no one would dare attack them.

With the help of William Courtenay's mediation and a placatory message from Princess Joan to the citizens of London, conveyed to them by Simon Burley and two other knights, the rioting ceased, but it was not the kind of insult a man of Gaunt's imperious nature could accept. In his turn he attacked the city.

The mayor and aldermen found themselves summoned to appear before King Edward who, himself too ill to speak, expressed the royal will through his chamberlain. The dignitaries were scolded for the disorder they had permitted inside their jurisdiction and advised to beg John of Gaunt's pardon, with the unspoken but underlying threat that, if they refused, the city might be deprived of its precious privileges; a fear which could always bring it to heel, and this time was no exception. The Londoners hastened to obey, erecting by way of apology and peace-offering a marble pillar in Cheapside, bearing a shield of Gaunt's arms the proper way up.

On his part too, the duke made conciliatory gestures. Later, in King Richard's presence at Sheen palace, shortly after King Edward III's death, he kissed the mayor and each alderman in turn, a scene of reconciliation rounded off by a fanfare of trumpets and a herald's proclamation that peace had been made between the duke and the city. Prompted by Gaunt, Richard released from prison the speaker of the Commons, Peter de la Mare, who on his return to London was rapturously greeted by the citizens.

Unfortunately, it was not so easy to end popular hatred nor the rumours of treachery. These were repeated in the ale houses, fairs and markets, travelling the wooded roads of England with pilgrims, wool merchants, pedlars, minstrels and friars, who reported that the duke of Lancaster was so proud he had designs on the crown; he intended to poison Richard or have him declared illegitimate.

In vain did the great duke humble himself in Richard's first parliament in October, the dignified middle-aged man suddenly falling on one knee before the ten-year-old king, a diminutive figure in his robes, seated on the dais under the canopy of state. As the lords spiritual and temporal were struck silent with surprise he begged to be heard in his own defence. The rumours were lies, he said. 'None of his ancestors had ever been a traitor; they had all been true and loyal subjects of the crown. He himself had more to lose by treachery than any other man in England; apart from this it would be a marvellous thing if he could so far depart from the traditions of his blood.'

Gaunt's emotive and dramatic plea evoked a clamour of reassurance from Lords and Commons alike: they knew he was innocent; of course, the rumours were lies.

But the rumours persisted. Unfairly, in view of Gaunt's constant attempts to bolster the monarchy, he was to be dogged by suspicion of treason for nearly ten years, during which time he was suspected even by his own nephew King Richard himself. He who fostered the suspicion in the royal mind was evidently none other than that same youth who had joined the royal household with Henry, earl of Derby: the 'king's kinsman', Robert de Vere. This young earl's hostility to Gaunt was probably rooted in jealousy of the older man's influence on Richard, for the duke of Lancaster too had a room in the palace and still exercised great power.

While the king remained a small child, governed by Princess Joan who was Gaunt's friend, the duke was safe, but he was to be in actual danger of his life when Richard came to make his own political decisions as a youth. If De Vere's attempts to poison Richard's mind against Henry's beloved father started, as they may well have done as early as 1377, this would have provoked many a bitter argument between the boys. It would also explain Henry's future enmity to de Vere which was to become so overwhelming as to lead him into rebellion, contrary to his oath of fealty to his king and the loyal tradition of his own family.

From December 1377, when together the little princes visited the abbey of St. Albans to June 1381, the date of the outbreak of the Peasants' Revolt, the records provide us with no further glimpses of Henry in King Richard's company. So we may presume that for some reason his stay at court came to an end and from the age of eleven to fifteen the earl of Derby grew up in his father's castles, where he was once more living with his sisters Philippa and Elizabeth, with his stepmother Constance and her little blonde daughter Catherine, as well as with his father's mistress Katherine Swynford and her legitimate and illegitimate children, Thomas, Blanche and the growing family of young Beauforts. Although doubtless he would have visited court on special feast days in common with other peers of the realm.

During this period, tutored by William Montendre and his chaplain, Hugh Herle, Henry blossomed into a youth accomplished in ways still unusual for his rank; he became skilled not only in the gentlemanly accomplishments of 'courtesy' (manners and etiquette), jousting, 'venerye' (hunting), dancing singing and piping (playing the flute), the arts possessed by Chaucer's squire, but also in matters more often left by nobles to their scribes at this time. He learned to read and write in both English and French and to understand some Latin, the excellence of his education being one quality he had in common with his cousin and ex-playmate, King Richard.

Gaunt did not fail to provide his heir with anything that could add to his happiness or well-being, even acquiring a wife for him when he was fourteen. At this age then a boy was considered ripe for matrimony, although sometimes the marriage was not consummated for a number of years. For his precious, only legitimate son Gaunt had picked a prize in the marriage market, Mary de Bohun, a rich heiress. She was no more than eleven years old, but one of the two daughters and co-heiresses of Humphrey de Bohun, earl of Hereford and Essex, hereditary constable of England, who had conveniently died in January 1373; in her marriage portion Mary would bring her husband the earldoms of Hereford and Northampton, as well as a collection of illuminated manuscripts.

According to Froissart, an attempt to thwart the marriage had been made by Gaunt's youngest brother, Thomas of Woodstock, who although he had acquired half the de Bohun fortune in marrying Mary's co-heiress and elder sister, Eleanor, in 1377, was still plagued by lack of money, and an income too small to pay for the magnificent style of life his rank required. In an attempt to solve this problem and lay hands himself on the whole of the de Bohun inheritance he tried to persuade Mary to enter a convent. If the report of this attempted double-dealing is true - and Thomas's ambitious and ruthless nature makes it seem all too credible - his intentions were speedily frustrated by Gaunt, who on 27 July 1380 bought Mary's marriage from the king for 5,000 marks.

By the following March the little heiress was safely married to Henry at a jubilant ceremony in her mother's favourite house, Rochford Hall, Essex, a substantial part of which can still be seen today now converted into the headquarters of Rochford golf club. As wedding presents from Gaunt and his daughters Mary received a ruby ring costing sixteen marks, a hanap or wine cup, and a silver ewer, while to celebrate the occasion Gaunt provided a tun (225 gallons) of Gascony wine and a vat of Rhenish. The festivities must have been merry indeed and they were further enlivened by two companies of minstrels, one sent by Richard and one by Edmund of Langley, earl of Cambridge, Gaunt's younger brother. Needless to say, Henry's other uncle, the baulked Thomas of Woodstock, sent nothing.

In selecting Mary as his son's bride, Gaunt had chosen well, for the young couple proved immediately compatible, indeed their liking for each other soon became almost embarrassingly obvious. In view of the bride's youth it had been agreed that they were not to live together. She was to remain with her mother at Gaunt's expense until she was fourteen, but this arrangement they seem precociously to have defied because within a few months eleven-year-old Mary was pregnant. Henry had proved his manhood, this being one of the qualities for which he was eventually to be chosen king in preference to his cousin Richard many years later. A live boy was born to Mary at Rochford on 26 April 1382, her sister Eleanor being in attendance.

By now Henry had his own accounts, still extant for this year; and they record his pride in his son's birth. Immediately on receiving the news, the youthful father took horse for Rochford Hall, where within two days he had appointed a nurse at 26s. 8d. a year, and a governor for his son's household at 40s., princely sums both to be paid from his own coffers.

Sadly, after this entry the little boy disappears from Henry's records, and we must assume that he became another victim of one of the many causes of the high infant mortality of the day.

For the king of England, even more than for Henry, the earl of Derby, an early marriage was important. A new heir to the throne was urgently needed, since should Richard die now the succession might well be in dispute. If the usual custom of primogeniture were to be followed the dead duke of Clarence's grandson, the earl of March, should inherit the crown, but in the absence of any written law on the subject his succession was by no means certain. The relationship between Richard and March was unusually distant, the custom of primogeniture had not always been followed, and the unpopular Gaunt was considered by many people likely to become the next king.

By this date a bride had been chosen for Richard too. Anne of Bohemia was a few months older than the king, merry, sweet-natured and well educated, able to read and write in both Latin and German, she was also, to judge from her effigy in Westminster Abbey, very plain; although Richard, who came to love her, would always see her as 'fair'. She had been chosen not for beauty, but for rank and political advantage. Beside such qualities good looks were little regarded.

As the sister of Wenzel, King of Bohemia and Emperor of the Holy Roman Empire, Anne was a grand match for the monarch of such a small insignificant country as England then appeared. Besides, the marriage cemented a useful alliance between countries that shared allegiance to the pope in Rome, rather than to his rival pontiff in Avignon, a crucial matter at a time when the Church and Europe were rent by the great schism. In emotional terms the marriage of Richard and Anne was to be as successful as that of the earl of Derby, although it was never to be popular with Englishmen, who grudged the money it had cost.

For this impressive match the royal council agreed to pay 100,000 florins into Wenzel's empty coffers. Richard's subjects would have preferred them to settle for an earlier suggested bride, less exalted but richer, Katherine, daughter of Bernabo Visconti, duke of Milan, who in his turn had been prepared to pay well for the honour. The English commons were never to forgive Anne for her lack of dowry and her arrival in their country bringing with her nothing except the new fashion for riding side-saddle, and a large train of frivolous and expensive Bohemian attendants whose unorthodox behaviour at court caused ripples of disapproval that have lasted into our own times. They feared she would prompt royal requests for more taxes but were unable to make their views felt strongly enough to change the council's decision.

In the spring of 1381 a German embassy led by the duke of Saxe Teschen arrived in England, and on 2 May the terms of Richard's marriage with Anne were agreed. It was to be a testing summer for England. Within weeks of the conclusion of the marriage negotiations the Peasants' Revolt had broken out, an uprising that set at risk all the country's institutions and threatened to topple the whole pyramid of social hierarchy at whose apex was the king. With reason Froissart called it a 'great mischief, a rebellion of moving of the common people by which deed England was at a point to have been lost without recovery'.

At this terrifying moment for England's ruling classes Henry, earl of Derby, is to be found again in Richard's company. The cousins were to be in the eye of the storm together in an experience that was to have a lifelong effect on their relationship.

III BETRAYAL

'The king ... proclaimed ... that they might go through all the realm of England and catch all traitors.' *Anonimalle Chronicle*

The king was staying at Windsor Castle, and Henry was probably already with him when the Peasants' Revolt began, an uprising that from a twentieth century viewpoint seems inevitable, but which in 1381 took the governing classes completely by surprise. It had not occurred to this handful of nobles and gentlemen whose splendid lives were made possible by the vast majority of villeins and labourers that such insignificant people could, or would rebel. Clad in coarse, inexpensive materials, all that was permitted them by Edward III's sumptuary laws, they were an accepted part of the landscape, living in wattle and daub cottages with unglazed windows clustered humbly below the lord of the manor's great house or castle.

They tended his sheep, and cultivated his strips as well as their own in the largely wide open fields that surrounded the village. With oxen and primitive tools, they ploughed, spread dung, sowed and harvested his crops so that the lord could keep his garderobe replete with silk, satin, velvet and fur-lined gowns, his stables full of fine horses, his mews alive with hawks, and his high raftered hall supplied with viands, wine and ale plentiful enough to extend hospitality to all comers. Supported also by peasant labour was the lord's big household of servants, his minstrels and a band of armed retainers sporting his livery, a badge on their doublets, or a distinctive cap. For although wealth was created in the growing towns, most of the affluence of the nobility and gentry still came from the land and the people who worked on it.

Ironically, as sometimes occurs with revolutions, this one came at a time when social conditions had actually begun to improve and villeinage was already on the wane, when increasing numbers of serfs were becoming freemen who paid the lord of the manor for their cottages with a small money rent and services, perhaps two days' work on his lands a week, or at especially busy periods of the year. Those who were already freemen and cottars were better off too, for the scarcity of labour, created by repeated ravages of the plague, had forced up labourers' wages, although two attempts had been made to control them. The Statute of Labourers of 1351, declaring it illegal to pay anyone more than was customary before the Black Death in 1348-49, had been reinforced ten years later, under pain of branding, for any man who left his home district to seek higher wages elsewhere.

Measures of this nature seem terrible to us today, nevertheless they had a bright side in that they were deemed necessary, thus indicating that the law was being evaded; and we have other evidence of this besides in the records of King Edward III's new buildings at Windsor Castle. For this work, because other employers were paying more, William of Wykeham, in control of operations, could not find enough builders, even though he had the power to impress them.

There are records also of adventurous serfs successfully achieving freedom by their own actions, of individuals who escaped their manors, hid themselves in towns and took advantage of the law which granted freedom if a man managed to stay out of his lord's clutches for a year and a day, provided he was never foolish enough to return home, for if found on the manor he could be arrested and returned to serfdom.

However, this gradual improvement in their wretched lot was too slow for many peasants who, having caught sight of the promised land, were understandably in a hurry to reach it. Labourers wanted the repeal of the Statute of Labourers, cottars wanted to commute all their services into rent. While the most oppressed section of all, those who were still serfs, wished to be free of this anachronistic, intolerable and shameful bondage, which made them and their children the property of the lord for ever, to keep or sell as he wished.

By 1381 the peasants had a ready-made bonfire of discontents that only awaited a spark to ignite and this came in the form of a new poll tax. A charge of one shilling a head on everyone, except beggars, over the age of fifteen, at a time when 'the wages of a carter, ploughman or shepherd only averaged 13s. 4d. a year', it was impossibly onerous. Nevertheless, revolt did not follow at once, the peasants at first tried a more peaceful means of evasion. Since they were not represented in parliament, whose house of 'Commons' then consisted of no one lowlier than a burgess or knight, they defended themselves in the only way they could. They lied about the number of adults in their families, so that the commissioners' returns to the exchequer in January 1381 showed an absurdly small number of people over the age of fifteen. It was a picture repeated right across England, and since all governments in the final resort depend on consent, a form of unanimous, spontaneous protest the king's council would have been wise to take as a warning that its policy could not safely be enforced.

But at this date Richard's councillors, led by his chancellor-archbishop of Canterbury, Simon Sudbury, and his treasurer, Sir Robert Hales, appear to have been out of touch with the people they ruled. Instead of mitigating the burden of the poll tax in some way, they appointed new commissioners and instructed them to ride round the villages, seeking out and punishing those peasants who had made the false returns, and since this meant nearly everyone, fear and indignation united the populace as nothing else could have done.

The revolt which the extremists were to take over began in mere self-defence with riots in Essex and Kent. On 30 May 1381 the inhabitants of three villages obeyed an order to appear at Brentwood to be examined as to their tax statements. But when the commissioner, Thomas Bampton, appeared, he was firmly told by the villagers that they would pay no more than they had already paid, and when he attempted to arrest their spokesman, a baker, Bampton and his clerks were chased out of the district with flung stones.

Given the task of punishing these rioters, Robert Belknap, chief justice of common pleas, arrived in Brentwood on 2 June to find the villagers armed and in no mood to co-operate. They forced him to 'swear on the bible that never again would he hold such a session, nor act as a justice in such inquests', then put him ignominiously to flight. A humiliating experience but one which he survived, more fortunate than three of his jurors and three of his clerks; for these scapegoats for the royal policy were set upon by the angry mob, who cut off their heads, stuck them on poles and marched round the villages, triumphantly displaying their gory trophies before seeking refuge in the woods from the punishment to come.

All over the south-east similar incidents were happening. Also on 2 June 1381 a mob burst into the monastery of Lessness and forced the abbot to take an oath to join the peasants' cause. The insurrection snowballed at an enormous rate. Two days later the peasantry assembled in such numbers at Dartford, in Kent, that their leaders found it necessary to order all those who dwelt near the sea to remain behind to defend the coast against the French, an illustration of the interesting fact that at no stage of the revolt was the peasants' movement totally anarchic. They wanted to remedy their own lot, but not at the price of destroying England.

On 6 June there was a more ambitious attack. Hearing that an escaped serf belonging to Sir Simon Burley had been arrested and imprisoned in Rochester, the peasants broke into the castle there and set him and his fellow prisoners free. At Maidstone they sacked two houses, murdered a townsman, opened the archbishop of Canterbury's gaol, releasing that extraordinary character, the priest, John Ball, who had been imprisoned there since April for preaching his egalitarian ideas in the market places. At North Cray a manor house was destroyed, four gentlemen were seized and forced to swear fealty to 'King Richard and the true commons of England'.

It was a significant development, for in a matter of a few days the revolt had altered its character, ceased being a matter of mere self-defence and an attempt to secure better conditions, and developed into a movement with a radical purpose; this was nothing less than to establish an entirely changed, egalitarian society under the rule of the king with all intermediate classes abolished, this worthy ideal unfortunately, like most ideal societies through the ages, to be founded in blood.

Whereas the revolt at this stage brought no threat to Richard's life - since the fourteen-year-old king was to be head of the peasants' new commonwealth - Henry's position was far more perilous, for he represented to the peasants the barons who were to be destroyed, some of them executed. The rebels had begun to plan the execution of those councillors they believed to blame for the economic problems that had led to the iniquitous poll tax: Simon Sudbury, chancellor and archbishop of Canterbury, Sir Robert Hales, treasurer, and the ever unpopular Gaunt, among many others appeared on the list of victims they were beginning to draw up. As the hated duke's son, Henry was in especial danger, since Gaunt himself was beyond reach, leading an expedition into Scotland.

All over the south-east the peasants were now up in arms, inflamed by John Ball and his obscure, semi-coded messages of which the following, echoing Langland's already well-known poem, *Piers Plowman*, reads like an incantation to violence:

> Iohan the Mullere hath ygrounde smal, smal, smal;
> The Kynges sone of heuene schal paye for al.
> Be war or ye be wo;
> Knoweth your freend fro your foo;
> Haueth ynow, and seith 'Hoo';
> And do wel and bettre, and fleth synne,
> And seketh pees, and hold you therinne;
> And so biddeth Iohan Trewman and alle his felawes.

Though much of this is double-Dutch, its gist is clear. The ominous figure of John Trueman represents the peasant who had had enough of his unfair lot in life and plans to put a stop to it. Like the mills of God, his corn has ground slowly but now justice is about to be done. It is time for everyone to beware or suffer the consequences, to know their friends from their foes, to live a more Godly life and seek peace. Clearly, the peace John Ball had in mind was not immediate, that happy state of affairs would only follow a complete revolution of society accompanied by a good deal of killing.

Grown into a vast horde, armed with farm tools and the longbows they were encouraged to practise with by law, on 10 June the peasants burst into the walled city of Canterbury with help from the citizens themselves. It was to be one of the most alarming features of this rebellion that, once started, the most downtrodden members of society everywhere made common cause, artisans and poor townsmen joining the peasants in the hope of remedying their own grievances, too, of which they had many.

Henry and Richard would have heard of the rebels' success and blood-thirsty deeds in Canterbury with mounting anxiety. The peasants had turned their attention to this city as being the see of one of their chief enemies, the chancellor, Simon Sudbury, and once inside the gates they made for the cathedral, bursting in during High Mass. With that curious mixture of good intentions and cruelty that characterised them throughout the uprising, they first knelt in reverence, then roughly told the terrified monks it was time they elected a new primate from among them, 'for he who is archbishop now is a traitor and shall be decapitated for his iniquity'.

Next after the chancellor and the other king's councillors, the rebels resented those who had drawn up the legal documents in which the details of their manorial bondage were enshrined. Pouring into the lawyer's offices, they took from the coffers armfuls of parchment documents and flung them out on to the street, piled them into heaps and set light to them. By now the rebels had a 'wache worde': strangers were questioned, 'With whom haldes yow?' And those who failed to make the correct reply which was, 'Wyth kynge Richarde and wyth the trew communes', lost their heads. With these gruesome objects carried aloft before them, the men of Kent, several thousands strong, set off for London the next day. They marched under the leadership of Wat Tyler and the inspiration of John Ball, with his unforgettable slogan,

> Whanne Adam dalfe (dug) and Eve span
> Who was thanne a gentil man?

Soon afterwards, from Essex, under the leadership of Jack Straw, a similar motley horde also began to march towards the capital. The revolt flamed into existence so quickly that there was no time to organize resistance. For the government, it could hardly have come at a worse time, for of two recently mustered armed forces both were out of reach. Edmund of Langley, earl of Cambridge, had just set sail with a considerable army, bound for the Iberian peninsula where he meant to join the Portuguese in an attempt to oust the usurper, Henry of Trastamare, from the Spanish throne; while Edmund's elder brother, Gaunt, had recently led a smaller force to Scotland with a commission to settle the latest border incident, preferably by peaceful means, but if that proved impossible, by war.

For us today, accustomed to the fact of standing armies, it is hard to visualise a government caught totally without defences, as happened to Richard and his council in June, 1381. By the time his advisers realized the gravity of the situation it was already totally out of hand.

All Richard's council could do was play for time and negotiate. He sent messages demanding to know the rebels' intentions and offering to meet them to hear their grievances. Then he, too, set off for London, taking this route for several reasons. The city militia could be quickly mustered; and London also held the Tower, which with its elaborate defences reconstructed by King Edward I was probably the strongest fortress in the land. But undoubtedly he was impelled by a more altruistic reason as well. In time of war it was the duty of a medieval monarch, even if only fourteen, to protect his capital city.

So as the rebels moved in a westerly direction from Essex and Kent, the king was moving eastwards. At about the same time as he rode over the moat into the Tower of London the two rebel hordes set up camp outside the city walls, the men of Kent on the wide expanse of grass and scrub that was then Blackheath on the south side of the Thames; and the men of Essex on the north side of the river in the park called Mile End.

Seeking refuge with Richard inside the thick walls of the fortress, whose central white keep was then adorned with weather vanes of gilt crowns above conical blue-grey turrets, were members of his household, including Henry, earl of Derby, and Robert de Vere, as well as Simon Sudbury, chancellor, Robert Hales, the treasurer, and most of those who regularly sat on Richard's council and formed the government of the country. In all there crowded into the stronghold some six hundred people, including the mayor of London, William Walworth; although two prominent members of the royal entourage were missing. Richard's tutor, Simon Burley, who had left London for Bohemia in mid-May to make final arrangements for Richard's marriage to Anne of Bohemia, and the king's mother, Princess Joan, who was on pilgrimage to Canterbury when the revolt broke out.

Desperate to reach her son's side in this crisis, the princess decided to make a dash for it, having herself driven in a 'whirligig' through the very middle of the encampment on Blackheath. Fortunately, the peasants had warm feelings for the Fair Maid of Kent; we are told that she was seized and kissed - an alarming experience for a great lady of her time but not fatal - and then allowed to complete her journey to the Tower.

For those lords and their servants whom the peasants regarded as enemies, to be executed at all costs, the fortress of the Tower had now become their last sanctuary, presenting a very different aspect from the one we are familiar with from the jewel-like illumination in the poems of Charles, duke of Orleans. This shows a peaceful and pretty River Thames, enamelled with little boats, decorated with the wide arches of London Bridge and the myriad spires of the city churches. The duke, clad in luxurious robes, writes at his ease in the White Tower, a prisoner of war who nevertheless knows there is no danger to his life, for he is to be ransomed.

By contrast, that June week of 1381 was to be full of the fear of violence, although the first night appears to have been quiet enough, if one disregards the threat implied in the mere presence of thousands of rebels camped just beyond the city walls.

For the ministers and councillors in the Tower, frantically debating their best course, the Peasants' Revolt was in many ways more terrifying than any French invasion. Because this army was governed by none of the usual rules of chivalry whereby the lives of the rich and powerful were spared, later to be exchanged, like the duke of Orleans, for fat ransoms. In this revolt the rich and powerful knew that they were the ones most in danger, for the rebels had made that clear. In their message answering Richard's demand to know their intentions they had replied, 'that they had risen to deliver him and to destroy traitors to him and his kingdom'.

Chief among the 'traitors' the rebels wanted was John of Gaunt, and they had a new watchword: 'We will have no king called John'. Hatred of him was not confined to the armies lying in wait outside London. At Hertford a mob broke into the cellars of the duke's castle and drank his wine, while in Cambridgeshire the peasants destroyed two manors simply because they belonged to Gaunt's steward, Thomas Haselden, also fortunately for him, in Scotland at the time. They then sold all the poor steward's crops, horses and farm animals. So dangerous was it to have any connection with the duke that his terrified duchess fled north to Pontefract Castle, only to be humiliatingly refused entrance by the duke's own officers, ungallantly mindful of the safety of their own skins; she was forced to ride on that same night all the way to Knaresburgh Castle before she could find refuge. While the abbot in Leicester was so terrified of provoking the mob's anger that he refused a request to take into safekeeping the treasures from Gaunt's castle there.

If the times were dangerous for Gaunt's friends and servants, how much more so for his only legitimate son! It was almost certainly because of this widespread feeling against his father that throughout the revolt Henry was to keep such a low profile compared with Richard and the 'king's kinsman', Robert de Vere, for one of Henry's prime qualities was bravery.

Admittedly he was in good company. By now it was not only the little group of important people in the Tower who had need of protection. The radical sermon that John Ball is said to have preached to the horde encamped on Blackheath - again echoing the language, if not the tone, of *Piers Plowman* - was a recipe for the massacre of all the upper and middle classes. Now God had given the people the chance to throw off the yoke of servitude, he declaimed to the attentive peasants. England was like a field with both good wheat and weeds and it was time to root out and cut away the latter, beginning with the lords, judges and lawyers, so that afterwards all men would share the same freedom, rank and power.

To be a weed in John Ball's field of folk was to invite execution, and while it is true that the English peasants were actually to claim far fewer victims than their French counterparts in the Jacquerie of 1358, whose atrocities have been so vividly described by Froissart, their intentions were certainly terrifying. There appeared to be no way of frustrating them except through the king, and since he was the only authority the rebels would recognise and respect, there was no escaping a meeting between them and Richard. But aware that they had no boats, his council found a way to make the interview slightly safer.

Probably on the same day as Ball preached his alarming sermon a flotilla set off from the Tower. First, the royal barge containing the fourteen-year-old king, the archbishop, the treasurer, the earls of Warwick, Salisbury and Oxford and the other members of the council. Robert de Vere was included, unlike Henry whose red hair made him too easily recognisable as Gaunt's son. Four more boats followed, gleaming with men-at-arms from the Tower garrison, the soldiers giving the royal party some protection, as did the river itself. Nevertheless, most of the occupants of the barge were nervous, especially when they reached the heath and saw the vast number of rebels massed on the bank, and they were not reassured by the peasants' attempt at a display of order and loyalty.

In an appealing attempt to reassure the boy king they had drawn themselves up under pennons and banners of St. George. But so excited did they become when the barge rounded the last bend that this intended impression was ruined. According to Froissart, they 'began to shout and made such a cry as though all the devils of hell had been among them'. To make the situation even more nerve-racking, someone threw into the barge a petition which contained the names of the 'traitors' they wished executed, those of fifteen lords who were with Richard in the Tower, and one who was not, the list being headed by the name of John of Gaunt, duke of Lancaster.

Judging that in such a mood the rebels were capable of anything, Richard's councillors decided on retreat, although according to one chronicler, Richard himself had wanted to land. So his barge stayed for a few moments, rowing up and down between the banks crowded with insurgents, then suddenly turned and began hastily to pull back towards the comparative safety of London, making the rebels angrier than if the king had never offered to come and listen to their demands.

The whole operation had been appallingly mismanaged. The rebels felt Richard had broken his promise to treat with them. Their tempers mounted as the shining little flotilla rowed away from Blackheath, and it was pursued by shouts of 'Treason! Treason!'

Not long after the royal party thankfully regained the Tower, rebels began to pour after them along the south bank. Arrived at Lambeth and Southwark, they were joined by artisans boating across from the city. Together they opened the prisons of Marshalsea and the King's Bench, setting free the inmates; they burnt to the ground the house of John Imworth, warden of Marshalsea prison, and sacked the archbishop of Canterbury's Lambeth Palace. (Perhaps it was at this point that Sudbury himself escaped to join the king in the Tower.) Then they turned their attention to the city.

The mayor, William Walworth, had ordered the drawbridge raised in the middle of London Bridge, which was then the only bridge over the river, but this did not halt them for long. Through either fear or treachery - it is impossible to decide which - the drawbridge was lowered. Meanwhile, the Aldersgate on the east side of London wall had also been opened by the men who were supposed to be guarding it. Without a blow being struck Wat Tyler's and Jack Straw's armies were in the city. Once in, their numbers were swollen by London artisans.

With its own drawbridges, moat and curtain walls the Tower was a citadel within a citadel, and it was just as well for Henry that he was inside it, for the rebels were bent on destroying everything and everyone belonging to his father.

On entering London one of their first goals was Gaunt's wonderful palace of the Savoy, built by Peter of Savoy, uncle of Henry III's queen, and said to surpass in splendour even the royal palaces of Westminster, Sheen and Eltham. They rushed through Ludgate, down Fleet Street and the Strand, burst through the gates and made their way to the splendid rooms within.

'They took all the torches they could find and lighted them and burnt all the sheets and coverlets and beds and headboards of great worth ... and all the napery and other things that they could discover they carried to the hall and set on fire with their torches.'

His treasures they systematically destroyed, his store of gold and silver pots they broke with axes and threw in the river or the open drains; gold and silk cloth they tore and trampled under foot, rings and other jewels and precious stones they flung into mortars and ground to powder.

Unable to wreak their wrath on Gaunt himself, they set up a substitute - a 'jack' found in his wardrobe (a jacket of leather or buckram, stuffed with wool, probably brightly coloured and embroidered with jewels). Stuck on a lance, this was used for target practice and shot full of arrows, then in a frenzy pulled down and hacked to pieces with axes and swords. Finally, the peasant mob completed the ruin of the 'fairest palace' by enthusiastically rolling three barrels of gunpowder into the flames, regardless of the fact that thirty of their own kind were still inside and perished in the ensuing explosion. It was lucky indeed for the duke that he was in Scotland at the time.

While some rebels thus razed the Savoy others released prisoners from the Fleet Prison, burned surrounding houses, residences of lawyers in the Temple, and the Hospitallers' Priory of St. John of Clerkenwell, whose prior was the Treasurer, Sir Robert Hales. Finding in the priory church seven Flemish merchants, who aware of their unpopularity had sought sanctuary there, they dragged them outside and beheaded them. Thirty-five more Flemings were to be among the hundred and forty or so men killed the following day in a rebellion which, like all civil wars, presented an opportunity for everyone to pay off old scores.

By Thursday evening a sea of insurgents lapped round the Tower in camps behind it on Tower Hill and to the east of it on St. Catherine's Wharf. As the June darkness fell there arose shouted threats to storm the Tower and clamours for the blood of the 'traitors' within.

In this impasse the onus again fell on the boy King Richard to try to negotiate. 'Pensive and sad', he went up into a turret overlooking St. Catherine's Wharf and made a proclamation. No doubt he had been told what to say, but his words fell on deaf ears. When he offered free pardons if they would go 'peaceably to their homes', the rebels refused and 'all cried with one voice that they would not go before they had captured the traitors who lay in the Tower, nor until they had got charters to free them from all manner of serfdom'.

Richard redoubled his efforts, sending out a bill repeating and elaborating on his offer, presumably in the hope that when they saw it in writing, signed with his personal signet, it would carry more weight. The royal envoy stood on an 'old pulpit' on St. Catherine's Wharf to read out the message. The king gave them all a free pardon and promised, if they put their grievances in writing, that he would provide a remedy 'with the aid of his loyal lords and his good council'.

He begged them again to go peaceably to their homes, but his efforts were in vain. Such a vague promise was not what the rebels had left their manors and risked their lives for. They wanted no less than a radically changed society from which all their enemies should be eliminated. They pronounced the bill 'nothing but trifles and mockery' and promptly issued their own chilling proclamation, having it 'cried around the city that all lawyers, and all the clerks of the chancery and the exchequer and every man who could write a brief or a letter should be beheaded, whenever they could be found'.

The men of violence were gaining control. The darkness was punctuated not only by the torches of the rebels but also by the sinister brilliance of more houses in flames. Richard climbed a turret to observe the destruction and although he appeared in great distress of mind throughout the short night, he alone, according to the *Anonimalle Chronicle*, kept his head while his councillors panicked. Perhaps more clearly than he, they realized the utter helplessness of their position.

As dawn approached they decided in desperation that the best Richard could do was to try to persuade the rebels to leave the vicinity of the Tower for a few hours, long enough at least for their intended victims to escape. A proclamation was made in the king's name that 'every man between the ages of fifteen and sixty, on pain of life and members' should go to the park outside the city at Mile End where he would meet them at seven o'clock that morning. And in the belief that he intended to agree to their demands, most of the rebels obeyed, gradually marching away from Tower Hill and St. Catherine's Wharf to make their way to Mile End. Everyone's hopes now rested on the fourteen-year-old king, those of the beleaguered group in the Tower no less than those of the peasants.

Preceded by Aubrey de Vere, holding the sword of state, and followed by only a small escort, including his grown-up step-brothers, John and Thomas Holland, and Robert de Vere, Richard rode across the drawbridges and out through the main gate. It seems to have been decided that he would agree to the peasants' most vociferous demand, 'freedom from every manner of serfdom', while doing everything he could to protect his friends' lives, a tall order for anyone of any age in the nerve-racking circumstances, but one that the young king began by fulfilling bravely.

As Richard left the Tower a man called Thomas Farringdon sprang forward, seized the royal bridle and demanded immediate vengeance on the treasurer, Sir Robert Hales. It was with both tact and spirit that

Richard replied, saying the rebels should have all that was just, then broke away and rode on. But later in the morning when he faced the terrifying hordes that awaited him at Mile End, his resolve was to crumble and give way. For his promise to grant charters of manumission to everyone did not satisfy the majority of peasants, and expressions of pleasure were drowned in a rising tide of demands for the heads of the 'traitors'. Richard was virtually helpless among them, the very small escort with which he had left the Tower having been further diminished when, for some reason now lost to us, the Holland brothers had fled on the way to Mile End. In this very frightening situation it seems that he weakened and granted them, if not exactly what they asked for, the next best thing. The *Anonimalle Chronicle*, which is generally favourable to Richard, tells us he replied that: 'They might go through all the realm of England and catch all traitors and bring them to him in safety, and then he would deal with them as the law demanded. Under colour of this grant Wat Tyler and the commons took their way to the Tower to seize the archbishop ...'

According to the city corporation's account, Richard's betrayal went further: 'Our lord the king granted that they might take those who were traitors against him and put them to death, wheresoever they might be found.' Whatever the exact words of Richard's reply, the rebels took them to mean royal assent, and on hurrying back to the Tower they had no difficulty in convincing the guards that they had permission to enter.

They streamed across the lowered drawbridges and into the keep. Here their terrified victims were awaiting them, having been foiled in their attempt to escape while the coast was clear by rebels who had remained behind to watch the Tower while their fellows went to Mile End. When soon after Richard's departure for the meeting, Sudbury and several others had pushed off in a boat from the Little Watergate 'a wicked woman raised a cry against him and he had to turn back'. The manner in which at this point the royal councillors abandoned themselves to despair, making no further effort to save their lives by flight, suggests that they were indeed inept.

The archbishop led them up the spiral staircase to the chapel in the White Tower. Here, in the room which with its aisles and gallery and semi-circular east end can still be seen today, he gathered those whose lives, like his, were at risk, heard their confessions, then passed the remaining time preparing them to die according to the pious standards of the day. Their number would certainly have included Henry. 'He heard two masses or three, and chanted the Commendacione and the Placebo and the Dirige and the Seven Psalms and a Litany ...' Appropriately at about eleven o'clock he had just reached the too apposite words, 'Omnes sancti orate pro nobis', all saints pray for us, when the rebels burst into the chapel.

Sudbury himself, Hales, Gaunt's surgeon, Friar William Appleton, and two others were seized, buffeted, hustled out to Tower Hill and there cruelly beheaded. And then it was the turn of Henry, earl of Derby.

At fifteen, the boy could not possibly have been considered responsible for any of the government's policies but he still would have died for them had his assailant's hand not suddenly been stayed by one obscure man, John Ferrour of Southwark, who thus in a moment changed the course of history.

The miraculous nature of his rescue was to linger in Henry's mind so that nearly nineteen years later he would refer to Ferrour as having saved him 'in the midst of that commonalty in a wonderful and kind manner'. When he no longer expected it, he had escaped death by a hair's breadth. But it was no thanks to his cousin. Such would certainly have been Henry's indignant feeling. Richard had betrayed him, panicked and agreed to his death. Knowing that his own life was sacrosanct - since he was to be an intended part of the rebels' new society, 'King Richard and the true commons' - he had not saved his friends.

Looking back across the centuries at the history of the revolt, one's pity for the peasants is balanced by admiration for Richard's role in bringing the uprising to an end at yet another meeting with the rebels at Smithfield the following day. For no one has ever questioned the fact that it was his presence of mind and bravery which then saved the situation. A moment of terrible danger to the royal party arose when the mayor of London, William Walworth, lost his temper and thrust his sword through the clamorous Wat Tyler, filling the peasants with a sense of outraged betrayal. As their leader fell to the ground they set arrows to their bows and drew them. And it was in that second before they loosed that the boy king rode boldly forward with the famous words: 'You do not wish to shoot your king, do you? ... I am your king, I am your captain and your leader; follow me into the field and you shall have anything it pleases you to ask.'

This speech was so effective that the rebels immediately relaxed their hands on their bows, trustingly replaced the arrows in their quivers and obeyed, while taking advantage of this sudden lessening in tension the royal escort fled. Quite alone, Richard led the horde of suddenly docile rebels into Clerkenwell fields nearby, where he held them in parley for a considerable length of time. It was the strangest situation imaginable, an armed force seemingly held in check only by the power of the concept of kingship embodied in a frail youth, and Richard showed an extraordinary degree of courage.

He kept the rebels' attention long enough for Walworth to reach the city and return with an army which must have been mustering in the wards secretly during the past few days. And as the peasants in their turn fled for their lives before this sudden nightmare apparition of soldiers where no soldiers should be, Richard showed another quality of nobility. Those rebels who had not already taken to flight be ordered 'two knights to conduct ... through London and over London bridge without doing them harm, so that each of them could go to his own home'.

But this heroic impression was not the one likely to have remained uppermost in Henry's mind. For him, his cousin's behaviour in the Peasants' Revolt would have meant first and foremost a betrayal of trust, so that henceforth something valuable had gone from their relationship which could never be recaptured.

IV   VENGEANCE AND MURDERS

'It is ignoble for a king ... to take
vengeance by private murders.' John of
Gaunt, *Monk of Westminster's Chronicle*

In the eyes of the world Henry remained on the friendliest terms with the
king in an association whose closeness was to be splendidly displayed in
January 1382 when Richard's royal wedding festivities distracted the
country's attention from the tragic aftermath of the Peasants' Revolt. The
late summer of 1381 had been a bad time for the rebels. With Richard's
proclamation on 2 July that all charters of manumission 'lately issued in
haste' were withdrawn, all their high hopes seemed to have come to
naught, and worse. Their leaders were executed, swung from gibbets
shadowing the green countryside. And, although other justices in other
counties put down the rebellion far more mercifully, in Essex and
Hertfordshire the fiendish chief justice, Robert Tresilian, exacted a terrible
retribution; at Colchester alone he hanged nineteen men from a single
beam. And the king, who presided over Tresilian's courts, was rumoured to
have uttered a discouragingly vengeful jibe: 'You have been and are
villeins; in bondage you shall remain not as up to now, but incomparably
more debased!' So it was a relief when on 30 August he ordered that all
arrests and executions should cease, and when later in the year parliament
declared a general amnesty. By Christmas this sad chapter in social history
had been brought to a close, all the turmoil and all those lives lost
apparently for nothing.

In the nuptial ceremonies and celebrations Henry played a
spectacular part, first meeting the queen on her triumphant entry into
London. After running the gamut of winter storms in the Channel and
danger from hostile French and Spanish ships, fifteen-year-old Anne of
Bohemia had finally arrived outside London to be welcomed, among other
notabilities, by the earl of Derby and the younger of his two sisters, the
flighty Elizabeth of Lancaster, later to be renowned for her skill in singing
and dancing, and reviled for her lack of sexual morals. Henry was
disporting new long-pointed spurs in bronze, she perched on a red velvet
saddle embroidered with leopards. Brother and sister rode in the young

queen's escort over London Bridge, through the city and down the wide avenue of Cheap, past a wondrously ingenious wooden castle erected for Anne's delight with fountains that spouted wine, and towers from which damsels blew gold leaf that fell shimmering before her horse's hooves.

Four days later at Anne's coronation in Westminster Abbey - which followed her wedding in St. Stephen's chapel, Westminster Palace on 20 January - Henry was resplendent in a gown of 'gold cloth of damask' beneath a cloak of satin, charged with the gold leopards of England, both garments being presents from Constance, his Spanish stepmother.

In looks and demeanour during the ceremony he seems almost to have challenged King Richard; and in the celebrations afterwards he outshone him by jousting in a tournament. With silver-gilt spangles like roses on his armour he made his first recorded appearance of many in this much admired, but still sometimes hazardous sport; for flung violently from his horse, a man could suffer serious if not fatal injury. Richard is recorded as having ventured to joust once only, several years later, but Henry took to it with relish, his prowess in the jousts at Smithfield in 1386 even winning a mention in the *Chronicle of London*. In later years his prowess and daring in the lists were to become part of the reason for his popularity with the commons.

Henry now had all the possessions and accoutrements of an adult, a fashionable young lord, as we can see from the accounts of his receiver, the faithful Hugh Waterton, whose records for September 1381-82 happily still survive to give us a glimpse into the earl's style of life for this crucial year. No longer did he need to live with the other members of his family; he had a choice of several places of his own, a substantial house in London, St. David's in Fleet Street; and a 'wardrobe' in Coleman Street, in which to store the considerable paraphernalia required to maintain a fourteenth century great house. (It included such items as reserves of candlewax, spices, arms, harness and packs of cloth). Henry also owned three manors, Soham in Cambridgeshire, Daventry and Passenham in Northampton-shire. And to care for all this extra property his household had expanded to include a treasurer, yeoman of the chamber, clerks, squires, a keeper of the palfreys and an attorney.

But this appearance of total independence was an illusion. Unlike Richard, in most aspects of his life Henry remained very much under his father's control. The duke of Lancaster continued to subsidize his finances both in large and small ways, making up Henry's annual income of £426 9s. 11¾d. with a grant of 250 marks, and even contributing to Henry's largesse to the poor, as we learn from a revealing and fascinating entry.

On Thursday 3 April 1382, at Hertford Castle, Henry starred in a ceremony performed only by the monarch today, but which until the

Reformation was also carried out by noblemen and their families: the distribution of Maundy money, then a far more exacting ritual than it is now. His silken clothes well protected with an apron, he personally washed the feet of fifteen poor men, the number chosen to match his age, and when from his own money he gave alms of 12 pence each to two of these men, the accounts tell us it was 'by direction of my lord of Lancaster', who produced the 12 pence each for the other thirteen. Gaunt clearly was undertaking his son's education in such vital matters as the duty of the rich to bestow charity on the poor.

He was personally training his heir in other ways as well. On Gaunt's death Henry would acquire the greatest inheritance of any subject in the kingdom, lands which Gaunt had inherited through his father-in-law, the first duke of Lancaster. It is undoubtedly why most of Henry's time that year was spent, not in his own houses, but in one after another of his father's strongholds. Pontefract, Leicester, Lincoln, Kenilworth, Tutbury, Hertford, the great Lancastrian castles that strode in all directions across the kingdom, were visited in succession by the red-haired young earl. Henry was getting to know the wide lands that would one day be his and, more important, their tenants and retainers who would owe him feudal dues, rent or manual labour in return for protection against their enemies. It was a lesson Henry learned almost too well, to the extent in later years of protecting his own men even when they committed murder, rape and robbery, crimes for which he was personally to demand and receive their pardon from the king.

More justifiably, in the summer when he was sixteen we see him despatching Hugh Waterton to plead the cause of his tenants at Passenham before King Richard after they had been beaten in an affray initiated by Aubrey de Vere's tenants from neighbouring Stony Stratford.

The care that Henry bestowed upon the Lancastrian tenants during his tour of his father's estates this year was to pay rich dividends, for among those who lined the dusty roads to watch him ride past in 1382, were many who would hasten to join him when he invaded England in 1399.

In July we find Henry staying with his father at Lincoln Castle and presiding with him at a trial for heresy in Lincoln Cathedral to learn another lesson. Before the bishop stood William Swinderby, commonly known as 'the hermit', accused of spreading the Lollard doctrine of the 'hooded men' who, clad in russet gowns, wandered from one market place to another preaching against the established Church and refusing to remove their hoods during Mass before the Host. Although he had supported one very influential heretic, John Wyclif, when it suited him, Gaunt regarded lowly heretics like Swinderby as enemies of the establishment, and he treated them accordingly. When in his lordly presence the bishop pronounced 'the hermit' guilty, and ordered him to make public recantation in the cathedral and all the churches where he had preached, Gaunt conveyed his approval of the sentence. He had fulfilled one of his responsibilities as a baron, to superintend the maintenance of peace and order in the kingdom, a function Henry too would be expected to fulfil.

The great lords of England, Henry was to learn, had a right and a duty to partake in the government of their country, which meant acting as royal adviser, diplomat and leader of armies. Shortly afterwards, again in Gaunt's company, he was to discover what two of these roles meant in practice.

In December 1383 he sailed to Calais with his father and young uncle, Thomas of Woodstock, to negotiate a truce with the French. The outcome was the truce of Lelinghen, concluded on 26 January 1384 and unfortunately to last for no more than eight months.

In the spring of the same year Henry took part in an expedition against the Scots, supposedly to punish them for their recent aggression in which two days after the expiration of the current truce with England they had recaptured Lochmaben Castle in Dumfriesshire. With his father, commanding the English force, and accompanied by his uncle, Thomas of Woodstock, in April he rode through the Lowlands of Scotland at the head of an army that set torches to a few undefended villages, then on reaching the gates of Edinburgh demanded and received a ransom to save the city from a similar fate. The punishment Gaunt had meted out was mild. At this date more interested in peace than war with Scotland, he forbade all looting of the capital, and as an extra precaution allowed the citizens to remove their property before the English army entered the gates.

Henry's first military experience was soon over. He was back in England by 23 April, in time to attend the feast of St. George at Windsor with his father, stepmother and three legitimate sisters, all of them equally resplendent in violet furred with miniver and lined with scarlet, the robes issued to the Knights of the Garter and their families for that year.

When still only eighteen Henry acquired the finance needed to live up to his high rank; from 22 December 1384 he was able to claim the lucrative revenues of the earldoms of Hereford and Northampton, his wife, Mary de Bohun's, inheritance. These increased his yearly income to over £2,000, and in November of the following year he at last set up house with her in very grand style.

For much of the time they lived at Monmouth Castle in Wales, but should they tire of that, Gaunt had put at their disposal another castle gloriously situated on its great man-made defensive lake, Kenilworth, in Warwickshire. They had, besides, Henry's house called St. David's in Fleet

Street, London, and especially favoured by Mary, a manor at Peterborough. While to see to their comfort and draw attention to their importance, they were attended by a large retinue of retainers, including two trumpeters, wearing livery of red and white, the royal colours, to which Henry was entitled by virtue of his nearness to the throne. Senior officers of his household wore the silver-gilt collars patterned with the letter S, already a favourite Lancastrian badge.

Through Waterton's accounts for 30 September 1387-88 we learn something of the appearance and interests of the two young people. Henry ordered for himself a gold garter adorned with hawthorn leaves, another of his favourite badges; also gowns of satin, red cloth and scarlet, jousting armour and a grey courser, perhaps the first of the 'white' horses that were to become one of his distinguishing marks. At the same time Mary bought an armilaus, or cape, adorned with harebells, yet another of Henry's badges. And as an indication of how this young couple spent their leisure time together, there are records of a set of silver chess men, and for Mary a pet parrot and little dogs adorned with collars of green and white check silk with silver-gilt letters and bells. Most revealing, for the light it sheds on their relationship, is the fact that they shared a love of music, Mary playing a cithar and a canticum, and Henry a ricordo, or flute.

In the late summer of 1387 the second of their seven children, the future King Henry V, was born, to be followed the next year by Thomas, born in London. Both babies were wrapped in gowns of scarlet and red tartaryn for every day, and red and white satin for best.

So by the age of twenty-one Henry was a great lord in his own right, yet the accounts list an item which shows him still curiously under the influence of his father: numbered among Mary's household and clearly put there to rule over it, was Gaunt's mistress, ex-governess of Henry's sisters, Katherine, Lady Swynford, who had such a gift for organising noble households that she was eventually in her old age to be put in charge of the future Henry V's establishments. Among the countess of Derby's retainers she was a superior figure, wearing Henry's livery of red and white, but adorned with miniver, and with her came her legitimate son, Thomas Swynford, and her daughter by Gaunt, Joan Beaufort. It seems that even now Henry was not yet truly independent, that for all his splendour, he still lived to a certain extent in the shadow of the great duke.

Richard's position as he emerged from boyhood was naturally very different. No one blocked his light; quite the contrary. Used as he was since the age of ten to presiding on a dais while even the most exalted of his subjects bent the knee to him three times, he had been encouraged by the men around him to make this appearance of power a reality as soon as possible. They taught him to regard any attempt by parliament to control his choice of ministers or his expenditure as a trespass on his royal prerogative, a view for which some of the blame must go to Gaunt, but most undoubtedly should rest with Richard's tutor, Sir Simon Burley.

Generally considered to have been the chief influence upon Richard in his childhood, and described by Gervase Mathew as 'possibly in some sense' his mother's 'lover', Burley was well liked by those who really knew him. Froissart regarded him as 'a gentle knight and of strong good sense', while Richard described him as 'our beloved and faithful knight' and was devoted to him. A lover of culture and luxury, he possessed an exceptionally large number of books for the day, no less than twenty-one, all in French except for one single manuscript, *The Romance of the Forester and the Wild Boar*.

He had acquired in the royal service castles, manors, lands and lucrative offices, and he flaunted his wealth, riding about the country with a band of retainers clad in gold and fine scarlet, attending on his pupil in gowns so resplendent that the *Kirkstall Chronicle* tells us he had 'no peer in the splendour of his apparel'. His vast wardrobe included 'eight fur cloaks or gowns ... five long and six short gowns ... a tabard of scarlet with a sleeve embroidered with the sun and letters of gold and lined with white tartarine; a coat of white leather, embroidered with stakes (his heraldic badge) and with fifty-four gilt buttons', apart from surcoats, doublets, hats, sleeves and gilded jousting armour.

Revelling in such personal splendour and importance for himself, in a similar manner he aimed at the maximum possible authority and magnificence for his charge. Richard's tutor is generally regarded by historians as having been the chief architect of the manoeuvring for monarchical power that took place between the years 1381 and 1385, measures which were to lead to the Appellants' Revolt of 1387, and the first serious confrontation between Richard and Henry.

The manoeuvring began in response to parliament's actions when it met that November in the wake of the Peasants' Revolt. Alarmed at the catastrophe that had so narrowly been averted, parliament sought to solve the problems that had led to the uprising by imposing new controls on the king. Believing that maladministration of the royal finances had led to the need for the disastrous poll tax, it turned its attention to the running of the king's household, complaining of the 'outrageous' number of people living there and insisting on the appointment of a commission of enquiry into the influences on the young king. A dual role, summed up in the records as 'pur survere et examiner en prive conseil si bien l'estat et governaill de la persone nostre di seigneur come de son dit hostiel, et de lour adviser des remedes suffisantz'. Illustriously headed by Gaunt and the archbishops, the commission appointed two guardians, the earl of Arundel and Michael de la Pole, to live with, 'counsel and govern' him.

It was an imposition indeed for the self-willed royal youth, and one he must have found both offensive and ungrateful. For it was through no action of parliament's that the Peasants' Revolt had been quelled. He alone had saved England by his resourcefulness and courage at Smithfield. It seems that Burley found the new restrictions forced on his charge, who had acquitted himself so well, equally insupportable. For efforts were soon successfully made to get rid of them.

By the following year Richard had somehow dispensed with one of his guardians, the tactlessly crude and aggressively nationalistic earl of Arundel, who was to become one of his most hated enemies; while the other guardian, Michael de la Pole, had yielded to royal blandishments to become his lifelong ally.

Within three years the regal power had taken another dramatic step forward: all five of the great officers of state, chancellor, treasurer, chamberlain, keeper of the privy seal and the steward, who with the king's councillors substantially governed the country, were now the king's men, willing to take orders from no other source. And there had been instituted a radically new department, the signet office, in which highly educated clerks of the Chapel Royal used the king's own personal seal to authenticate documents, thus enabling him to bypass the officers of state whenever he wished.

What has been called Richard's 'first tyranny' was thus established. While his cousin Henry continued to be dominated by his father, Richard was well on the way to becoming an autocrat.

But his adolescence was not all such serious stuff. Under Burley's tuition Richard had learnt well how to enjoy himself. Freed from parliamentary restraint on his expenditure, he was able to lavish grants of lands and lucrative offices on his friends, much needed comforts on his primitive palaces, adding to these rambling, draughty, insanitary abodes a little basic plumbing, heating and new kitchens. Most fastidious of English medieval kings, he gave to Sheen a magnificent room, 'the King's Bath', decorated with two thousand painted tiles, and in his courtiers' rooms there, constructed private latrines and even fireplaces. In Eltham he installed a new bath house, as well as 'spicery', 'saucery', and, ultimate refinement, a 'private saucery'. At King's Langley the bath house was enlarged to include ten glazed windows and a large oven beneath to heat the water. There were more glamorous items as well - at Eltham Palace a painted chamber, a dancing chamber, windows of stained glass and a new garden 'for the pleasure of the king and queen'; at King's Langley, chambers for de Vere and Mowbray and a 'queen's garden'. While across the water from Sheen Palace on the island of La Neyt in the Thames, there arose a luxurious timber-framed dwelling where the king, the queen, whom he adored, with her Bohemian ladies and their friends could enjoy themselves hidden from the public eye.

There they led a life of parties, flirtations and extravagant fashions in manners as well as in dress that appealed to Richard's sophisticated taste for colour and drama. They celebrated not only the love of women but also brother love between men, that medieval ideal so misunderstood today, and described by Geoffrey Chaucer in his *Knight's Tale* of Palamon and Arcite. Recreating Eleanor of Aquitaine's court of love, they played mysterious games of the leaf and the flower, while the king at the same time made an elaborate display of his affection for de Vere. It was a frivolous, hedonistic atmosphere, observed with disgust by that vitriolic, warmongering Benedictine monk, Walsingham, who believed the proper place for any self-respecting king was on the field of battle in France, winning back the lost empire. In his chronicle he summed up this young court as 'more knights of Venus than of Bellona (goddess of war), more valiant in the marriage bed than in the field, better armed with the tongue than with the lance'.

Careless of such old men's carping, Richard's courtiers swaggered about in gowns so voluminous that their hems trailed on the tiled floors, or doublets so short that they offended current standards of decency; in sleeves that touched the ground and collars that seemed to stretch the neck 'as though preparing it for the axe'. So long and pointed were their spurs, a contemporary poet scoffs, that they dared not kneel in chapel for fear of spiking their hose and they 'staggered when they walked as though buffeted by the wind'. Richard himself was responsible for what seemed at the time one of the strangest of new fashions. Listed among his expenses are: 'parvis peciis factis ad liberandum domino regi ad portandum in manu suo pro naso suo tergendo et mundando', for small pieces (of cloth) made to give to the lord king to carry in his hand to wipe and clean his nose; his courtiers were content to use their sleeves.

It was in vain that parliament, on 20 October 1385, criticized Richard's expenditure once more, forcing him to agree to the establishment of a committee of enquiry into the royal finances, for parliament's power then lasted only as long as it sat. It was up to the king in the fourteenth century to decide when to call it again. And when the parliament of 1385 was dissolved Richard's chancellor, de la Pole, simply saw to it that the committee Richard had been compelled to give his assent to was never able to meet. De la Pole, like Burley, was a key member of what has come to be called the curialist party, believing in the supreme authority of the king in anything to do with the royal household, a party not as undemocratic as it might seem today, since at this date parliament represented such a tiny proportion of the English people.

But influenced and advised by these men though he was, Richard was far from being merely their pawn. Maturing in understanding far more quickly than Henry, he had learned by the age of seventeen to consider the government of England to be his own particular responsibility, as we can see from the fiery and undignified exchange between him and the earl of Arundel in the parliament that met at Salisbury in April 1384.

The earl, who had become by the export of wool one of the wealthiest of English subjects, felt he had a right to a voice in the government of the kingdom, and by virtue of having been briefly Richard's guardian may also have felt entitled to criticize his ex-charge. Now he roundly accused the seventeen-year-old king of misgovernment. His royal pride deeply hurt by what he regarded as the earl's impertinent and insulting manner to God's appointed minister, Richard told the earl to go to the devil, adding for good measure that he was a liar.

Fortunately, John of Gaunt had been able to calm them both down, but the king was not grateful for his uncle's interference. Indeed, this attempt to dominate him as Gaunt dominated his own son filled the touchy, headstrong Richard with loathing in place of gratitude. This feeling was encouraged by the ever present Robert de Vere and other young royal favourites, like Thomas Mowbray, earl of Nottingham, known at this date as the king's 'consodalis et coaetaneus', boon companion and contemporary.

Richard's ungrateful treatment of Henry's beloved father was to be yet another spur to the growing hostility between the cousins, for although Gaunt was struggling to do all he could to fulfil the oath he had made to his brother, the Black Prince, to 'comfort and defend' his royal nephew and 'to maintain him in his right', all his efforts met with rudeness, and worse. Richard was soon deliberately to put Gaunt's life in danger. It seems that the king's confident young friends, anxious to keep him to themselves and infuriated by a member of the older generation who was always giving him advice, whether or not it was requested, had by one means or another persuaded him that the duke was a traitor, aware that rumour had already made the king susceptible to this suspicion.

Richard was an even more than usually hot-headed youth. At seventeen suspicion alone was enough to cause him to act suddenly and violently, and in April 1384 Gaunt narrowly escaped execution at his command, according to the Monk of Westminster, who describes what appear to be two plots against the duke's life, one of which is alleged to have had royal approval, if not connivance.

Describing the first incident, which occurred during the eventful Salisbury parliament in April 1384, the monk gives us an eye-witness report, that of Sir John Clanvowe, a knight of the king's chamber, who was later to become known for his heretical Lollard opinions.

Richard had gone into de Vere's chamber for Mass when suddenly the Irish friar who was to celebrate it asked permission to speak. This having been granted, he blurted out a terrible accusation. Gaunt, he declared, was at the head of a widespread conspiracy to murder the king,. At once, and without even demanding proof, Richard in a fury ordered his uncle to be put to death. Luckily there were other lords present of a more sober turn of mind, who managed to persuade Richard that the evidence should be examined. When this was done no facts were discovered to incriminate Gaunt, but neither was anything found to pinpoint the originator of the accusation. The sequel was even more disturbing.

The friar who had caused the trouble was placed in the custody of John Holland, who in the presence of Richard's chamberlain and seneschal tortured him so terribly that he died a few days later in Sarum castle, and without divulging the names of any confederates. An analysis of those involved in his arrest and torture makes it seem probable that he was deliberately killed before he could be persuaded to name de Vere, the obvious suspect. Strangely, the friar's torment greatly affected Richard who, on hearing it, 'uttered troubled groans and sighs from the bottom of his heart'; with sorrow for this pathetic victim of *hautes politiques*, or perhaps fear that his beloved friend might be implicated, but certainly with no sympathy for Gaunt, if we can judge from a series of incidents the following year. According to the Monk of Westminster Richard's favourite planned to murder the duke during a tournament there but was foiled when his intended victim, alerted just in time, fled secretly from the palace. On the facts becoming known, it was expected that the king would at least show public disapproval of the would-be assassins; but far from fulfilling this expectation, he continued to share his pastimes with them, demanded no explanations and made no public excuses, behaving as though the attempted murder of the greatest baron in England was of no consequence.

Even Richard's own councillors were shocked, and at a council meeting at Westminster took him to task for his shameful behaviour. Their spokesman, William Courtenay - the prelate Gaunt had once insulted in St. Paul's Cathedral, and now archbishop of Canterbury - accused the king of having been himself privy to the plot and warned him of the consequences. Through such a bad example, he declared, law and order would suffer and strife and trouble of all kinds would arise throughout the land ... he must abstain from such wrong doing in future lest the whole realm be injured.

Not surprisingly, Courtenay's words infuriated the hot-blooded young king, who leapt to his feet with wild threats. And when, by chance, he again met his critic afloat on the Thames - both were returning at the same time from dining out - reflection had not cooled his anger. As the gilded barges, bright with heraldic emblems, drew close, then came alongside each other, with more courage than sense the archbishop seized the opportunity to expand on his theme, shouting his disapproval from boat to boat.

In response, Richard drew his sword. And on being forcibly restrained by his companions, Thomas of Woodstock, Sir John Devereux and Sir Thomas Trivet, from striking Courtenay, the king in a fury turned the blade on them instead with a look of such purpose that all three jumped for their lives out of the king's and into the prelate's barge.

This unseemly scene on the river had a sequel. For like the archbishop, Gaunt was also to protest at Richard's attitude to the conspirators, and Henry would almost certainly have been a witness. The king was at Sheen on 24 February when his uncle suddenly arrived in armour with a large retinue, his visit planned like a military exploit, his retreat well guarded. Before entering the palace he posted sentries by the river bank, others to watch his boat, still others at the palace gates to prevent anyone entering or leaving, precautions that were a reproach in themselves.

However, once in the royal presence his words, as given by the chronicler, reveal beneath the indignation a deep loyalty to Richard, and more interesting and illuminating still, a belief in the king's independence of all other authority. To his erring nephew Gaunt is reported to have said: 'It is ignoble for a king ... to take vengeance by private murders, when he is himself above the law and has it in his power to grant life and limb and even if he chooses to take them away at his pleasure ... so excellent a person should have about him good and faithful counsellors.'

From the tone of this speech we can presume that among the lessons Gaunt taught his receptive son was belief in the royal prerogative, and duty to the king. If so, the latter was to be severely tested once again that year. For although Richard is said to have replied to his uncle's lecture with soft and sweet words and promised to act more justly in future, beneath the mild facade the hidden hostility festered, to burst out again that August during yet another punitive expedition into Scotland, a more genuine one on this occasion, led by the king himself. Marching with the army were both Henry and de Vere, the latter still busy poisoning Richard's mind against the great duke.

As before, the Scots avoided the hazards of pitched battle, while the English on this *chivauchée* burnt not only crops and houses but also three magnificent abbeys, Melrose, Newbattle and Holyrood, on their way to Edinburgh. Having reached this city, the king called a council to decide what should be done next, declaring that he himself was anxious about his supplies, and was in favour of turning back. Gaunt insisted that they should, on the contrary, proceed across the Firth of Forth, and argument flared. Richard, losing his mercurial temper, shouted that he and his men were going back. Gaunt could please himself, he was a traitor who cared only for his own purse, not the king's. One can imagine the violent feelings such an unjustified accusation would have evoked in Gaunt's son.

While the duke was prepared to forgive this vicious jibe, indulgent as ever to his nephew's youth, Henry's reaction is likely to have been one of towering resentment, especially as his father's situation, through no fault of his own, was now almost intolerable. Richard clearly distrusted him and was prepared to use any means at all, however dishonourable, to oust him from power. Perhaps some confrontation between the cousins might have erupted at this point had not luck, always the duke's friend, stepped in to rescue him.

When it looked as though Gaunt's role as the most important man on the political stage was finished, that he would be forced to abandon the limelight he loved to retire to obscurity in his country castles, developments in the Iberian peninsula transformed his situation.

On his return to England with the army, envoys from Portugal awaited him with a proposal that offered a chance to fulfil his greatest ambition, to transform his dreamed-of castles in Spain into reality. Edmund of Langley's expedition in 1381 had brought this no nearer, but now everything was changed.

In August 1385 Portuguese forces under the regent, the future King John I, had vanquished the Spaniards under King Juan I in a battle at Aljubarotta, the envoys announced. The position could not be more favourable to their joint interests. Should Gaunt at this time come to their aid, together they could follow up this victory to their mutual advantage: the Portuguese could inflict total defeat on their enemy; Gaunt could finally make good his wife's claim to Castile and Leon. With little argument, Gaunt agreed to their proposition.

For Richard the Portuguese proposal was a godsend, an opportunity to rid himself of his overbearing uncle for many months. Overnight his attitude to Gaunt became changed apparently from cold to effusively loving and approving, and the feeling was catching; suddenly with the prospect of seeing the last of him for a while every one liked the duke of Lancaster.

During the next few months Henry saw his father fêted instead of reviled. The time passed in euphoric preparations. The parliament voted him a subsidy for his expedition, Richard lent him money - a thousand marks from his own coffers - and treading in the footsteps of his grandfather, Edward III, he presented Gaunt and Constance with crowns of gold. With commendable foresight he even had a treaty drawn up between the King of England and the 'King of Castile and Leon' which bound their descendants to perpetual alliance.

The Pope in Rome was quick to take advantage of the situation, too. Urban VI, unwilling to miss a chance of harming his rival, Pope Clement in Avignon, who held the allegance of the Spaniards, sent Gaunt a holy banner, pronounced his expedition a crusade and declared that those who helped to finance it would earn special remission of their sins. Throughout England town criers proclaimed the papal message, while the bishops of Llandaff and Hereford, riding up and down the kingdom, eagerly exchanged papal indulgences from their servants' packs for more immediately obvious benefits, money to pay soldiers and buy weapons.

Gaunt himself impressed ships, carpenters and sailors, while the women of his family excitedly prepared their wardrobes. No less than five of them were to accompany him: Constance, of course, whose claim to the throne he was about to make good, and his three legitimate daughters, because new ambitions had blossomed in the duke's mind. For Catherine and Philippa he planned royal marriages; and Elizabeth he probably took with him to prevent her from getting into even more trouble in his absence. Far less amenable than his other daughters, although for years the promised bride of the earl of Pembroke, Elizabeth was now scandalously pregnant by the king's half-brother, John Holland, and Gaunt had to take time off from his preparations to see them respectably wed. Not that Gaunt himself took such moral peccadilloes too seriously, to judge from the identity of another member of his party: his illegitimate daughter, Blanche, with her husband, Sir Thomas Morieux, also travelled with him. It was a truly representative family expedition.

Although Henry was left behind, he was not left out of the preparations, since he was to look after the Lancastrian lands and the administration of the County Palatine in his father's absence. The only one of his father's legitimate children not to accompany him, Henry rode with his father to Plymouth and saw him set sail on 7 July 1386. When the sails of Gaunt's fleet of seventy-seven ships dwindled into the summer sky, Henry, at the tender age of 20, and with every reason to feel hostility towards the king, had the great Lancastrian power at his command, a power that could shake and even topple the royal throne.

V THE FIVE LORDS MARCH

'I saw the host of the five lords march
through the city on their way to London
from the battlefield; whereof the earls of
Warwick and Derby led the van.' Adam
of Usk, *Chronicon*

Gaunt's departure for Portugal removed the most dominating personality
from the stage of English politics, so that hitherto minor characters were
suddenly free to take his place in the limelight. There strode to the fore
three barons, one of them closely related to Henry and so bound to have a
strong influence on him in the absence of his father. Chief among these
three was Henry's youngest uncle, the aggressive thirty-one-year-old
Thomas of Woodstock, duke of Gloucester, last of Edward III's five tall
sons to reach maturity, but far from the least significant. The fact that in
Gaunt's absence Gloucester was the most powerful lord in the land was a
matter of personality as much as status; for although he was thirteen years
younger than his next brother, Edmund of Langley, duke of York, he was
more impressive, described in Hardyng's chronicle as 'full of corage',
where Edmund is represented as 'full of gentylnesse' and 'a prince who
loves his ease and little business'. Unlike the mild tempered York, his
younger brother was perpetually engaged in angry confrontation.

Gloucester was a man of strange contrasts, which are well summed
up in the little illumination in the *Liber Benefactorum* of St. Albans, painted
after his visit to the abbey in February 1388 and still to be seen glowing
forth from old vellum in the British Library. This shows him gorgeously
clad in a pink gown with a white-fur-trimmed, blue mantle, a gold coronet
in his fair hair, offering to the abbey an object of rare beauty, 'a gold circlet
in the middle of which a white swan (his favourite badge) has its wings
outstretched as though about to fly'. But the face between the fashionably
curled hair and forked beard is strangely grim. Gloucester was a man with
a taste for beautiful objects. His favourite abode of Pleshy Castle in Essex
was full of splendid things. There was a bed said to be worth the princely
sum then of £182 3s., with blue satin curtains patterned in gold garters,
and there were numerous fine tapestries depicting romantic or religious

subjects: sets describing the crusades of Godfrey of Bouillon and Charlemagne; portrayals of "the history of the battle between Gamalayn and Launcelot"; ... jousts; a mythical knighting; "the history of an assault made on ladies in a castle"; and "the history of a discomfiture of a Wodewose (wild man of the woods) and a Lion and other histories". In Pleshy Castle alone his library held eighty-three fine books, a great number for the time, mostly in French and Latin - apart from those in his chapel there and in his house in London.

Yet nothing satisfied Gloucester. Certainly not his finances which came largely from royal grants, instead of that more certain base, great estates of his own; and certainly not the government of the country. He was convinced that he could do better, outspokenly criticising Richard, whom he despised as an incompetent ruler. It seems that even his grand status gave him little pleasure, for in later life he was to become austere in his personal habits, a man who 'sat little at dinner and supper'. His redeeming qualities included intense patriotism and a great loyalty to Gaunt. When, after the friar's accusation at Salisbury in 1384, Richard had ordered Gaunt killed, Gloucester had rushed into the king's room, drawn his sword and threatened to kill anyone who accused his elder brother of treason.

From a twentieth century viewpoint a curiously unattractive character, at the time his honesty of purpose was to make him seem to many of his compatriots 'the best of men' and 'the hope and solace of the whole community of the realm'. Gloucester's closest political ally, the earl of Arundel, lacked his cultural interests but otherwise was of similar temperament, for both men became very pious, each founding next his castle wall a college of secular priests, dedicated to the Holy Trinity. Even more austere than Gloucester, Arundel was to stipulate in his will that he was to be buried without pomp, an unusual request at a time when elaborate torchlit funeral processions were the fashion for the rich. Like Gloucester, the earl of Arundel disapproved of Richard whose guardian he had been appointed when Richard was fourteen and whom he was inclined to scold in public as if he were a naughty boy.

But unlike Gloucester, Arundel possessed great landed wealth. Processions of wooden wheeled carts and barges, laden with sacks of wool from his vast estates in Sussex, Surrey and the Welsh Marches, regularly travelled the roads and rivers of England to be shipped over to the wool staple in Holland or Calais. Though not as closely related to Henry as his uncle of Gloucester, Arundel was connected to the young earl by marriage, his sister being the countess of Hereford, Henry's mother-in-law.

The third baron in what was to be described by the chronicler, Favent, as 'the indivisible trio' of lords was Thomas, earl of Warwick, some years older than Gloucester and Arundel and a more genial and generous character than either of these men. In his will the earl was appealingly to order for himself, not only a sumptuous funeral, but also a good supper to follow for everyone who attended. He is best known for Guy's Tower, his romantic addition to Warwick Castle, which has survived the ravages of time and the Civil War to delight us still on the green banks of the river Avon, a tower that was probably named after his mythical ancestor, Guy of Warwick, whose adventures were embroidered on the castle's tapestries. If we can believe the illumination in the *Liber Benefactorum*, which shows the earl kneeling beside his wife in a plain red robe, his short brown hair unfashionably straight, he was an honest and simple man, although as was later to become apparent, sometimes easily manipulated by his two friends. All three of the 'indivisible trio' were eminent members of the nobility. Warwick had been brought up at court and had held high command in Edward III's wars in France under John of Gaunt and Edmund of Langley, then in 1377 he had been appointed admiral of the north. In his youth Arundel had been a knight of Edward's household, so devoted that he had made the king a substantial loan in March 1377. Appointed admiral of the west that same year, he had joined Gaunt in his unsuccessful siege of St. Malo the following summer, and in June 1381 he had been made chancellor after Simon Sudbury's murder by the peasant rebels.

Gloucester, appointed constable of England in 1376, had been created earl of Buckingham by Richard the next year. In November 1378 he had commanded the naval expedition that relieved Brest and captured eight Castilian ships. Having commanded the forces that suppressed the Peasants' Revolt in Essex, two and a half years later he had conducted diplomatic negotiations with the French. Richard had created him a duke the following year.

The three barons were typical of the old nobility who felt themselves unjustly and offensively elbowed aside by the new men at court, the clever and fashionable curialists whom Richard now called to his council in their place, and on whom he lavished his favour at their expense. To one of his new men, his receiver of the chamber, John Beauchamp of Holt, Richard had even given manors, lands and offices in Worcestershire and North Wales, regions that the earls of Warwick and Arundel regarded as their own spheres of influence. It seemed to them that no position was too high for Richard's upstarts to aspire to, and they had humiliating evidence of the revolutionary new royal policy in this regard.

When in 1385 Richard had created his two younger uncles, Edmund of Langley and Thomas of Woodstock, respectively dukes of York and Gloucester, he spoiled the taste of this honour for them by bestowing an earldom on a man of much lower rank, a mere banneret. His chancellor, Sir Michael de la Pole, became earl of Suffolk, acquiring at the same time many of the estates of William Ufford, earl of Suffolk, whose death without issue at Westminster in 1382, had brought the direct male line of this noble family to an end.

No less offensive to establishment figures like Gloucester, Arundel and Warwick, had been the elevation in the same year of Robert de Vere, earl of Oxford, who, although already higher in rank than de la Pole and so in their eyes more suited to the highest honours, had nevertheless done nothing whatsoever to deserve them. The career of the 'king's kinsman' had so far been distinguished only by the king's favour; yet Richard had created a whole new rank for him, that of marquis, a title never before used in England; and in parliament had bestowed the gift so lovingly that it must have made most of the other lords writhe. The parliament rolls record that he commanded him 'with a glad countenance to sit in a higher place among the peers of parliament, between the dukes and earls, and the marquis at once gratefully did this'.

One can visualise the smile that flashed between the two high-born youths, feel the outrage of the displaced earls and the disapproval of the dukes and, in particular, the disgust of Henry, earl of Derby who is unlikely to have enjoyed the sight of this unjustifiable elevation of his father's enemy only such a short time ago involved in a plot to murder John of Gaunt. In this atmosphere it would be easy for Gloucester and Arundel (Warwick was to join them later) to organize opposition to the king and the curialist party. However, it would be wrong to ascribe to the two lords motives purely of jealousy and pique, for these were only a small part of the picture. They sincerely believed that what stirred them to thoughts of revolution in the autumn of 1386 was evidence of misgovernment so bad that the existence of the country was imperilled. Certainly appearances were on their side, for within weeks of Gaunt's sailing to Portugal in July disaster had loomed over the horizon.

While Richard with his young friends in fantastic summer clothes paid tribute to the goddess of love on the island of La Neyt, across the Channel the god of war was being entertained by his enemy and near contemporary, the seventeen-year-old King Charles VI. The young French king was raising a vast army to invade England, and by 11 August he himself was on the move for the port of Sluys in Flanders, where his forces were to embark. So confident of success was he that he had already had built a portable camp of huts made of oak in Normandy and Brittany, which he planned to ship over the Channel and set up on the English shore to accommodate his troops. Seemingly it would only be a matter of weeks before this great force set sail and then, with Gaunt and his army out of the country, it would be England's turn to have her crops and villages burnt and her people slaughtered in a retaliation for the bloody havoc she had visited on France.

Although King Richard must have been aware of French intentions, he moved to defend England only at the eleventh hour, and even then, the preparations were ill-planned. Placed in charge of defence at this late stage were de la Pole and the royal favourite, de Vere, both lacking military experience and hopeless choices for the task.

Gloucester and Arundel, whose experience of soldiering in France made them natural leaders in Gaunt's absence, were given only the comparatively humble task of heading the county 'commissions of array' to help raise the army de la Pole and de Vere tardily ordered mustered. (As his own personal offering, Arundel was able to bring a small retinue of 95 men-at-arms and 341 archers, and Derby 249 men-at-arms and 314 archers, little enough, but a worthwhile contribution of trained soldiers.) Desperately de la Pole and de Vere ordered the posting of sentries on the south coast and beacons piled high to signal news of the invasion from hilltop to hilltop. Evidently they were from the start resigned to the prospect of French troops landing on English soil, for they stationed the newly mustered army near London, thus in effect surrendering the whole of southern England before an arrow was shot, or a knight unhorsed.

So real was the fear of invasion that the houses and other buildings which during the long years of peace had been allowed to grow up on the exterior of the city walls were hastily demolished and cleared away so as not to give aid to an attacking force; and at Canterbury, the jewelled shrine of St. Thomas Becket was lovingly dismantled, packed in a wagon and trundled over the rutted roads to Dover Castle for safety. The abbot of Westminster and two of his monks bought themselves suits of armour and prepared to defend the coast by themselves.

It was in the end luck, combined with muddle and jealousy among the French, that saved England. A storm sank a number of French ships as they approached the rendezvous at Sluys, and the cargo of wooden huts, bound by sea for the same harbour, was captured as it sailed past Sandwich by an English fleet commanded by the earl of Northumberland's son, later to achieve fame as Henry Hotspur. The huts were triumphantly carried back to Sandwich and there pressed into use as defences. But most important of all, the troops of the royal duke of Berry failed to arrive at their rendezvous, he being envious it was said of the authority of his brother Philip, duke of Burgundy. Berry did not lead his men into Sluys until 14 October, when it was too late in the year to risk the French fleet in the uncertain weather of the English Channel. With his deliberately delayed arrival the danger of invasion was over.

But this near escape had underlined the inadequacies of Richard and his advisers, and it had been costly. The crisis receded, but left an aftermath of sullen unease that autumn. To begin with, there was the problem of the soldiers who, mustered to fight the French, were now roaming through the home counties in search of food and plunder. Then there was the problem of money. The soldiers would need to be paid before they would go home. So Richard's subjects would have to find more taxes in addition to all they had already paid during his reign, and if the French were to be deterred from massing again for invasion next spring more money still would be needed to mount an English expedition against them. The king's coffers were nearly empty as usual, the English economy was in a mess. In the Middle Ages a king was expected to pay the expenses of government from his own revenue, applying to parliament for extra taxes only in national emergencies, but throughout Richard's reign, although taxation became increasingly burdensome, he had nothing to show for it. Unlike Edward III, whose tax-expensive armies had at least resulted in the great victories of Crécy and Poitiers, with a stream of spoils flooding into the country.

Good government in the fourteenth century was based on careful management of the royal finances, but it seemed to Gloucester, Arundel and their friends that Richard's were being squandered and embezzled by his favourites. It seemed that men like de Vere and de la Pole were ruining the country. They must be removed; there were plenty of other people, both lords and commons, to agree with this judgement.

So Gloucester, Arundel and their faction prepared to attack the royal entourage in the parliament that a desperate need for taxes had forced Richard to summon to Westminster on 1 October 1386.

The so-called Wonderful Parliament opened in the White Hall with the customary speech from the chancellor. Michael de la Pole made what was intended to be a popular announcement. Owing to rumours that he was personally reluctant to go to war the king had decided of his own will to cross the sea to lead an army against the French. To pay for this he asked parliament to grant him four fifteenths, that is, four times the subsidy usually demanded at the time for such military expeditions.

Parliament was not impressed and instead of the plaudits and eager offer of money that Richard had hoped for, the Lords and Commons responded with loud complaints of maladministration of the royal funds, and demands for reform of the royal household, not at all what they had been summoned for. In a fury at what he regarded as their impertinence, Richard behaved in a most unkingly way. He ordered his attendants to pack and moved out of Westminster, leaving parliament to continue its debates without him, in so doing, since the king was an integral part of parliament, robbing it of the power to interfere with his household.

Richard then rode to Eltham Palace, whose tranquil appearance today belies its bustling medieval origins, with buildings then ranging round seven courtyards and two chapels, brilliant with painted glass. In this strategically placed dwelling from which he could view the grey spires and towers of London city in one direction and the main road to Dover in the other, the king prepared for a long and patient stay. Eltham, with its park for hunting, its little town at the bottom of the hill for supplies, and its gardens full of vines, was one of his favourite palaces and agreeable at all seasons of the year. Here he planned to wait until parliament made a move. It came almost at once. In the political game of chess that followed, envoys from both sides were to clatter constantly to and fro across the wooden bridge that spanned the moat between the Great Court and the Green Court. (A stone bridge still in existence was to replace it in the fifteenth century.) First, parliament sent a petition demanding that the king dismiss both his chancellor, de la Pole, and his treasurer, John Fordham, bishop of Durham, because 'they were not to the advantage of the king or kingdom'. The envoys added ominously that they had charges to bring against de la Pole that could not be made while he remained chancellor.

To Richard, the right to appoint his own chief officers of state was part of his almost sacred royal prerogative and, bursting into one of his characteristic rages, he declared that he would not at their demand dismiss even the meanest scullion in his kitchens. He added that instead of meddling in matters that were the king's business, parliament should concentrate on its own, meaning the raising of taxes. Parliament countered with the statement that they would proceed with nothing until the king himself returned to Westminster and consented to the dismissal of de la Pole. To this message, in a slightly more accommodating tone, the king replied suggesting that they should send forty of their members to negotiate.

Meanwhile, on 13 October he further infuriated the lords by raising de Vere's rank yet again, from marquis, a creation which had been unpopular enough, to duke of Ireland, and with this dukedom de Vere was granted palatine powers like Gaunt's. It did not matter to the lords that in Ireland these lofty sounding powers were only theoretical, the country being dominated by the chiefs of the 'wild Irish', all except for the very small area round Dublin known as the Pale, which England controlled. The grant still appeared to bestow on the 'king's kinsman' entirely unmerited acclaim, and at a time when de Vere was unpopular for another reason too. The new duke of Ireland had recently had the temerity to petition the pope for an annulment of his marriage to Gloucester's niece,

Philippa de Coucy, grand-daughter of Edward III, and this so that he could marry a mere queen's lady, Agnes Lancekrona, one of her frivolous, side-saddle riding Bohemians. Gloucester, and even his mild brother, Edmund of Langley, duke of York, regarded this as an insult to the blood royal and an outrage.

Under the influence of Gloucester and Arundel parliament decided on harsher measures. Instead of the forty representatives for which Richard had asked, there rode across the bridge just two lords with parliament's next message. They were the duke of Gloucester and the earl of Arundel's forceful and astute younger brother, Thomas, bishop of Ely, later to play an important part in restoring the fortunes of Henry, earl of Derby, when they were at their lowest ebb.

The continuation of *Knighton's Chronicle* has left us a full report of the dialogue between these lords and the king. Gloucester and Thomas Arundel began with comparative moderation. They begged Richard to return, but pointed out that if he did not do so parliament was entitled to disperse after forty days, without granting the taxes he needed; a threat, according to the chronicle, which Richard opposed with another more violent and extremely unwise one.

If parliament intended to refuse him the help he had asked for he would be compelled to seek it from his cousin, the King of France, he retorted impetuously. The implications of this for the kingdom were full of menace. And it was apparently in a mood of incredulous, furious indignation at the prospect of a king of England attempting to use French money, or perhaps even French troops, against his own parliament that its emissaries resorted to the last, most terrible weapon in their armoury.

Either he return to Westminster, or they would depose him.

It was quite feasible, they told him, for there was a precedent. An ancient statute stated the chilling concept: that 'if the king ... should alienate himself from his people, and should not be willing to be governed ... by the laws ... of the realm, with the wholesome advice of the lords and peers ... but should headily and wantonly by his own counsels work out his own private purposes, it should then be lawful for them ... to depose the king himself from the royal throne and elevate in his place some near kinsman of the royal line'.

What was probably the first hint of Gloucester's own royal ambitions was also checkmate for the king, who was forced to realize that the lords and knights of his parliament had seriously made up their minds to get rid of him if he would not do as they wished. Loath as he was to lose such officers as de la Pole and Fordham, he had no choice but to submit to parliament's demands. According to one chronicle he toyed briefly with the desperate notion of inviting to dinner all the lords opposing him, and there murdering them, but rejected the idea as impracticable.

So the king returned to Westminster to swallow the distasteful draught prepared for him. With deep reluctance he agreed that his two chief ministers should be deprived of office, that Thomas Arundel, bishop of Ely, and John Gilbert, bishop of Hereford, should be respectively appointed chancellor and treasurer in their place; and that his loyal ally, de la Pole, should be impeached. (Fortunately he was to suffer no worse punishment than to be confined for a period to Windsor Castle.)

But for the king there was even more painful humiliation to bear when, wrapping the steel of their demand in the customary velvet glove of respect, the Commons begged him 'most humbly for the honour of God and in maintenance of his crown and for the profit of his demesne ... that he would please to ordain and establish' a commission with powers to control the government of the kingdom. Although only to last for a year and to include moderates like Courtenay and Wykeham, the commission's mere existence was a defeat for what Richard with all his heart believed the monarchy should be. Even after the Peasants' Revolt parliament had not imposed on him a commission to govern the country. Even as a boy of fourteen, he had been burdened with fewer shackles.

The petition to which now, at the age of nineteen, he most unwillingly gave the required response 'le roy le voet', the king wills it, was to him an injustice and an insult, yet ringed round by politely hostile subjects, he made only one protest. 'By his own mouth' he declared that 'anything done in this parliament should not prejudice himself or his crown, so that the prerogative and the liberties of the said crown should be saved and guarded'.

It was decisive. He had been forced to agree to what he believed was nothing less than revolution but this declaration saved his freedom of action. Soon after parliament dissolved in November he made plans to restore the supremacy of the monarchy by every means in his power. Although first, he made plain his feelings about parliament. Choosing to celebrate his Christmas at Windsor, where de la Pole was confined, he singled out the disgraced chancellor for special honours, seating him next to him throughout the festivities, the jousts, banquets and disguisings. And as a further gesture of defiance, when the important office of steward fell vacant, he ignored his promise to choose another with the commission's advice and instead presented the white staff of office to Sir John Beauchamp of Holt.

In the New Year he prepared for more militant action. Gathering round him a group of intimates and advisers, which included Alexander Neville, archbishop of York, a member of the commission whom he had won over to his side, as well as his own unpopular favourites, the disgraced de la Pole and Sir John Beauchamp of Holt, Sir Nicholas Brembre, ex-mayor of London, and the justice, Sir Robert Tresilian, who had so cruelly punished the peasants in 1381, he bound himself with a special secret oath to follow their counsel until death.

With most of this group in February he then withdrew from London and for the next ten months travelled the country, leaving the commission to contact him when necessary by messenger, an arrangement that was very frustrating and tedious for them, since the royal consent was needed before any measure could be taken.

Under the guise of an extended royal progress, Richard's travels were in reality far more purposeful. Secretly, he was gathering the strength to provoke and this time win a renewed clash with his opponents. Visiting York in March, by July he had reached Cheshire, where he planned to raise a royal army. He needed first and foremost an army of his own to counterbalance the vast armed retinues of the barons. Cheshire was his own earldom, an ideal recruiting ground for another reason as well: ever since the start of the Hundred Years' War, fighting had been a way of life for the people of this poor country, and now that so few expeditions were mounted against the French, many men were without work.

In the urgency of his need, the king and his beloved 'kinsman' split company, de Vere, with the office of justice of Chester and North Wales, remaining in the royal earldom, where he established himself in style with his mistress, Agnes Lancekrona. (Among the possessions he is known to have had with him were her side saddle and his bed of blue camaca embroidered in gold with owls and fleurs de lis, valued at £68 13s. 4d.) Publicly and mendaciously proclaiming that he was collecting an army to lead against the unruly inhabitants of his Irish dukedom, he began to recruit the force that would give Richard the military power he required.

Meanwhile, reaching Shrewsbury and Nottingham in an August heatwave, the king attempted to rally the country behind him. We know that secretly he had sent out agents to try to recruit men willing to fight for him, because that month one of them was arrested in Cambridge and imprisoned there for distributing Richard's livery, badges of gilt and silver crowns, throughout Essex and East Anglia. The event suggests that even at this early date the country as a whole was unsympathetic towards Richard's autocratic policies.

At the same time he attempted to find armed support by a slightly more orthodox method. To Shrewsbury he summoned a number of sheriffs and asked them the critical question: how many men in their shires could they assume would be willing to fight for him in the event of a confrontation with the lords? He received the disappointing answer that since all the people were behind the barons it was impossible to array any military force at all. Asked also whether they would be willing to ensure that only those knights agreeable to the king and his council were elected to the next parliament, the sheriffs declared chillingly that they did not wish to abandon the custom of free elections. An indication of popular feeling that the king unwisely chose to ignore.

Brave to the point of rashness, Richard was not discouraged but began instead to try to use the law against the barons. At Nottingham he assembled those justices he believed favourable to him, and asked them to pronounce on the legality of the actions of the so-called Wonderful Parliament. It appears the document they were thereupon asked to sign was already drawn up. One by one, led by Robert Tresilian, these eminent men set their seals on a momentous declaration, it stated that the commission imposed on the king in the past autumn was illegal. And everyone responsible for its establishment, or for compelling the king to accept it, was worthy of a traitor's death, unless the king wished to extend his grace to them. The sealed statement amounted to a new definition of the capital crime of treason.

The meeting with the justices had been held in secret, but inevitably news of a decree so threatening to so many of the nobility leaked out. The archbishop of Dublin, who had been present at the conference, sent word to Gloucester, who in turn alerted his two friends. It was at this stage that Warwick joined Gloucester and Arundel to create the so-called 'indivisible trio'. Like them, he realized that so long as this document existed no man who had assented to the measures of the Wonderful Parliament could feel himself free of the shadow of a barbarous end by drawing, hanging and dismembering.

In view of this frightening discovery attack appeared to be their only means of defence, attack on Richard's counsellors who had placed them in danger of death. These men, they decided, must be killed before Gloucester and his allies could feel themselves safe. Even if it meant such drastic and treasonable action as rebelling against the king. As summer ripened into autumn, from their estates in Essex, Sussex and Middlesex, the 'indivisible trio' began to gather their private armies.

Meanwhile, Richard had found a fresh possible source for a royal army, for Nicholas Brembre had successfully rallied the Londoners to his cause, and in October he had received the welcome news that the leading citizens had sworn an oath 'to stand with the king' against his enemies.

Relying on this promise, and in the knowledge that there was a ready-made royal army in Cheshire, Richard mistakenly believed that he was strong enough to take on the barons. Accompanied by de Vere and de la Pole he returned to his capital city on 10 November 1387 to a reassuringly loyal welcome by the civic dignitaries, clad in the royal livery of red and white.

His entry into London was a solemn preparation for the struggle which lay ahead. Led by the archbishop of York bearing a cross, he and his companions rode to Charing Cross Mews, where they were met by the abbot and convent of Westminster Abbey; they dismounted. Between the two places a carpet had been laid. On this, barefoot, Richard, de Vere and de la Pole, preceded by the monks, walked in procession to the abbey where they performed their devotions. Spiritually, at least, he was prepared for whatever might happen.

By now Gloucester, Arundel and Warwick had gathered their forces. Provoked beyond bearing, on 13 November in Harringay Forest, Middlesex, they assembled their archers and men-at-arms, each lord's retinue distinguished by his badge on their doublets, Gloucester's swan, Arundel's horse, Warwick's bear. That night was spent camped in the forest, and the next day, raising on high their heraldic banners and Gloucester's special emblem, a fox's tail fixed to a lance, they marched on to Waltham Cross in their first move against the king in London.

Richard sternly forbade the citizens to supply his adversaries with food and ale, at the same time sending a deputation, led by the earl of Northumberland, to demand why the lords had armed themselves thus against their allegiance and their king. It was an accusation of illegal action to which the three lords replied firmly: they were not rebels, they were the king's loyal lieges, they had united and assembled for his own good and that of the kingdom, because England was in danger while the king was ruled by false counsellors.

With a long list of charges they 'appealed' of high treason de Vere, de la Pole, the archbishop of York, Neville, the ex-mayor, Brembre, and the justice, Tresilian.

Richard had been taken by surprise. With an army at the gates and no troops of his own in London to challenge it, he was at their mercy. He decided to consent to nearly everything the rebel lords, called 'appellants' demanded, and play for time. He received them at Westminster Palace and although they strode into his presence there wearing armour with three hundred armed men waiting, drawn up under their heraldic banners threateningly in the courtyards outside, he suffered without protest this terrible breach of royal etiquette. He agreed to their demand that his five friends should be tried before parliament and that he would summon it to meet at Westminster on 3 February 1388, on which date, he promised, the appeal would be heard. Meanwhile, he declared, he would take the case into his own hands, placing both accused and accusers under his protection. He would be responsible for the safe keeping of the accused.

Anxious to preserve the fiction of their respect for the king's authority and aware of the danger of stepping outside the law more than was absolutely necessary to achieve their ends, the three barons accepted Richard's promise and prepared to leave their cause to parliament. Triumphantly believing they had won, they rode away from the city and foolishly disbanded their armies.

But Richard had no intention of throwing his friends to the wolves by keeping an agreement imposed upon him under duress. Behind his fair skin and long, curling auburn locks, the face 'beautiful as Absalom', lay cunning and resolution.

No sooner had Gloucester, Arundel and Warwick withdrawn their forces from the outskirts of London than he seized the opportunity to save his favourites; far from setting a close guard on them as he had sworn to do, he allowed them to escape. Neville and de la Pole got clean away by ship to France. The chancellor, however, disguised as a poultry seller, was recognized in Calais, captured and forced to return to Hull before he again finally escaped also to France. Tresilian hid himself in an apothecary's shop in Westminster, where he concealed his identity behind rough clothes and a long, unkempt beard.

At the same time Richard sent Robert de Vere posting up to Cheshire - allegedly with five companions all disguised as humble yeomen with bows and arrows - to collect and bring south the army he had mustered there. Brembre remained behind to try and rally the Londoners. Disappointingly, the second force Richard had relied on was to prove an illusion. While encamped outside its walls the appellant barons had sent into the city a letter explaining their case so convincingly that the Londoners' feelings were wholly changed. Richard must have been horrified to hear that when asked to make good the November oath to 'stand with' the king, the new mayor, Nicholas Exton, replied bluntly that the citizens were merchants and craftsmen, unskilled in fighting, and they would not be willing to fight except in their own defence. He then asked to be relieved of his office.

Richard's hopes now were pinned on de Vere's army marching south from Cheshire. But the appellants had got wind of his activities and were again mustering their forces, this time to meet at Huntingdon, their numbers swollen by the retinues of two new very important recruits to their cause.

Throughout the turbulent events of the past thirteen months Henry, earl of Derby, had lain low. Neither in the peaceful revolution attempted by the Wonderful Parliament nor in the armed revolt of the appellants in November had he played an active part. Perhaps loyalty to the king - deeply ingrained, despite his hostility to Richard as a person, coupled with respect for his father's wishes - had kept him from joining the barons, whose interests he shared. Now suddenly with the advent of his childhood rival, Robert de Vere, as commander of an army, all was changed. This was an enemy Henry could not resist.

Sporting the glinting Lancastrian SS collar on his breast, he led his men to the appellants' rallying point at Huntingdon. With him, distinguished by his badge of the crowned feather, rode Thomas Mowbray, earl of Nottingham, with whose fate Henry's henceforth was to be fatally entwined. A ward of court and once one of the king's closest companions, the young earl had fallen out of favour when he married, without the king's permission, the daughter of the earl of Arundel.

The coming of these two powerful new allies was indeed a blessing for the 'indivisible trio'. Henry's adherence being particularly valuable, since he set the mark of respectability on their enterprise. While there is no proof that he brought with him any of his father's retainers, the mere fact of his presence among the appellants suggested to the kingdom as a whole that the movement had the blessing of the great duke of Lancaster.

From Huntingdon the appellants, as all five lords were now known, led their considerable forces west to Northampton to cut off de Vere from his intended route to London, and as they marched they published a proclamation. They were no rebels, but loyal subjects of the king who meant only to drive away the traitors that surrounded him.

Soon, the rough country roads of England were alive with armed men. Seeing the five lords as the champions of ordinary people's rights, large numbers flocked to their banners. While others, more peaceably inclined, formed religious processions instead, praying for the avoidance of civil war.

Against the combined military experience of the appellants, the brave but untried de Vere had no chance. Within days he allowed himself to be driven into a trap. As he moved south through the Cotswolds they pressed behind and around him, until he was left with only one possible route to London, across the upper Thames.

Although this part of the river was narrow enough for men and horses to swim, de Vere needed a bridge to take the army's baggage, 'carts packed with gold and silver, clothing, bedding and utensils', not to mention armour, weapons and provisions.

By 19 December 1387, when the king's favourite was at Stow-on-the-Wold in Gloucestershire, four of the rebel lords had slipped behind and around him, deploying their forces at Bourton-on-the-Hill, Blockley, Chipping Camden, Brailes, Banbury, Chipping Norton and Witney, thus cutting off his retreat to the north-west, north and east. It was a serious threat and to evade pursuit and reach London, de Vere decided to cross beyond Burford at Radcot Bridge, but unknown to him, the earl of Derby waited for him to make just such a move.

The fact that de Vere made such a fundamental error as to send no scouts to reconnoitre first suggests that Walsingham's judgement of him was indeed right, he was better in the marriage bed than on the battlefield, elegant and sophisticated, but with little practical sense.

A born military leader, Henry, on the other hand, had made prudent preparation, cutting the bridge in three places so that no more than a single horseman could ride across at one time. He also stationed archers and men-at-arms at the head of the bridge. And as usual in his youth, luck compounded his skill; thick fog allowed his forces to remain hidden until the last moment when on 20 December the royal army approached.

De Vere's men were almost at the bridge before they saw the trap. Surprise was complete. 'We are deceived,' de Vere is reported to have shouted before too late he gave the order for the unfurling of the royal standard and a trumpet call to action.

In the thick moisture-laden air neither the glimmer of the great flag nor the muffled trumpet blasts had much effect. Besides, the hearts of de Vere's followers were not in the battle. They had been mustered under false pretences to fight the 'wild Irish' and they had no stomach to kill fellow Englishmen. When they heard the approaching hoofbeats of Gloucester's men hurrying to help the earl of Derby, they threw down pikes, lances, bows and baggage and fled.

Deserted, de Vere had no choice but to spur his horse and flee alone downstream through the forest to Newbridge, which is today the peaceful site of two country pubs in pretty gardens but which then bristled with Henry's archers. Mercifully for de Vere he saw or heard them first in the fog and no one gave the alarm as he slipped past and rode on down river. Somewhere between Newbridge and Bablock-Hythe he unbuckled his costly armour and, throwing it on the grass, urged his horse into the water and swam across. Then, the 'king's kinsman' turned his back on his friends and rode for his life towards the coast where somehow he found a ship and escaped across the Channel to France.

Henry had won his first battle, a decisive one, for Richard had no more forces at his command. The king was once more at the mercy of the appellants, and this time they had the country behind them. United in triumph, the five lords rode the next day to Oxford and paraded their victorious army through the streets. The chronicler, Adam of Usk, then a student of canon law, was in the crowd that saw them pass, Henry and Warwick leading the van, Gloucester the centre, and Arundel and Nottingham the rear. Riding on to St. Albans, they rested a week, piously putting off the final confrontation with Richard until Christmas was over.

Not until 27 December did they move again, to encamp outside the walls of London, in St. John's Fields, Clerkenwell, at the same time blockading the Thames so that Richard, who had taken refuge in the Tower, could not escape.

During the last few days feeling in the city had hardened against the king, and the appellants were welcomed like heroes, the dignitaries riding out to proffer them the great keys of the gates, while the citizens sent out bread, meat and ale.

Wisely, the appellants responded with a show of respect. On entering the city three days later on their way to their first audience with the king in the Tower, they stopped at the Guildhall and, to the prominent citizens gathered there, formally explained their reasons for coming armed amongst them. They knew that to keep the friendship of the Londoners, it was essential to observe their liberties and privileges, a lesson Richard was never to learn. Having thus appeased their hosts, they rode on up to the Tower where Richard awaited them.

Deserted by his capital and his subjects, deprived of the company of his closest friends, who had gone into hiding or into exile, the twenty-year-old king had only one defence left: his royalty. But 'the divinity that doth hedge a king' was a potent force as he knew well. With this in mind he had displayed himself in the chilly, open air where he could be seen by as many of his subjects as possible, seated on a royal throne before a pavilion draped in cloth of gold.

With his fellow appellants Henry rode into the inner bailey. But before this imposing vision of kingship he dismounted and knelt the prescribed three times. For although Henry had just defeated the royal army at Radcot Bridge, Richard was still his king, and Henry the king's loyal subject, at least in theory.

VI 'TO DEPOSE THE KING'

'If the king ... should alienate himself
from his people ... it should then be
lawful for them ... to depose the king
himself.' The duke of Gloucester and
Bishop Arundel, *Knighton's Chronicle*

Although the five appellants had gained this confrontation in the Tower
with Richard by an act of war against him, they still firmly denied that they
were rebels. They remained on their knees before him in a show of
deference, until at his nod they rose 'modestly', but their squeaking armour
and clanking swords menacingly denied their pretence. No less than
Richard, they were playing to the gallery, their own followers and his
attendants observing with suppressed tension the dramatic scene within
the fortress, while outside the citizens crowded the green slope of Tower
Hill, or waited, oars resting on the water, in crowded wherries, eager for
news of the momentous events.

Even men as confident and determined as Gloucester and Arundel
knew that the same people who shouted their support today might call
them traitors tomorrow, in which case their heads might be the ones to
decorate London Bridge.

But these shouts now gave them the excuse they sought to withdraw
into the relative privacy of the nearby chapel where they could more easily
drop their masks of humility. The Monk of Westminster tells us: 'They
spoke severely to the king about his deeds: first, that he had contravened
his own oath by not performing what he had promised them; secondly, that
he had recklessly attempted to kill them, contrary to his dignity and
position; thirdly, that he had defended false traitors, to the undoing of his
own safety and the weakening of the whole realm. And they said much else
to him there which has not become public knowledge.'

Richard, who had once drawn his sword on William Courtenay,
archbishop of Canterbury, for less offensive words than these, was forced to
listen to this stern lecture, and there was worse to come when the massive
wooden gates and portcullises of the Tower closed on the outside world.
The appellants had seized the great keys. He was a prisoner, almost alone

except for the queen, all his remaining friends and attendants having been ordered, it appears, to Westminster.

In the illumination that adorns the poems of Charles, duke of Orleans, the Tower is open to our view. We look through a doorway so wide that it reveals a hall and its occupants, the guards with red crosses on their breasts and the duke seated at a table; but the width of the arch is the artist's licence. In reality the medieval Tower was a secret place, where windowless cells and instruments of torture existed in terrifying proximity to the stately, comfortable rooms and pleasant, vine-adorned garden of the royal apartments, a place where a few generations later the little princes, King Edward V and his brother, Richard, duke of York, could disappear without trace for centuries. With King Richard II we are more fortunate. He was to disappear from public view for no more than three days, and during this time the chronicles allow us glimpses of his sufferings.

Richard was forced to face the grave reality of his situation, first by Henry, then more brutally by Gloucester. *Knighton's Chronicle* tells us that when Henry of Derby drew him to the ramparts of the tower and showed him the vast congregation of the appellants' supporters pressed angrily round the grey stone walls, 'the king marvelled at so great a multitude', then Gloucester, true to his merciless type, told him roughly, 'This is not a tenth of the people who want to take our part to destroy and exterminate false traitors to the king and kingdom.' By traitors, of course, he meant the king's friends.

The execution of Richard's five counsellors was the prime object of all the appellants, since only with these men out of the way could they feel their own lives to be secure. But this object was to prove unexpectedly difficult to obtain, for the king would not give his consent. Helpless prisoner as he was, he still proved infuriatingly difficult to bully, one moment agreeing 'with sobs and tears' to his captors' demand, the next altering his mind. They could not pin him down and, driven to distraction by his shilly-shallying, the older appellants concluded he was impossible to deal with, and the only answer was to implement the threat they had made in 1386 and depose him. This was indeed a treasonable resolution, which they later attempted to keep secret, but it is recorded in the *Whalley Abbey Chronicle*, substantiated by Gloucester's confession of 1397: 'I was in place ther it was communed and spoken in manere of deposyl of my liege loord, trewly I knowlech wele that we were assented thereto for two days or three ...'

So, for three days the indivisible trio's' decision held sway, and in that time Richard lived in a world of nightmare, seeing himself at the age of twenty, a man on the threshold of life, treading in the sad footsteps of his great-grandfather, King Edward II, first deprived of his crown, then secretly murdered in Berkeley Castle. And for Richard, who believed he had a mission to be a great and powerful king, the fear would have been worsened by the sense of failure. He had failed to live up to the marks of regality which he believed the unction at his coronation had imprinted on his body for ever.

There is little doubt that the nightmare would have become reality had it been left to the senior appellants and that King Richard's tragic end would have come then instead of nearly twelve years later, had it not been for Henry and Mowbray. More moderate than their seniors, the two young earls now felt things had gone far enough. Their purpose in joining the rebellion had been solely to get rid of the five counsellors, not to destroy the king, and they took what action they could to protect him, as the parliament rolls of 1397 laconically report. These inform us that the 'indivisible trio', 'continuing their malicious, false and treacherous purpose' to depose the king from his 'royal estate and majesty' and take his crown into their custody, 'would have treacherously performed the said purpose had they not been prevented by Henry of Lancaster, earl of Derby and Thomas Mowbray, earl of Nottingham.'

Thus to stop their seniors was no mean feat for the two younger earls, barely of age and newly recruited to the cause. According to the *Whalley Chronicle*, the prime mover was Henry, using a trick that was both logical and cunning. The prospect of Richard's deposition raised the question: who was to replace him as king? And when Gloucester advanced his own claim to the crown, Henry seized his opportunity, arguing that he himself had the better right, the one argument which he knew could save Richard. For conflicting claims would cause dissension and division in the appellants' ranks, something they could not afford, their power, like that of their army, being based on unity. That Henry seriously put forward his claim is not credible. For even if already attracted by the lure of the golden round - and all the evidence suggests this temptation came later - he was too intelligent to believe he could hope to become king in his father's lifetime. Because after the descendants of the duke of Clarence, Gaunt had prior right, and though in person far away in the Iberian peninsula, in spirit the great duke was still close to his son.

The key to what went on in the earl of Derby's mind at this time lies in his accounts. Throughout the crucial months, from Michaelmas 1387 to 1388, these show communication between him and his father. We must presume that, just as Gaunt sent his son word of Philippa's marriage to King Joao of Portugal in the spring and of negotiations for Catherine's marriage to the Infante of Castile in the autumn, Henry replied describing his part in the rebellion in England. And the exchange was of the most amicable nature, for the messengers were rewarded by Henry with presents of gold-embroidered stuff in red-and-white and other brilliant colours. The accounts give no hint of the row that would have developed had Henry announced he seriously intended to claim the crown. Tormented as he had been by the royal favourites, Gaunt may have been prepared to wink at a rebellion that would sweep his enemies from the political board before his return, but it is inconceivable that he would have consented to the king's deposition. The accounts establish Henry's bona fides.

Alarmed at the prospect of divided ranks, the 'indivisible trio' reversed their decision. Richard was reprieved, he remained king. But at least the appellants gained their object, fear of losing the throne having finally persuaded Richard to submit to their demands as the lesser of two evils, and he was grateful to Henry for his intervention. Walsingham tells us that after making terms in the Tower that day, he invited Henry to dine and stay the night with him in his apartments 'as a pledge of his love'. And it is tempting to see those hours they stayed together as an oasis of mutual affection and loyalty in the doomed relationship of the cousins, when the love their grandfather, King Edward III, had tried to nurture between them proved stronger than the forces that pulled them apart.

Richard's rescue, however, was far from total. Henry's action had only mitigated the agony the king was to suffer, for submitting to the appellants' demands was still to prove very painful. Henry was to do a little, but only a little to lessen it. During the next few days he was too busy savouring the agreeable taste of power himself to have room for much sympathy for the king. As one of the appellants, now again united, he was among the rulers of England.

Finally on 31 December, after what must have seemed a lifetime to Richard, he was released from the Tower and allowed to make his way to his palace of Westminster, sadly and discreetly, perhaps by barge. The five victorious lords rode out from the Tower, through the city, along Fleet Street and the Strand, greeted as popular heroes by the waiting crowds. They entered the great gates of Westminster like monarchs themselves. Through the courtyard paved with Flanders tiles, past the conduit and the clock tower, with its great bell known as Edward of Westminster, they strode, and into the royal apartments, whose painted chamber had been adorned by King Henry III with images from Old Testament battles. There they behaved as masters, examined the accounts, expelled certain officials and courtiers, and arrested others. Men who had lived their lives in the sunshine of the royal favour and had shared the king's pastimes, played the games of 'the leaf and the flower', listened to Chaucer reading aloud his poems, and danced with the queen and her Bohemian ladies, suddenly felt rough hands seize their silken garments and chains weight their wrists. Marched off to prison like felons were Richard's chamber knights: his old tutor and vice-chamberlain, Simon Burley; his steward of the household, John, Lord Beauchamp of Holt; as well as Nicholas Dagworth, William Elmham, James Berners, John Salesbury, usher of the chamber, and Thomas Trivet; also the ex-mayor of London, Sir Nicholas Brembre.

Banished summarily from court were John Fordham, bishop of Durham, Thomas Rushook, bishop of Chichester and Richard's confessor, expelled once before after the Peasants' Revolt, Aubrey de Vere, uncle of the infamous 'king's kinsman', and five lords, de la Zouche of Haringworth, Lovel, Beaumont, Burnel and Camoys, as well as Sir John Devereux, Sir Thomas Blount, Sir John Clanvowe, Sir Nicholas Devereux and Sir John Golafre. Expulsion was not confined to men; the ladies Mohun, Poynings and Molyneux had to pack and go too. The appellants then appointed a committee, including members of the so-called Wonderful Parliament's commission, whose mandate had now run out, to govern the realm. And to all this arbitrary and brutal intrusion in his household and his government, as yet unsanctioned even by parliament, Richard could do no less than give his assent.

So gross an assault on the royal prerogative did not go unmarked by the chroniclers. Walsingham and the Monk of Westminster, at least, were not behind the actions of the appellants. They saw all around portents of divine displeasure. They reported whirling wheels of fire in the night skies of November and December, a storm in January in which snow, hail and strong wind mingled, contrary to the laws of nature, with thunder and lightning, and the sudden mysterious drying up of the Thames under one of the arches of the bridge at Abingdon.

But the appellants' dictatorial behaviour so far was only a curtain-raiser to the more harrowing drama in which Richard was about to play his melancholy part.

On 3 February 1388 in the White Hall he presided over the opening of a parliament which had met with the express purpose of trying his dearest, most trusted friends for treason. That Henry approved of these trials we know from an item in his accounts in which he ordered despatched to each of the other appellants stuff of which to make a rich gown of Cyprus gold with a black ground, to wear as a symbol of their unity during the coming parliament. For Henry, twenty-one, thus to set his seal on a rebellion by some of the most powerful lords in the land would have been a satisfying triumph, and it was presumably in these shimmering garments that they strode into parliament together on 3 February. Favent, thought to have been one of the black-gowned royal clerks who kept a record of parliamentary proceedings, has left us a full description of the scene.

The White Hall was crowded with people right up to the corners, the king sitting in his chair of estate, on his right the lords spiritual, on his left the lords temporal, the chancellor on his scarlet wool sack before him, while the appellants performed their charade of loyalty. Arms linked and dressed alike in shining robes, they entered and knelt all together. Firmly, in the still customary French, their spokesman, Robert Pleasington, began by scotching a dangerous rumour, that the appellants had discussed killing Richard. He declared that the five lords had 'never imagined or consented to the death of the king'. There was no one present to contradict; on the contrary, Thomas Arundel, who had replaced de la Pole as chancellor, stood up and replied directly to the most prominent of the appellants ostensibly on Richard's behalf: 'My lord duke, you come from such an honourable line and one so close to the king's that no such intentions could be suspected of you.' A statement which it is hard to believe was made entirely without irony.

A clerk of the crown, Geoffrey Martyn, then spoke for the lords. 'As loyal subjects of our lord the king, for the profit of the king and kingdom', they begged to bring forward the appeal first made at Waltham Cross on 14 November against Alexander Neville, archbishop of York, Robert de Vere, duke of Ireland, Michael de la Pole, earl of Suffolk, Robert Tresilian, 'false justice', and Nicholas Brembre, 'false knight of London'. The accused were charged with 'high treasons made by them against the king and his kingdom', and the appellants 'begged that right and justice should be done in the present parliament'.

There followed a recitation of the thirty-nine articles of appeal in which Richard was humiliatingly portrayed as a puppet king who had misbehaved but only because his strings had been pulled by the five false counsellors, who were blamed for all his most unpopular acts, in which allegedly he had had no free choice.

The long list of these counsellors' supposed crimes sheds a fascinating light for us on the medieval ideal of kingship. They were accused of taking advantage of 'the tender age of the king and the innocence of his person' and of usurping to themselves the royal power, so that where the king should be 'of freer condition than anyone else in the kingdom', they had 'placed him in servitude against their allegiance.' They were said not to have suffered the nobles of the kingdom or the good counsellors to talk or approach him 'except in the presence of the accused... Thus the grace which the king should show to nobles and people had been checked and the king hindered from his duty and his heart estranged ...' The five were stated besides to have enriched themselves with royal gifts and impoverished the king and to be guilty of corruption. While at their instigation those nobles and sage counsellors who remonstrated had been forbidden by the king to speak of it, or banished from his presence.

Still other charges were more specific, relating to the past year. The five were accused of advising the king to order the mayor of London to raise a force against the 'loyal' appellants ... of keeping the king from meeting parliament and falsely advising him that the commission of 1386 was against his royal prerogative ...

They were also accused of advising him to question the justices, of keeping the king away from his appointed council and of drawing his heart and goodwill from those who set up the commission of 1386. They were declared to have plotted to put to a shameful death the lords and commons responsible for the commission, to have sent letters to the King of France offering to cede him territory in exchange for aid to destroy the lords. And they were said to have extracted an improper oath from the craft gilds of London that they would side with the king ...

The old French fell from the lips of the clerk for two hours, piling accusation upon accusation until men wept, a sign of the hysteria of the occasion.

The excitement and fear generated by the revolt and the powerful personalities of the duke of Gloucester and the earl of Arundel resulted in an emotional momentum that nothing, it seemed, could stop. Both Lords and Commons were entirely behind the appellants. When the judges objected to trial by appeal before parliament on the grounds that this process was itself revolutionary, their objection created only a momentary check. The Lords declaring that 'in such high crimes' which 'touched the person of the king and the welfare of the kingdom' judgement could be given in no lower court, the proceedings rushed on remorselessly.

The trials began. The four 'traitors' who had fled were summoned to the bar, and on their failure to appear to answer the charges, the suggestion was made that they should be pronounced guilty by default. Recovering his nerve at this point, the young king attempted to fight for his friends. He succeeded in postponing their condemnation for several days by insisting that 'an honourable and profitable judgement could not be passed without examination of the facts', but when the examination was made it revealed only what the appellants wished.

On 11 February 1388 a verdict of guilty was pronounced, followed by the inevitable sentences. Robert de Vere, Michael de la Pole and Robert Tresilian were condemned to a cruel death by drawing and hanging, while Archbishop Neville, saved from a similar penalty by his cloth, was deprived of his temporal goods and handed over for further punishment to the Church. Pope Urban was to deprive him of his see of York and appoint him instead bishop of St. Andrews in Scotland, a cynical fiction since

Scotland only recognized Urban's rival pope in Avignon. Like the sentences on de Vere and de la Pole, Neville's amounted to perpetual banishment. However, there existing then no extradition treaties between countries, Richard's friends were safe so long as they remained abroad.

Sir Nicholas Brembre, in the Tower, was less fortunate, being within reach of the law. He was, besides, generally hated. Many people in London held against him his attempt to uphold the monopoly of the fishmongers' gild, of which he was a member, thus excluding competition and keeping the price of fish high. And the appellants were bitterly hostile to him for trying to raise an army in the city to oppose them.

They had decided he was to die. On 17 February 1388 Brembre was taken before parliament to be tried by an irregular process, all arguments in his defence, including vociferous ones from the king, being disallowed, as also was a verdict that amounted to 'innocent' from the twelve peers first appointed to try him. When these lords announced that they could find nothing treasonable in the accusations against the ex-mayor, their finding was ignored; they were replaced by one committee after another, until something approaching the required verdict was reached by a committee that included the new mayor, the aldermen and the recorder of London.

These dignitaries pronounced that they thought Brembre more likely to be guilty of treason than not, and on this inconclusive judgement the man who had done so much to support Richard was condemned to death. His last slim chance vanished when he requested to be accorded his privilege as a knight to prove his innocence by mortal combat. Although no less than three hundred and five gages were tossed at the king's feet in the White Hall by lords and knights keen to take up the challenge, the request was refused. Not only the appellants, but the assembly in the White Hall as a whole, wanted the ex-mayor dead, true to the title by which it has ever since been known, the Merciless Parliament.

Further to whet its appetite for blood, on 19 February 1388 in the middle of Brembre's trial, the chief justice, Tresilian, was discovered close by in the apothecary's house in Westminster precinct, where he had been hiding all this while disguised as a poor and aged man. Before the hue and cry for him began he managed to make his way into the abbey, where had his right of sanctuary been observed he should have been safe. But even more than Brembre, Robert Tresilian was loathed. By the barons because he had advocated the terrifying new interpretations of treason that had set their lives at risk, and by the common people for the cruel number of executions he had ordered after the Peasants' Revolt.

On hearing of the justice's discovery, the members of parliament rushed to the abbey door in a crowd, and there they paused, all except Gloucester and Lord Cobham. The duke was not to be balked of his prey by a taboo so often defied for reasons of state. Armed with a cudgel and assisted by Lord Cobham, he burst into the sacred buildings, strode up the aisle and arrested the unhappy fugitive.

The end had come for the chief justice. Having been already sentenced to death in his absence, he was forcibly marched to the Tower, and thence drawn along the cobbled roads on a hurdle to Tyburn. There, the executioner stripped him of his shabby clothes and hanged him naked, cutting his throat, to the delight of the mob, who perceived, as they expected, marks of the devil on his poor twitching body. In a less sensational execution Brembre was beheaded the next day.

The task for which parliament had originally been summoned was now done; the five 'traitors' appealed at Waltham Cross had been tried and sentenced, Richard's most influential counsellors were destroyed for ever. But the lords appellant had gone too far not to go further. Richard had more friends, more supporters, and if these were not also killed they might seek revenge. In the interest of the appellants' own safety more men must die.

Six times more the executioner's axe or the hangman's rope found victims, six times more the beggars who lined the way when a prisoner went to execution, hopefully stretched out their hands. The Merciless Parliament was to sit for five months until 4 June 1388, in which time thirteen more men were convicted of treason and sentenced accordingly. Of these, seven were granted their lives. Like Neville, the bishop of Chichester was saved by his cloth, but deprived of his temporalities, his see and his office of royal confessor. Sentence of death on the judges who had appended their seals to the document at Nottingham was commuted to exile at the plea of the queen and the archbishop of Canterbury, and instead of suffering execution they were banished to Ireland, where with a final twist of the knife, their wives and families were forbidden to join them. Of the six men on whom sentence of death was carried out, two were drawn on hurdles from the Tower and hanged at Tyburn on 4 March: John Blake, who had drafted the questions put to the judges at Nottingham; and Thomas Uske, the poet, author of *Testament of Love*, who was accused of drawing up false indictments for treason against the lords and knights who had been responsible for forming the commission in the Wonderful Parliament of 1386.

Also to suffer death were four of Richard's chamber knights, Sir John Beauchamp of Holt, Sir John Salesbury, chief royal usher, Sir James Berners and Sir Simon Burley, who had fallen so ill in prison that he had to be supported at the bar in parliament by his nephew Sir Baldwin Raddington, controller of the royal wardrobe, on one side, and an esquire,

John Durant, on the other. Before these men died, however, there had come another division in the ranks of the appellants.

Favent's history of this parliament makes clear that the brutal punishment meted out to this second lot of victims stemmed from the violent and ruthless 'indivisible trio' rather than from the appellants as a whole. Henry was sickened when he saw Richard's old tutor, pale and fainting, pathetically propped up at the bar and accused of treason, a sentiment shared by many of his fellow peers.

Although considered to have been chief architect of Richard's 'first tyranny' Burley was a respected and popular figure at court. He had campaigned with Gaunt and the Black Prince in France, had been a friend and servant of Princess Joan; he was Richard's vice-chamberlain and before that he had been his chamberlain in the days when Richard was Prince of Wales; he was a Knight of the Garter. And even the acid-tongued Walsingham had a kind word for him, a 'powerful nobleman - gentle in deeds and gracious - and a longtime courtier of the king'.

Many of the peers now attempted to save his life, and feeling mounted so high that a fight nearly broke out between the royal dukes. Abandoning his wonted passivity, Edmund of Langley, duke of York swore that Burley 'had been a faithful man in all affairs both to the king and kingdom' and if anyone wanted to contradict this he himself would prove Burley's innocence in a duel. Whereupon Gloucester also rose to his feet. Burley was false to his allegiance, he asserted, he would prove it with his right hand. His brother lied, retorted York, and the two dukes would have rushed at each other had the king not calmed them down.

The peers were divided, but unhappily, Richard's old tutor was unpopular with the Commons, who disliked him for living as they thought above his station, with his flamboyant clothes and costly retinue. They complained in the prevailing atmosphere of hate and revenge that his style of living was more like that of a duke or a prince than a soldier. A petition presented by York and Lord Cobham, begging them to save Burley's life, was rejected.

The king, needless to say, was distraught at the prospect of thus losing the man who had been almost a father to him since the Black Prince died. He declared forcibly in parliament that his old tutor was guiltless of all the crimes of which he stood accused, and afterwards in the privacy of the Bath House pleaded with the earl of Arundel to show mercy, only to be told in brutal fashion that he must either agree to Burley's death or lose his crown.

Queen Anne, on hearing of this, was overcome with emotion. She demanded to see Arundel, pleaded for Burley's life, even humbling herself by falling to her knees before him and remaining thus, it is said, for three hours, but to no avail, for these pleas served only to prolong the trial still more. After a month of it the 'indivisible trio' had their predetermined way. Burley was found guilty in the presence of the king and, despite his age and long service, he was condemned to death with the three other chamber knights.

The guards pushed Burley roughly to his feet and began to march him away, but Henry could contain his indignation no longer. He sprang to his feet and, says Walsingham, 'tried with all his might to prevent him from being dragged away, which caused great dissension between him and the duke of Gloucester'.

It was too late to alter the sentence. Though sick and infirm, on 5 May 1388 the king's former tutor, ringed by guards, stumbled through the streets of London to the Tower in heavy chains. On Tower Hill his head was struck from his body, Beauchamp and Berners suffering similar deaths seven days later, while the wretched Salesbury was forced to suffer the full penalty of being drawn on a hurdle to the place of execution and then hanged. With the falling of the axe at Tower Hill a whole era of Richard's life abruptly ended. He had lost all the men upon whom he most relied, for friendship, companionship and advice. Even those who had escaped he would never see again, for Neville, de la Pole and the beloved de Vere could never return to England. He was alone and surrounded by enemies. In this bleak moment even the smallest kindness would have brought him comfort. And Henry's brave attempt to save Burley would be remembered by the king many years later when the time came for him to avenge his friends.

In the last few days of parliament the possibility of such a revenge at some future date greatly occupied the minds of the appellants, and they did their best to protect themselves against it with every conceivable sanction of sacred oath, legislation and threat of excommunication by the Church. On 20 March 1388 all members of parliament swore an oath on the cross of Canterbury, to bind themselves until death to keep the peace, and to 'maintain and sustain' the appellants with all their power. And throughout the country sheriffs and burgesses were forced to swear the same oath. Completely in their pocket, parliament passed an act pardoning the appellants for the 'assemblies, ridings, appeals, and pursuits' which had been done 'for the honour of God, salvation of our lord, maintenance of his crown and salvation of all his kingdom'. And it voted them the enormous sum by contemporary standards of £20,000 for the 'great expenses they had incurred for the salvation of the kingdom and the destruction of the traitors'.

Finally, the appellants attempted to repair what they had shattered, the bond of loyalty and service between the king and his lords, broken when he was deposed during his three-day imprisonment.

Quietly in Westminster Abbey both sides renewed their coronation oaths; for what had happened in the Tower was to be covered up and concealed as much as possible. All suggestion of the treasonable deposition, as of rebellion, was hidden in a bouquet of euphemisms in Favent's account of this extraordinary ceremony:

> The king, queen, all the nobility, both lay and clerical, and the commons, came to Westminster Abbey to prorogue Parliament, and the Bishop of London, as it was his diocese, celebrated mass. After mass, the Archbishop of Canterbury gave a sermon about the forms of oath-taking, and the perils attaching thereto.
>
> Then, although the king had previously at his coronation sworn the royal oath on his own soul, and the nobles and commons of the kingdom had done homage and sworn allegiance to him in due form, nevertheless, that very same oath was then solemnly renewed in the same form and manner as at the coronation, accompanied by the homage and oaths of the nobles, because it had been sworn when the king was a minor; and also because it seemed necessary to remove and obviate certain heart-searchings and hesitations both on the part of the king and on the part of the nobility.
>
> When this had been done, the said primate of England lit a candle and with all the bishops who were present, beneath a single stole, solemnly ex-communicated each and every person who should, either by himself or through the agency of others, oppose or interfere with any and every act, settlement or decision of the present parliament, or in any way impugn their validity, force and authority: whereupon the candle was extinguished.

The quenched flame, symbol of the Christian sacraments that would be denied anyone who offended, was also the symbol of the end of a parliament rightly termed the 'Merciless' for its cruelties. The appellants had taken every possible measure to forestall retaliation, but they had reckoned without two things: the explosive hatred they had created in Richard, and the very real power that a medieval king could command. Both were formidable forces.

They had misjudged Richard's quality. It was to prove an error for which they would pay dearly.

VII   RICHARD FIGHTS BACK

'Y am of fulle age to governe my selfe, my howseholde, and my realme.' King Richard, *John of Malvern's Chronicle*

Sickened as he was by Burley's execution, Henry could not but find satisfaction in the increase of his own power through the appellants' actions. It was something to set in the balance against the magnificent achievements of his sisters, both of whom would now be queens, his favourite sister, Philippa, some six years older than he, already married to the king of Portugal, his half-sister, Catherine, betrothed to the infante of Castile.

Throughout that summer power lay in the hands of the five barons. They, and not parliament, had appointed the committee of two bishops and three lords that assisted the chancellor, treasurer and lord privy seal to govern England. They dominated the royal council and its decisions, while one of their two leaders, the earl of Arundel, appointed admiral of England, set sail in June with a naval expedition against France.

Unfortunately the appellants, so successful in rebellion, were no statesmen; they failed to fulfil a basic function of government, to protect the country's borders. They tried, but were unable to renew, the current truce with the Scots, who promptly took advantage of the absence in France of Arundel and his men-at-arms to attack. Within ten days of the truce expiring, on 29 June 1388 two Scottish armies, one on the west and one on the east, invaded England. They devastated the northern counties as far as Tynemouth, murdering the inhabitants, burning crops and villages in an attack that the Monk of Westminster described as the most savage for fifty years; and to add insult to injury, the English were unable to do anything to stop them. A hastily gathered force of 9,000 men meeting the Scots under the earls of Douglas and Murray at Otterburn on 15 August 1388, was defeated despite its superior numbers and the dash of its leader, Henry Percy, who for his prowess in this battle was dubbed Hotspur by his enemies. Percy was taken prisoner and some two thousand English were killed. The battle, gloatingly and fancifully commemorated in the Scottish *Ballad of Chevy Chase*, was a sad humiliation for the English.

The Scots withdrew of their own accord and were safely back over the border by 3 September 1388 when Arundel sailed into Hastings, his holds crammed with booty. Although he had destroyed no less than eighty enemy ships his triumph could not heal the suffering of the northern counties.

Having failed to protect the land they ruled, the lords appellant were by autumn no longer the popular leaders they had been in the spring. The new critical feeling towards them was reflected in the voice of the Commons in the parliament that met in Cambridge on 7 September 1388. The Commons, without whose consent no taxes could be raised, were already proud and forceful, even though they had become an integral part of parliament only as recently as the reign of Edward III. Consisting as they did largely of shire knights and burgesses, moneyed men with more or less the same interests as the nobility, they usually, but not always, agreed with the Lords. That autumn was one occasion when they chose their own path.

Assembling at Barnwell Priory, their mood was very different from that of February, when they had fiercely supported the five lords. Now they rounded on them, insisted on an enquiry into the way Arundel had spent the money allocated for his naval expedition and demanded an end to the private armies of the barons, their retainers who terrorized the countryside, murdering, robbing, corrupting juries, secure in the knowledge of their lord's protection. Although this was an attack on all the lords it was directed primarily at the appellants, who had been swept to power the previous winter by just such armies under their badges of the swan, the horse and the bear, the SS collar and the crowned feather.

Now the Commons demanded a law forbidding the wearing of such liveries, which, they declared, exalted men with pride, enabled them to commit extortions without fear of punishment, and prevented poor men from getting justice.

It was an amply justified complaint. Henry himself, earl of Derby, was in that very year successfully to sue to Richard for pardon for seven of his retainers accused of homicide, and it was at his plea that another of his retainers, who had taken part in a barbarous incident at midnight on 28 September 1387, was pardoned. With a band of followers Sir John Pelham had stormed a manor house at Fulbourn, four miles from Cambridge, and removed an heiress, whom he then married, whether with or without her consent we do not know. This lawless aggression may have been one of the reasons why parliament was summoned that autumn to the unwonted venue of Cambridge.

Indignant at the prospect of a law that would destroy the chief basis of their power, the Lords declared that the Commons were impertinent to suggest it. It was precisely this sort of situation for which Richard had been waiting.

The agonizing experience of the past months had not been entirely wasted, it had exercised a salutary effect on his political skills. Robbed of his chief friends and advisers and forced for the first time to rely on himself, he had become harder, more cunning, above all determined to regain his lost power by whatever means he could find, no matter how devious, and now he saw his opportunity. As the gap widened between Commons and appellants Richard made it still wider. He offered to abolish his own badge of a gold crown, the badge his agent had been imprisoned in this very town for distributing in 1387. Considering that his one successful effort at recruiting a private army had ended in the disastrous battle of Radcot Bridge, this involved no great sacrifice for the king, and one would have thought the appellants might have seen and avoided the pit that he had dug for them. Instead they fell headlong into it. Stupidly, they did just what they were meant to; by angrily refusing to make similar sacrifices, they antagonized the Commons and created a new alliance between them and the king.

From this point on, the power of the appellants melted away. That winter Richard felt strong enough to expel their nominees from his household and restore in their place his surviving favourites, including some who a bare few months ago had narrowly escaped execution for treason. Once again the old and new palace yards at Westminster Palace saw a great coming and going of courtiers and their baggage, chests, canvas bundles, wooden carts in such a commotion that our black-robed anonymous chronicler from his abbey cloisters nearby believed Richard had 'ejected from his household about four hundred persons'.

Although the number involved in the change-over was really far smaller, this development was important, since the men who returned to Richard's household were members of the royalist party, his chamber knights, who had the royal ear, and whom he trusted. Back through the great palace gates rode Sir John Lovell and the Lollard knight Sir John Clanvowe, author of a famous heretical treatise; Sir Nicholas Dagworth, Sir John Devereux, Sir Thomas Blount - whose loyalty to Richard in 1400 was to make him a leader in the revolt against the usurper; even Sir John Golafre, who had been accused by the appellants in 1387 of carrying letters asking for armed help from the French, was allowed to return. Richard Medford, 'released from prison in June on condition that he kept away from court', had already quietly resumed his post as king's secretary.

Then, in a more openly aggressive move on 3 May 1389, Richard took the war into the enemy's camp, formally declaring his independence of any authority except his own. To the Marcolf Chamber at Westminster, bright with wall paintings, he summoned a great council of magnates, and when these lords and other notables were all assembled, he swept into the room in his long robes, seated himself on his chair of estate, and abruptly demanded of the company how old he was. It was a rhetorical question; nevertheless he waited for an answer, deliberately creating a theatrical pause to add emphasis to his intended speech.

The calculated drama of the scene, so typical of Richard, is marvellously caught in a sixteenth century translation of Ralph Higden's *Polychronicon*

> ... hit was answerde he had xxti yere in age. Then the kynge seide, 'By that y may conclude that y am of fulle age to governe my selfe, my howseholde, and my realme, for me thenke hit is not ryzhtefull that y scholde be of moore vile condicion then eny person in my realme. For every heire of my realme havynge xxti yere in age after the dethe of his fader is permitte to governe hymselfe and his londes ...
>
> Beholde y knowe y have be governede unto this tyme by lords and tutors that y myhte not do eny thynge withowte theym; wherefore from this tyme y ammove theyme from my counsayle, and y wylle take to my cownsayle men after my wylle and pleasure as an heire of lawefull age. Wherefore y commaunde first that the chaunceller resigne to me his seale.' The archbishop of Yorke delyverynge hit, the kynge putte hit in his bosom and wente furthe ...

Speechless in their places, the appellants sat trying to digest their dismissal from the royal council, as Richard 'wente furthe' with the Great Seal of England tucked firmly inside his robes. There was nothing they could do, any resort to force being out of the question now that Richard had the Commons behind him. So simply, by this straightforward declaration had he turned the tables on them. His victory is embodied in a proclamation which he made in Latin on 8 May 1389, stating that: 'Desirous of the good and prosperous rule of his kingdom of England, and for its peace and prosperity and good government,' he would henceforth take upon himself 'the rule and full government of the aforesaid kingdom'. And so that his intention should be quite clear, he signed it 'by the king himself'.

It was a dramatic turnabout in his fortunes and the vicissitudes of kingship. He seemed to have the whip-hand. Nevertheless, he was resolved to proceed cautiously. His recent experience had taught Richard a useful lesson. He would not make himself unnecessary enemies among the barons. For the time being he would do all he could to set their fears at rest.

Moderation was the keynote of his new rule. He dismissed only the two chief ministers, the Arundel brothers. Richard, earl of Arundel, one of the leading appellants, was dismissed from his post of admiral of England and keeper of the privy seal, while his younger brother, Thomas, was forced to resign from the office of chancellor, although he remained archbishop of York.

King Richard also dismissed the treasurer, bishop Gilbert, and forced five of the judges to resign, but this was only to demonstrate his right to choose his own officials; he reappointed all six men soon after. He was even to reappoint Thomas Arundel as chancellor in 1391, and in his proclamation he reassuringly declared that he intended to abide by the oaths he had made during the Merciless Parliament. He promised that he would uphold all pardons and that he would listen to the advice of the leading men in the kingdom.

In the months that followed he forgave every one of his recent adversaries, no matter how terribly they had hurt him and those he loved. He showed that he harboured no grudges, had abandoned all personal feelings in the interests of a peaceful kingdom. He was a changed man from the emotional monarch of former days who had displayed such affection for his friends. Impossibly changed, it might be thought, but gradually his enemies came to believe what they wished to, that this really was a new Richard.

The first of the lords appellant to be accepted back into the fold was his one-time close friend, the earl of Nottingham. By the autumn Mowbray was once more included in Richard's circle of young courtiers, and he had been confirmed in the pleasantly lucrative offices of warden of the East March and keeper of the royal castle of Berwick on the Scottish border. Desperate to win back to his side the least hostile of the rebels, Richard even tried to persuade the council to increase the earl's pay, and when they refused lost his temper. 'To your peril be it if any evil arise from this,' he exclaimed, then abruptly left the room in mid-meeting and rode off to his manor at Kennington.

Though awarded fewer personal marks of favour, Henry also was soon apparently forgiven, his name, as well as Mowbray's, occurring in the minutes of a council meeting of 13 September, while no one could think it strange if, after the torture they had inflicted on Richard, the 'indivisible trio' had to wait a little longer. They did so in anguished suspense. Would they ever recover their former influence in the country? Had Richard really forgiven them? A fellow peer, the earl of Northumberland, pleaded their cause at that same council meeting of 13 September.

His petition expressed the great desire of the three lords appellant 'that love and unity ... might be established between the king and the lords of the council on the one part and the said duke of Gloucester, earl of Arundel and earl of Warwick on the other. And that neither party should have the other in any suspicion.' Only a few weeks later they too were welcomed back into the fold. Instead of being tried as they might justifiably have been for treason, for taking up arms against the king, all five of the men responsible for the exile and executions of the king's friends were summoned to attend on 10 December a council in Reading Abbey. The abbey gateway, flanked by towers, albeit heavily restored by Sir George Gilbert Scott, still survives to remind us of this historic meeting, although most of the once great complex of stone buildings has disappeared.

It was a very special council, not least because presiding at Richard's side was John of Gaunt, duke of Lancaster, newly returned to England and suddenly, miraculously high in the royal favour, his value as a pillar of strength in the shifting sands of English politics having at long last been recognized by a sadder and wiser king. Not only did Gaunt believe in the royal prerogative, he had the power and personality to control the rebellious barons as no one else could. Set in the balance against such assets, what mattered his uncle's manner that had seemed so insupportably overbearing to the teenage Richard of three years before? Then he had been delighted to see his uncle leave the country; now he had pleaded with him to return 'by land or sea' as quickly as possible.

Responding to this urgent royal request, Gaunt had sailed into Plymouth on 19 November in a glow of triumph as father-in-law both of the king of Portugal and of the heir to the Castilian throne, as well as the possessor of a vast fortune. He had returned with so much gold, showered on him in exchange for relinquishing his wife Constance's claim to the Spanish crown, that forty-seven mules, shipped for the purpose, were needed to transport it from his carracks to his castle. The gold was only part of the deal. He was to be paid an annuity of forty thousand francs in gold, and for the costs of the campaign, six hundred thousand francs in gold within the next three years.

Wealthy already, it made him seem rich as Croesus, and even after his death his influence would continue, through descendants who would reign over the major part of the Iberian peninsula. Gaunt's was a brilliant, dreamlike achievement and, in his aura, the lesser lights of Gloucester and Arundel paled into insignificance, as did the hatred Gaunt himself had once inspired. He had become a legendary figure admired by nearly all, and with this new image went a new, more sober approach to politics. In England from now on he was to play the part of the most respected elder statesman.

Gaunt's first known appearance in public after his arrival in England shows him in the role of the most venerated of Richard's councillors, his status underlined by the greatest honours. Arriving for the council at Reading, he was met two miles outside the town by the king who welcomed him with a kiss of peace, then lifted the SS collar from Gaunt's neck and placed it round his own as a token of unity and affection. Gaunt was to be used to set the seal of reconciliation between Richard and his former enemies and he delivered the main speech at the gathering, urging a new accord between king and appellants. He himself set an example by becoming reconciled with Henry Percy, earl of Northumberland, with whom he had had such a violent quarrel in 1381 that it had nearly led to an armed affray in parliament between their supporters. Now the duke proclaimed his friendship with this once bitter enemy, to general acclaim.

If all the lords now loved the duke that winter, so did the commons of London. When he rode back from the council meeting in Reading to the capital, he was met outside the city by the mayor and aldermen, while the abbot and convent of Westminster, in black Benedictine gowns, led him in procession to the abbey and sang *Honor Virtus* as he proceeded to the high altar to make his offering. In such detail do the chroniclers report Gaunt's re-entry into public life.

Unfortunately they leave us guessing as to the nature of his re-entry into the private lives of Richard and Henry and how he excused the part in the recent revolt played by his beloved son to the king. It was a delicate predicament, in which a display of shock and indignation at the impossibly turbulent behaviour of a difficult son would have done more to mollify Richard than a spirited defence of Henry's actions. And this may have been the origin of one of a strange series of incidents described in the French poem, the *Chronique de la traison et mort de Richart Deux Roy D'engleterre*. This poem tells us, incredibly, that twice or thrice in Richard's reign he was urged by Gaunt to put Henry to death. Still at times a man of 'rough and bitter' words, did Gaunt perhaps advise Richard that Henry should be killed for such rebellious behaviour? If so, it would have been a wild remark, not meant to be taken literally. For throughout his life Gaunt's special affection for Henry never wavered, to judge by his accounts and his will where, heir in any case to title and lands, Henry is also left the most valuable furniture, including the 'great bed of red and white check camaca, embroidered with a gold tree and a turturelle (turtle dove) sitting below the tree ... and the great bed of cloth of gold'.

The incident in the *Traison et Mort* is a fragile clue on which to depend, but whatever Gaunt said of Henry's rebellion to Richard it was cleverly conceived, for Henry was to figure advantageously in the reward the king now made to Gaunt for his support. In the parliament that met on 17 January 1390 Richard first created his eldest uncle duke of Aquitaine, then on 16 February made him a gift so costly that future kings of England also might have to pay a share of the price. The dukedom and palatinate of the county of Lancaster, which made this large area of England almost an independent principality, had been granted by King Edward for life only. Now Richard made the title and the enormous powers that went with it hereditary, dismembering his own kingdom to satisfy Gaunt's ambition for his son. Surely this was a sign of deep trust and friendship. There were other signs, too.

These days Richard constantly made much of his uncle; still wearing the collar of SS on his jewelled doublets, he strolled with him arm-in-arm and hand-in-hand through the painted halls, and formal gardens. But Gaunt at least knew the king too well to be taken in. Having had a room perpetually set aside for him in the palaces during Richard's childhood and adolescence, he had seen the boy grow up and watched his ideas form and mature. No one knew better than he how fiercely Richard objected to attempts to interfere with the royal prerogative. No one knew better how devious his nephew could be, how cunningly and secretly he could act behind a friendly, smiling face. He might appear to have forgiven and forgotten the Appellants' Revolt, but Gaunt knew that with Richard appearances were often deceptive. By taking part in the 'ridings and assemblies' Henry could one day be in danger.

Obviously, it must have seemed to the duke, that while the king's grief for his friends was still raw, the safest thing to do with Henry was to remove him from court, so that his presence there would not remind Richard of their terrible fate and of his own royal humiliation during the Merciless Parliament. It can be no coincidence that between March 1390 and July 1393 Henry was to spend nearly two years in Europe, enjoying himself in a series of adult adventure holidays out of harm's way, heavily subsidized by his father.

Having played such a prominent part in English politics in 1387 and 1388, Henry was now to vanish tactfully from the scene. By an extraordinary stroke of luck the activities he undertook were to help prepare him eventually to play an even more prominent role, establishing him as a hero of the common people, and, above all, teaching him how to organize and transport across the sea a force of men not much smaller than that with which he was eventually to invade England. This dress rehearsal for future rebellion came about innocently enough.

The first opportunity to remove his threatened son for a while out of England had turned up conveniently at about the same time as Gaunt's own return from Spain, with the arrival of a French herald bearing a challenge that Henry and many other young nobles found irresistible. In March three renowned French knights offered to do battle for the honour of France against the bravest knights in Europe in a tournament to take place just outside the Pale of Calais.

Significantly, among those who eagerly accepted the challenge and set forth with Henry, was his special ally among the appellants, Thomas Mowbray, although this time the two young earls did not ride together. Led by the king's half-brother and Henry's brother-in-law, John Holland, Mowbray was one of a party composed of more than sixty knights and esquires who, with their jousting armour and their horses, disembarked at Calais at the beginning of March. Henry arrived about two weeks later with nine companions, including his illegitimate half-brother, John Beaufort, the ever present Thomas Swynford, and Henry Hotspur, who, captured by the Scots at the battle of Chevy Chase, had since been ransomed.

The fascination this tournament held for Henry's contemporaries is mirrored by the prominence given to it in the chronicles of Jean Froissart and the Monk of St. Denys, who turn aside from contemporary politics to describe at length the Jousts of St. Inglevert. They paint for us a scene decorated with banners, coats of arms and heralds and centred on three vermilion tents, one for each of the challengers, and displayed before each tent a white shield and a black.

To engage in combat with blunted weapons a knight sent his squire to strike the white 'shield of peace', while to engage with sharpened weapons, he struck the black shield of war. Most of the young men daringly chose the more dangerous option. Then trumpets blew, the ground thundered beneath the hooves of great horses, spear clashed against spear, and in a few thrilling moments a competitor became either victor or vanquished.

The first English arrivals acquitted themselves well, John Holland proving tireless and unbeatable, although Mowbray was unhelmed. But their prowess in the joust was surpassed by Henry's in the mêlée according to the Monk of St. Denys, whose habit did not prevent him from sharing the medieval zest for this hazardous sport. Riding onto the field with red-and-white, fringed taffeta pensels (tiny flags) fluttering from their lances, Henry and his knights engaged in 'a more dangerous fight', the monk informs us with robust enthusiasm, and 'were recognised as the bravest of all the foreigners'.

Such strenuous combats were interspersed with gentler pastimes, dancing, carolling (dancing and singing together) and banqueting, during which the talk inevitably turned to future chivalrous exploits, two 'crusades' that were to be got under way that year, one against the Moorish pirates of the Barbary coast of Africa, the other to be mounted by the

Teutonic Knights in Prussia against the heathen Lithuanians. Enthusiastically Henry decided to join them both.

Arriving back in England, on 6 May he appointed Richard Kingeston, archdeacon of Hereford, as his treasurer for war, for the 'voyages' in 'Barbarye' and 'Pruz'; and soon after he himself returned to Calais, accompanied by Thomas Swynford, about twenty esquires, three or four principal officers of his household and forty-one archers. With this small force, it seems, he intended to set out at once to join the Barbary crusade, which was to sail from Genoa in Genoese ships. But something - possibly an urgent plea from the Teutonic Knights for help - made him change his mind.

Having donated the presents he had brought - a palfrey and a saddle for the Sire of Sempy, his chief adversary in the jousts, and a saddle costing £6 13s. for the King of France - he returned again to England with Thomas Swynford. John Beaufort, accompanied by twenty-four English knights and a hundred archers, proceeded to Genoa without him.

Preparations for the Prussian expedition were to be on a far grander scale than the Barbary affair. For Henry was to take with him in his own ships a paid retinue of about two hundred men. (These were to include ten knights, eighteen esquires, his confessor and chaplain, Hugh Herle, his chamberlain and receiver-general, Hugh Waterton, and other household officers, Lancaster Herald, twenty-five valets of the chamber, grooms, miners, engineers, archers and six minstrels - two trumpeters, three pipers and one nakerer (drummer). It was his own little army that he would take with him across the North Sea.

In his lofty position Henry did not make the preparations himself, they were master-minded by his household officers who became welded into a team by this adventure. It was no coincidence that many of those who accompanied Henry to Prussia were to be found playing a leading part in his invasion of England in 1399.

The splendour and extent of Henry's preparations could not but help to fix his image in the memories of people living between London and Boston, Lincolnshire, where his three ships waited. In June and the first half of July peasants, whose villages bordered the road between these places, would have observed processions of wagons rumbling past piled high with provisions for the earl of Derby; corded canvas bundles of bows and arrows, sacks of corn, ten cauldrons, six spits and two racks to hang above the cauldrons, wax for candles, cages of chickens, forty-eight sticks of eels, barrels of beer, flitches of bacon, a barrel of whale oil, empty barrels, empty hogsheads, rolls of cloth, dried cod, barrels of white and red wine, sacks full of comfits (sweetmeats), preserves and spices, saffron for colouring, 'flat sugar, red and white', and - to be used as both flavouring and digestive - four-and-a-half hundredweight of almonds. There were carts dragging whole trees to carpenter into cabins for the earl of Derby's ships - in his own quarters a miniature version of his chamber and hall on land. There was even a green corded tapestry to hang on hooks in his hall at sea and, most essential of all, a double coffer to hold his father's Spanish gold, twenty-five thousand of the duke of Lancaster's newly acquired gold florins of Aragon as well as £755 11s. 6d. in English money.

Scores of animals were being driven or ridden too: forty sheep on the hoof, horses of all kinds, Henry's favourite white steed, fine horses for his knights, sumpter horses and mules to carry the luggage and draw the carts. In fourteenth century England such unwonted traffic was a sensation, establishing Henry in the eyes of onlookers as indeed a great prince.

By contrast with all this luxury, only a few weeks later that summer it would become a familiar sight to see small children outside their cottages begging for bread, the result of a harvest so poor that it made corn too expensive for many people to buy. But in all the chronicles there is no criticism of Henry's extravagance. For what might seem a frivolous and amoral adventure to us today was regarded by his contemporaries as an almost holy act.

To fight the heathen was part of the chivalric ideal which we find embodied in Chaucer's knight. The poet could have been thinking of Henry when he wrote,

> In Lettow had he reysed and in Ruce,
> No Cristen man so ofte of his degre.

> (In Lithuania had he gone on crusade and in Russia,
> No Christian man so often of his rank.)

The expedition was to add enormously to Henry's stature in the eyes of his countrymen, his activities in Prussia being considered worthy of a long account in the Monk of Westminster's chronicle.

While his household officers busied themselves with the buying, carting and loading of provisions for the journey, the great lord himself rode first to Hertford to bid farewell to his father, then to Berkhamstead where his wife and children were staying. Although pregnant with their fifth child and son, Humphrey, who was to be born in Henry's absence, Mary de Bohun accompanied him all the way to Lincolnshire. We catch a glimpse of the couple making their offerings together in Lincoln Cathedral, praying perhaps for a safe voyage for him and an easy delivery for her. Happily married though she was to Henry, Mary would need to accustom herself to being alone.

However, more significant for Henry's future than his relations with his wife, were his relations with the king, which appeared at this moment to be almost equally good. He had of course received the royal licence to leave the country, and Richard had written several letters to foreign princes to speed his too successful cousin on his way. So when on 19 July 1390 Henry sailed from Boston with his three well-laden carracks he went, with Richard's blessing, almost as an English emissary.

VIII   KNIGHTS OF LOVE AND WAR

> 'And these were certainly more knights of
> Venus than of Bellona, more valiant in
> the marriage bed than in the field, better
> armed with the tongue than with the
> lance.' Thomas Walsingham, *Historia
> Anglicana*

While Henry set sail to fight the pagans in the 'Wilderness', which is the
term for Lithuania in the accounts of Kyngeston, his treasurer for war,
Richard planned his own more leisurely battle, a long-term campaign to
raise the royal status. He aspired to exalt the English monarchy to heights
far above that of the barons who had dared to challenge it so recently,
heights which he passionately believed fitted its special relationship with
God. He would begin by displaying its magnificence to the rest of
Christendom - the only world whose opinion then mattered to England -
through the type of spectacle the people loved. In October while his cousin
Henry, earl of Derby, was absent he would stage a tournament so grand it
would outshine even that of St. Ingelvert. So through the summer days
English heralds journeyed to Scotland, Germany, Flanders, Brabant and
France, delivering their challenge. And among the foreign knights who
packed up their colourful pennons, their lances, armour and crested
helmets and took ship for England, were such notable men as the count of
St. Pol, the king's step brother-in-law, and the count of Ostrevant, son of
the duke of Holland.

The opening day's pageantry rivalled the marvels of Arthurian
legend as, to a fanfare of trumpets, twenty-four Knights of the Garter, the
English challengers, emerged from the thick stone gateway of the Tower of
London to ride to Smithfield, just beyond the city walls. It was a pretty
picture, for beside each knight rode a lady leading him by a chain of gold
attached to his bridle. His accoutrements, his armour, coat armour, shield
and even his horse trapper were patterned with white harts, the animal's
neck encircled by a gold crown with a gold chain pendant.

This symbol, derived from the white hind device used by his mother,
Princess Joan, was henceforth to play a fateful role in Richard's scheme to

build up the power of the crown; it was to become his favourite personal badge, the livery of the king by which his supporters would make themselves known, and when the time came for his plans to be realized, the sign which the archers of his private army would proudly bear on their breasts.

The Monk of Westminster records that Richard himself competed in the first day's jousts, the only time a contemporary English chronicle mentions him as partaking in this fashionable sport at all. He was awarded the prize for skill, and having thus proved his valour, he spent the rest of the tournament playing patron, presiding over the jousts and *mêlées* by day and entertaining the competitors by night in the Bishop's House by St. Paul's Cathedral. Here he resided for the duration of the tournament with his beloved and high spirited queen, giving a banquet every evening of the week except on Friday, when Gaunt acted as host in his place, providing a dinner which Froissart describes approvingly as a large and handsome spread, 'bien étoffé'.

When the tournament ended the count of Ostrevant was made a member of the Order of the Garter at Windsor, a political triumph bitterly resented by the French, since the Netherlands were then among the possessions of King Charles's uncle, the duke of Burgundy.

Another even more significant outcome of the affair followed. When the tournament stands at Smithfield were dismantled and their silken hangings chested and carted away, when the foreign knights had packed their armour and sailed for home, the badge of the white hart remained to create a cult, so influential that its vestiges can still be seen today.

Richard's chained white hart, a captive beast from a magic land, is the origin of inn signs throughout England; it can also be found carved in York Minster, Westminster Abbey and Westminster Hall. In Richard's reign to wear a white hart badge was a sign of loyalty which as time went on a courtier would fail to don at his peril, and Richard distributed these brooches in great numbers to friends and members of his household. With pearls tipping the antlers, they are even worn by angels in a votive painting, the Wilton Diptych, in the National Gallery.

The promotion of such a personal livery, that eventually led also to a private army, was a radical change of policy for Richard, who in the Cambridge parliament of 1388 had actually supported the Commons' attack on livery and maintenance. In fact, Richard would have preferred to abolish the private armies of retainers that constantly interfered with law and order throughout the country, but he had tried to do this and failed. He had in the end been balked by the Commons themselves, who distrusted the new civil law procedures he had advocated using. So the plague of private armies could continue, with their symptoms of anarchy and armed revolt, for almost another century until Henry VII found means to abolish them. Unable to beat the system, Richard had no choice but to join it.

Until now an English king had possessed only a very small bodyguard of archers, barely enough to beat off attack when he rode through the outlaw infested forests that still edged so many of England's roads. The theory was that he needed no more protection since, according to the feudal concept, this would be provided by the faithful lords and commons. Richard had found them anything but faithful and himself at the mercy of any group of subjects that chose to rebel against him. 'Sovereign lord' though he might respectfully be termed, when it came to forces at his personal command, the king was in the invidious position of possessing far fewer than most of his barons.

It was not until 1394 that he began to assemble the infamous Cheshire archers, who proudly wearing his livery and owing allegiance to nothing and no one save their royal master, terrorized the countryside by their unruly behaviour, but there is reason to believe that he secretly laid plans for such a force many years before. It was a necessary part of any major design for the monarchy, but it would be a revolutionary and therefore inevitably unpopular move. Aware of this, the king knew he must prepare the ground carefully before putting such a scheme into operation.

Meanwhile he continued his new mild and tolerant rule, giving every faction its say. The former rebels were not only accepted back into his council but into the life of his court too, an essential development at a time when court and government were still so closely intertwined. In August 1390 Richard joined a hunting party given by Gaunt at Leicester, where among his fellow guests were three of his recent enemies, the duke of Gloucester, the earl of Arundel and the earl's younger brother, Thomas, now archbishop of York. The king appeared to bear him no grudge for having replaced in this see the king's exiled friend, Alexander Neville. And in December 1390 some of the lords were reappointed to commissions of the peace, from which they had all been excluded in July 1389 in Richard's bid to curry favour with the Commons. Although he insisted on his right to rule, in the years from 1389-97 Richard made no evident attempt to re-establish what has come to be known as his 'first tyranny', the autocratic type of rule that had been the chief cause of the Appellants' Revolt.

Instead, he tried to end the financial cause of discontent in England by lessening taxation, and inaugurated this new policy by collecting only half the subsidy that had been granted by the Cambridge parliament of 1388. But the keystone of his financial policy over the next few years was to be, he hoped, a peace treaty with France. Peace would save the heavy cost of equipping and paying English armies. It was a statesmanlike plan never fully to be appreciated by his subjects. In all aspects of government he gave the impression of a benevolent and dispassionate monarch.

Nevertheless, there were indications for the observant that this new Richard had not really forgotten his ordeal at the hands of the appellants, and that discreetly he was taking steps to prevent a recurrence. One of these related to Edward II, whose deposition had created a precedent with which Richard had been threatened by the 'indivisible trio': he resolved to have his great-grandfather canonised, not such an impossible task as it sounds, since Edward's incompetence as a ruler and suspected homosexuality had been largely forgotten by Englishmen, in sympathy perhaps for the terrible manner of his death, by impalement, in Berkeley Castle. By one of the ironies of history, the tomb built for him in Gloucester Cathedral by his conscience-stricken son, Edward III - adorned with a double canopy that symbolised kingship and a saintlike stone effigy - had become a focus of pilgrimage. Richard was quick to see the possible political advantages in this cult of a king whom in so many ways he himself resembled.

Ever since 1387, after he too had been first threatened with deposition, he had sent envoys, notaries, scribes and proctors to the papal court at Rome to plead Edward's claim to sanctity. And in the autumn of 1390 he rode to Gloucester to collect personally the reports of alleged miracles at the tomb, intending to include them in a book for the pope, to support the plea. The planned canonization was important because it would effectively armour Richard against his enemies. In the pious Middle Ages who would dare publicly to show approval of the deposition of a saint by using it as a precedent?

Unfortunately, once all the evidence had been collected, the final decision on Edward's sanctity, which would give protection as well as add lustre to the English monarchy, passed from Richard's hands into those of the papal lawyers, who were not renowned for their speedy conclusions.

Richard could achieve much more immediate results in his own court. He deliberately increased its magnificence to match developments across the Channel. Until well into the fourteenth century the English court had been mainly a centre of government and administration, little grander than a noble's house. Edward III had begun to transform it into a civilised centre of leisure, entertainment and elegance, and Richard II was to take this transformation much further. For the first time, women's light voices, women's laughter were part of the court scene, and whenever Richard moved from one palace to another they rode with him, cherished objects of courtly love, gracefully dressed, with low-belted, bright silken gowns sweeping prettily over their side-saddles, their hair braided and looped into gold cylinders under jewelled coronets or cauls. But their dress was inconspicuous compared with that of the men, who were brilliant as butterflies.

The royal apartments teemed with courtiers garbed in ever more flamboyant clothes, the hemlines of the voluminous robes known as houpelandes were often now 'dagged' into intricate shapes, the sleeves 'cut' or 'carved' to show another colour beneath. The belts that gave the appearance of tiny waists and the garters that adorned male legs, clad in all the colours of the rainbow, were hung about with tinkling bells, while gowns and abbreviated doublets alike were a riot of embroidered flowers, birds, jewels, heraldic mottoes. Sleeves grew so wide and long that they trailed on the ground. Men as well as women painted their cheeks and lips with dyes called brasil and greyn imported from Portugal, and the barber was forever in demand to tend men's small forked beards and curl their hair with tongs. By the 1390s these eccentricities were not only confined to the young. Of Gaunt, we are told by Hoccleve who seemingly disapproved of the young dandies, 'his garnements were not fulle wide', suggesting that such moderation of dress was the exception rather than the rule even among older men.

The fastidious, exuberant, sophisticated personality of the monarch had set its stamp on his courtiers' appearance. But in another important area as well Richard's increasingly splendid court bore the imprint of these royal attributes. His master cook described him as 'the best and ryallest vyander of all Christian kings', and we are lucky enough to have a roll of palace recipes that appear to support this estimate, at least as far as medieval monarchs were concerned.

Richard's dishes were the product of intellect as well as culinary skills. Concocted 'by assent and avysement (advice) of maisters of phisick and of philosophie that dwellid in his court', they were elaborate, digestible, delicious and beautiful to look at, with a subtle combination of flavours. The meat, usually cut small, they mixed with sauces and flavoured with herbs, wine, almond milk and more spices than we use today, while the whole dish was often coloured red, yellow, purple, white or black. It is worth quoting two such recipes from the *Forme of Cury* since perhaps, more than anything else, they waft to us across the centuries the very smell and essence of Richard's court.

For the dish named *Mawmenee Pheasant* the chef teased the meat apart with his fingers, mixed it with Greek wine, sugar, dates, cloves, cinnamon and ginger, then coloured it red, with sandalwood. In *Sawse Madame* he stuffed a goose with sage, parsley, hyssop, savory, quinces, pears, garlic and grapes. It was first roasted, then cut into tiny pieces. The stuffing also was cut up and mixed with wine, powder of galangal and sweet aromatic powder, then poured over the goose.

Extravagantly dressed and exotically nourished, Richard's courtiers enjoyed yet another aspect of culture, poems on the theme of courtly love read aloud to them in scenes typified by the frontispiece of Chaucer's *Troilus and Criseyde*. Another fascinating link with Richard's court, this illumination depicts courtiers and their ladies strolling or sitting in the garden of a many-turreted palace, men and women alike in gowns of pink, blue, red and gold, while the poet, also clad in pink, reads to them from a pulpit. This poem, and Chaucer's translation of the *Roman de la Rose*, it is worth noting, were written especially for Richard's court, as were Thomas Uske's *Testament of Love* and Gower's *Confessio Amantis*, the latter being composed at the direct command of the king, who regally invited the middle-aged Gower on to the royal barge and imperiously commanded him to do his duty and write 'som newe thing', as the poet himself proudly states in his record of that delightful event.

In poetry, as in dress, Richard wished his newly splendid court to be 'the glass of fashion and the mould of form'. But, inevitably, such costly novelty was bitterly criticised by many of his subjects, to whom the court's strange elegance seemed a sign of effeteness, an indication that his advisers could think of nothing more important than the cut of their clothes, a popular view that is summed up in the poem *Mum and the Sothsegger*, written anonymously in 1399.

> ... but if the slevis slide on the erthe,
> Thei woll be wroth as the wynde and warie hem that it made;
> And (but) yif it were elbowis adoun to the helis
> Or passing the knee it was not acounted.

> (unless the sleeves slide on the ground,
> they will be cross as the wind and scold those that made it,
> and unless the elbows hang down to the heels
> or past the knee the garment was not reckoned to be worth anything.)

The English commons preferred traditional monarchs with simpler, cheaper ways. And if his court culture was ahead of its time and so failed to win general appreciation, the same is true of his foreign policy. Most Englishmen would have preferred the glory and booty of a successful war to peace with France. Richard seemed to them soft, a man who 'shrank from personal exertion', and after its brief resurgence in the autumn of 1389, his popularity in the kingdom was quickly to wane.

He was their king and so as a whole his subjects were still loyal to him, but he was far from being their image of an ideal lord. For most of them the king's cousin, Henry, with his rumbustious skill at the tournament and love of fighting, came much closer to this ideal. And the 'crusade' he had sailed off to join in July 1390 was to enhance his reputation for manhood, that quality Richard was popularly supposed to lack. Henry's contemporaries saw this 'crusade' in a very different light from the one we view it in today. From the standpoint of modern ethics it was a particularly murky business.

To begin with, the Teutonic Knights were much changed since their twelfth century origin when they had been founded to look after sick and wounded Christian soldiers in Palestine and to fight the enemies of the faith. Forced by Moorish conquests to leave the Holy Land, they had degenerated into an aggressive territorial power on the Baltic, spreading Christianity by the sword while in the process acquiring rich new lands for themselves. Having conquered and Christianised Prussia, they were now fighting the Lithuanians. Sweeping into battle with the distinctive black cross on their white cloaks, in the name of religion they burned down villages, murdered the long-haired men and marched their shackled women and children away to be forcibly baptised. And the motive of greed behind their alleged crusading zeal in 1390 was plain to see, for since the king of Lithuania and Poland had just been baptised himself, Christianity would soon have come to this country without the need for compulsion. Instead of supporting the Christian Jagiello the Teutonic Knights had agreed to help a pretender, his first cousin, Vitold, to usurp his throne in exchange for the province of Somogitia if they were successful. This was the expedition dignified by the name of 'crusade'.

But to fourteenth century Englishmen, any fight against the so-called heathen was a holy act; whether Turks or Lithuanians, it mattered not, they were all 'panyms' and 'saracens' to Henry's countrymen, creatures without souls, so to go on a 'reyse' against them was a 'blessed viage', the crown of Christian knighthood.

The voyage alone was hazardous even in the middle of summer. Attempting to follow his nephew's example and go on a crusade to Prussia the following year, the duke of Gloucester sailed into a storm and lost ships, men, horses, jewels and nearly his own life before being mercifully driven ashore on the coast of Scotland. Fortunately, during Henry's journey the North and Baltic seas remained calm, allowing his little fleet on 8 August to anchor safely at Rixhoft where, impatient to get started on his adventure, Henry disembarked with a few of his men. Leaving the rest of his party to sail on to Danzig (now Gdansk) and without even waiting for his favourite white horse to be unloaded, he travelled in a cart to Putzig where he bought a mount, then spent the night in a mill, altogether an unusually humble proceeding for a man of his rank. Reaching Danzig himself on 10 August, Henry learnt that the army of the Teutonic Knights had already left for Lithuania, so after having sent a report of his arrival to Richard, he gathered together a force of some fifty lances and sixty archers and hastened after them.

It was at this stage of the expedition that the teamwork of Henry's pocket-sized army was most severely taxed. The success of the Prussian expedition was to depend a great deal on its organization. To begin with, the army had to carry all its own supplies through difficult, marshy, deeply forested country to the Lithuanian border. Using flat-bottomed boats called prames, which sailed down the conveniently placed River Memel, as well as the customary carts and pack-horses, a vast baggage train contrived to lumber after him. Incredibly, Henry's provisions for this journey were no less royally elaborate than had been loaded on to his three ships at Boston.

They included live sheep and cattle, barrels of food, canvas bundles of weapons and armour, cooking pots and spits; chests of hangings and tapestries for his hall and bed-chamber, his great bed, the silver and plate for his cup-board and the furnishings for his chapel. A prince must needs always show a prince's trappings. Mercifully for the success of the expedition fashions were less demanding in enemy country; at the border, everything not needed on the 'reyse' itself was stored in a local castle, and the little army travelled on less encumbered. Much of the organization can probably be attributed to the invaluable Hugh Waterton, still Henry's chamberlain and man of all work, who was also to care for his children during his exile in 1399.

Henry was fortunate in his choice of date to join a Prussian 'crusade' for the Knights were soon to find such raw young English nobles more nuisance than they were worth on these expeditions and to refuse to take them, thus depriving them of a useful introduction to military life at a time of truce with France. On catching up with the Teutonic Knights, Henry was received by their leader, Marshal Rabe, 'with a glad face and joyful expression' while a welcoming tune was played by the company of minstrels belonging to the Master of Livonia, a province possessed by the Knights.

So far, Henry's only worthwhile experience of military action had been the battle of Radcot Bridge in 1387, which although politically important, in terms of fighting was little more than a skirmish. But this present 'crusade' was to give him a chance to prove his expertise and courage. Together, the armies marched on to Trappohnen on the River Memel, where they learnt that under King Jagiello's brother, Skirjal, the Lithuanian force lay at the junction of the Memel and the River Wilia, defending the ford and blocking their passage.

Marshal Rabe decided on a surprise attack by a small detachment. He was clearly impressed by Henry since the English earl was allowed to accompany these troops on their difficult task. Leaving the main army behind to delude the enemy into a sense of false security, and loading their provisions on to pack horses, Henry and Marshal Rabe marched through the concealing forest for seven days. It is interesting to note that Henry had coolly taken his chess set with him to while away any moments of leisure. Unexpectedly emerging from the trees on 28 August, the little force fought its way across the Wilia, killing some three hundred men and capturing three dukes and eleven boyars. With the remnant of his army, Skirjal fled into the strongly fortified nearby city of Vilna, the capital of the country.

The laconic Monk of Westminster tells us that for this victory 'the earl with the help of his men and especially of his archers deserved many thanks'. During the siege of the capital that followed he also distinguished himself. The city on a hill, clustering around King Jagiello's new brick church, was divided into two parts, an inner citadel defended by a wall and a castle, and an outer district defended only by a wooden rampart. It was 'owing to the strength and courage of Henry and his men' that on 4 September the marshal's army successfully stormed the rampart, Henry's 'gunner archer' being the first man to reach the top, planting Henry's banner there, a feat for which he was rewarded with the princely sum of 6s. 8d.

The marshal sent his English ally thanks in the form of gifts, an ox, four sheep and two peacocks, to enliven Henry's diet, although anti-climax followed when the inner citadel held out under siege for nearly five weeks. It was in vain that, protected by a 'sow' of shields from the arrows and cannon balls of the Lithuanian defenders, sappers mined under the walls; in vain that Knights bombarded them until their powder ran out. Disease finally forced the marshal's army to withdraw. The retreat was a disappointment, but for Henry the 'reyse' as a whole was a success. He had played a key part in the winning of two victories.

As mementoes of his exploits, when he rode back to Prussia, he took with him a number of Lithuanian children. Perhaps it says something for Henry's character that, unlike the thousands of miserable prisoners trailing after the Knights, these little boys were not captured but 'bought' from their own countrymen. Travelling with them to Konigsberg, he had them well clothed, fed and boarded at his expense and also, of course, baptised. One he called 'Henry' after himself, and he took at least one back to England with him. The removal of these children from their families was to add rather than detract from his reputation, since, in the eyes of his fellow Christians, he was bestowing on them the priceless chance of eternal life. Although it has inevitably been suggested since, there was then never any suggestion that his motives were homosexual.

By the time he crossed the border it was too late in the year to embark for home, so Henry spent the winter in Prussia, renting a series of castles and grand houses at Konigsberg and Danzig, while being entertained in princely style. Clad in his favourite red and black gowns and wrapped in furs against the cold, he hunted, hawked, jousted, diced in moderation, listened to minstrels, watched the acrobatics of tumblers and accepted numerous presents, including horses, hawks, deer, three young bears and a wild bull. And in the spring, as a sign of special honour for the now famous Englishman who had helped to defeat the heathen, Pope Boniface himself prescribed Henry's penance for Easter week, a penance that was possibly designed to suit his abundant energy; the earl of Derby was instructed to visit and make offerings at no less than four different churches a day.

When at the end of April Henry with his 'family' sailed for home in two chartered ships and landed in Hull, he was greeted as a public hero.

From *Knighton's Chronicle* we learn that the twenty-six-year-old earl of Derby 'returned with great rejoicing and great honour after a fine campaign full of joy to all Christians', and the Monk of Westminster remarks that he looked 'healthy and cheerful', as though his appearance and well-being was suddenly of burning interest to the whole country.

Richard, striving to exalt the monarchy above the barons, now found this expedition to Prussia had made his cousin more than ever a man to watch. He had become a power in the land whom one day it would be essential either to conciliate or destroy.

IX THE PILGRIM

'Whan that Aprille with his shoures soote
'The droghte of March hath perced to the roote ...
'Thanne longen folk to goon on pilgrimages.'
Geoffrey Chaucer, *The Canterbury Tales*

After spending so many months abroad it might have been expected that Henry would hasten first to greet his wife and children at their Peterborough manor, but Mary de Bohun was obliged to wait a few days longer before she saw her lord, for he invariably put first things first. Straightaway he rode north to give thanks for his safe return at the tomb of John of Bridlington, at Bridlington Priory, in Yorkshire. Although, like Edward II, not officially a saint, John's death in 1379 had given rise to stories of miracles, of lame men, blind men and lepers suddenly cured while visiting his tomb. According to the beliefs of the day such cures were proof enough of sanctity, there was no need to wait for the papal seal on it, and people flocked to the priory on pilgrimages. Henry had caught the prevailing enthusiasm. He had already visited John's tomb a year or so before and had placed his eldest son, the future Henry V, under John's protection. He evidently felt special veneration for John of Bridlington, who was also a prophet, author of obscure utterances alive with mythical birds and beasts, a key Henry may have hoped to his own uncertain future. At the time there seemed little scope in England for a man of his energy and attributes, a man fully as capable and already nearly as eminent as his father, but unlikely now ever to be trusted in the same way.

An anonymous account written about 1429 says that Gaunt attempted to provide the necessary scope for his son, that he tried to have Henry recognized by parliament as heir to the throne, because although Richard had been married for nine years, he still had no child. But this is generally believed to have been no more than unfounded rumour as there is no record of the alleged attempt in the parliament rolls.

Since he had no political office, throughout most of that summer, autumn and winter Henry simply amused himself, indulging in expensive pastimes, for he now had plenty of money. He spent lavishly, nearly £2,000 in the eight months from March to December 1391, and much of it on his appearance in the tournament.

A glance into Henry's accounts for this year dispels for ever the belief that he was a plain figure of a man. Although stockier and not as tall as Richard, he was dashing, elegant and exhibitionist. Over this period we see him engaging in his favourite sport at Waltham, Kenilworth, Brambletye and Hertford, on one occasion riding into the lists bearing a red and white pennon and mounted on a horst trapped in red and white satin. On another, carrying a shield 'palez white, red and black, with white and red bands written with white and red letters', and wearing a helm with a 'busk ... painted with flowers'.

There was lavish expenditure also on a gilded barge, which waited at his landing stage in London with eight boatmen in red cloth and scarlet hoods ready to row him up or down the River Thames. And when he chose to ride through the country instead, he was preceded by a herald wearing his coat armour of red leopards and gold fleurs-de-lis with a blue label, and six minstrels in 'blood' striped liveries with tan facings.

His own dress was opulent, usually in the royal red and white or in black, the accounts revealing frequent orders for bales of velvet, silk and *or de Cypre* to be sewn up into billowing cloaks and sleeves, while his doublets and gowns were 'dagged', fringed and embroidered with the signs and emblems beloved by his age. As the earl of Derby strode through tapestried halls or danced in painted palace chambers, words, letters and patterns cunningly appeared and disappeared in the folds of his garments, such curious devices as his motto 'Soveyne vous de Moy' (remember me) and 'snags' and swans from his SS collar. While one stiffly shining gown, presumably worn only on occasions whose formality made movement almost unnecessary, was covered all over with gilt leaves of the forget-me-not, the 'lord's flower'. With this splendid attire went a manner amiable, graceful and less exaggerated than the king's. At Richard's court no man can have looked finer than this red-haired young lord.

What could be the future of an ambitious earl of such high calibre and reputation, a noble who might grow hostile if an opportunity for his energies was not found? Wisely, Richard decided to provide such an outlet. Indeed, at this date he had little choice but to cultivate this cousin whose father was his own apparently most trusted minister. At the king's instruction Gaunt's livery of the SS collar also now gleamed on the doublets of royal retainers above their white hart brooches. Gaunt's son, Henry, could hardly be thrust out of this aura of favouritism.

In the November parliament Henry was trier of petitions, and the following March he sailed to Calais as one of an embassy led by his father on the crucial mission trying to make a permanent peace with France. For

Henry, it was an embassy lit with a burning personal interest, for the means by which peace was to be accomplished would eventually make him almost as powerful a prince as the duke of Burgundy.

The chief bone of contention between these neighbouring countries had always been Aquitaine, owned by the king of England yet still claimed as a part of France, a situation giving rise to endless arguments about sovereignty and homage. Richard had decided on the one way to resolve them: English monarchs would simply relinquish the sovereignty of the duchy which had come with the marriage of Eleanor to King Henry II in 1152, and confer it instead on a new dynasty, the duke of Lancaster and his heirs, who would hold Aquitaine of the French king.

For England this was not such a sacrifice as might at first appear, since in the climate of growing nationalism across the Channel sooner or later Aquitaine was bound to become French. In fact, thus to anticipate the inevitable was a far-sighted and statesmanlike policy but a policy, Richard knew, that was unlikely to please his subjects, who still dreamed of a return to the time of England's great victories at Crécy and Poitiers. It would need skilled diplomacy and Richard had chosen his chief envoys with care. As well as Gaunt and Henry, who had a personal stake in the outcome, he had selected his pacific uncle, Edmund of Langley, duke of York; and his own half brother, John Holland, who though an aggressive and violent man was entirely loyal to the king.

In addition he had chosen Sir Thomas Percy, younger brother of the earl of Northumberland, and Walter Skirlaw, bishop of Durham, who were both fourteenth century doves. The hawks, the duke of Gloucester and earl of Arundel, who favoured a continuation of the war, were excluded from an embassy whose chief purpose was not mentioned even in its official reports. Richard showed the importance he attached to this mission and his anxiety for its success by providing an escort of a thousand horsemen and himself accompanying his emissaries to Dover, then awaiting their return in Dover castle.

Richard's scheme opened a golden prospect before Henry, at last a suitable scene for his talents and ambitions, a life in keeping with the rest of his family's achievements. On Gaunt's death he would receive an inheritance so grand it spanned the Channel, the Lancastrian lands and palatinate in England on one side, and the duchy of Aquitaine in France on the other. For him the whole visit to France must have shone with special meaning, and the French did their best to make his stay as agreeable as possible.

King Charles and his uncles were evidently no less eager than Richard for the success of a scheme that held so much for them. They received the English embassy with the greatest honours, the count of St.

Pol escorting them from Calais to Amiens, where the peace was to be negotiated, while equally courteously, Henry and his fellow nobles wore garments of dark green in mourning for his recently dead countess. The meeting was organized magnificently. As the embassy rode into the walled city of Amiens, a crescendo of music signified that the French king was simultaneously entering through the Paris gate accompanied by a vast escort.

Both retinues were to be lodged in the city, an arrangement that might have led to problems in the aftermath of war between their two countries. But the French were prudent. And so that no quarrels should break out, their citizens had been forbidden on pain of death to insult or provoke the visitors. In addition, the French king had promised to pay all the Englishmen's day to day expenses. As a result, the only battle that took place at the conference was one of courtesy between the French king and Gaunt. Charles VI, not yet subject to the distressing bouts of insanity that were so soon to make him a pawn in the hands of his brother and uncles, received the duke of Lancaster in the hall of the bishop's court, and on entering, Gaunt knelt three times, once on entering the room, once in the middle of it, and once before the throne, like the dutiful French courtier he intended to become in place of the English general whose main occupation had been to kill French soldiers and to burn and loot their villages.

Clearly just as anxious to forget the past, King Charles took him by the hand and said, 'Welcome to our kingdom; we rejoice at your arrival, which we have long ardently desired'. Lodgings had been prepared for the English lords in Malmaison, a shield with each lord's arms hung over his door, and in a purple gown sewn with jewels and pearls Charles entertained them all to a banquet where they were served by no lesser men than the king's own brother and maternal uncle, the dukes of Orleans and Bourbon.

Sadly, the negotiations were not at the time conclusive. Gaunt succeeded only in prolonging the truce made at Lelinghen on 18 June 1389. But they ended on a hopeful note with an understanding that talks would soon be resumed about the proposal to confer Aquitaine on a Lancastrian dynasty. And for their part the French negotiators had proposed a concession which should go a long way towards making the deal acceptable to Richard's subjects.

In exchange for England's sacrifice the French promised to increase Aquitaine's boundaries by returning to it on the death of the duke of Berry all those lands they had acquired since the Treaty of Bretigny, so that one day Henry would acquire not just a meagre strip of land from Bordeaux to Bayonne, but a sizable duchy. Riding back to Calais under trees just

107

breaking into leaf, Henry had every reason to feel happily loyal to his cousin Richard, who was looking after him so well.

In such circumstances it is not surprising that his accounts for this year list two brooches of the king's livery, a gold stag bought for himself and, for Mary, at a cost of £9, a gold hind with a collar, decorated with white enamel and set in a garter. There was also a gown fashioned for himself patterned with a design of harts and garters. Henry arrived home in time for the birth of his annual child - a first daughter, called after his mother, Blanche, and christened in Peterborough Cathedral. However, this excitement over, there remaining for the moment no further political role for him in England, he decided to return to Prussia.

His willingness to leave his wife and children again so soon does not indicate lack of affection. His accounts bear witness to his concern for them, listing such items as cloths from Champagne and Flanders to drape the font at Blanche's christening, six ells of stuff for Blanche's nurse's pallet, and the cost of mending two silver gilt collars for little Henry and Thomas, still far too young to be careful of their possessions. There were also kirtles bought for all four of his little sons. But, such energies as Henry's needed an outlet greater than the quiet domestic pleasures in Mary's favourite house at Peterborough.

Once more his father was ready to help. On 1 July at Leicester he granted him 2000 marks a year paid quarterly from the revenues of Tutbury and Bolingbroke, the payments to begin at Michaelmas 1392. However, it seems that this was not soon enough for the impetuous Henry, for on 15 July Richard Kingeston, archdeacon of Hereford, was called again from his ecclesiastical duties and appointed treasurer for war; and four days later Gaunt advanced the 2,000 marks for the first year and made a gift of an extra £1,000 with the express wish that it should be used for a second reyse. Henry was not put off by the fact that since his last visit several young nobles, including one of the powerful Percy family, who had journeyed to Prussia to help fight the unfortunate Lithuanians had been turned away by Vitold. His own reception, he was sure, would be different.

This time, he decided to embark at Lynn, to which little boats sailed up the coast with stores from Peterborough. When his three ships there were fully laden, they were towed by ten small boats fourteen miles north-east to Heacham, on the Wash, whence Henry set sail on 24 July, again with some two hundred men.

But an unpleasant surprise awaited him when he reached Konigsberg on 2 September. He was informed that his help was unwelcome, a blow the Grand Master of the Teutonic Knights tried to soften by contributing £500 towards his expenses. Undoubtedly disappointed, Henry simply switched plans, deciding to use his money for a pilgrimage to Jerusalem, a journey that would earn him special remission of his sins, besides offering the rare chance to see new countries and new courts.

Having sent home most of his men and stores, he set off across Europe from Danzig on 22 September and rode through Pomerania and Bohemia, then part of the Holy Roman Empire, reaching Prague on 13 October, where he was received by the emperor, brother of Richard's queen. With the dissolute Wenzel he spent eleven days, three of them at Zebrak near Pilsen, days whose revelry was interspersed with sightseeing and souvenir buying, a revealing sidelight on Henry's character, showing that even in his youth he kept measure in all things. He offered at the relics in the castle at Karlstein, visited the ancient castle of Hradschin and bought an ostrich from a traveller from Africa.

On 4 November Henry reached Vienna, where he stayed for four days, at the expense of Albert of Hapsburg, the duke of Austria, and met Wenzel's brother, Sigismund, King of Hungary, with whom he formed a bond of friendship, ordering a pair of hose embroidered with Sigismund's emblems of wounds and arrows.

Henry's high rank and amiable manner won him friends everywhere; through them he was to escape the discomfort experienced by ordinary pilgrims journeying to Jerusalem on stinking, overcrowded ships at risk from Turkish pirates. The duke of Austria wrote to the senate of the Republic of Venice requesting that a galley should be provided to transport Henry to Jaffa and back. The Venetians agreed, and when Henry entered their city on 30 November gave him a splendid ceremonial welcome at a cost of 360 golden ducats from the republic's treasury. In this most powerful Italian state filled with luxuries from the East, Henry had nothing to do but enjoy himself. While his officers bought stores in the countryside for his forthcoming voyage, their lord resided on the Isola di San Giorgio, facing the palace of the doge, with whom he offered at various Venetian churches, including the beautiful St. Marks.

Finally, leaving most of his remaining men to spend the winter at Portoguaro in north Italy, he set sail on the last part of his journey just before Christmas, travelling on one of the customary pilgrims' routes, down the Adriatic and through the Mediterranean via Zara, Lissa, Corfu, the Morea and Rhodes to Jaffa.

Arrived at this gateway to the Holy Land, Henry temporarily abandoned his princely pomp. Leaving most of his escort behind, he walked on foot the thirty miles to Jerusalem. Here for a fee its Saracen masters would show Christians the Holy Sepulchre, the Mount of Olives and the exact location of other important episodes in the Redeemer's life, the very spot where Jesus had picked up his cross and laid it down, even where he had raised Mary Magdalene from the ground. His visit retained a deep meaning for Henry throughout his life, and he would often express a longing to return; as with so many medieval men, a solid religious faith being part of the secret of his resolute character.

From the Holy Land he made his leisurely way back to England via Cyprus, Venice, Milan, Pavia and Paris, accumulating friends and keepsakes as he went, including a Turk who was baptised Henry like his Lithuanian predecessor, a leopard, a parrot, cups made of ostrich eggs and a case to keep them safe ... In Venice he bought for himself and his retainers new outfits all to match, one set of doublets in green and another in his customary red, as well as a set of short white mantles, the earl's own garments and those of his knights and esquires being made of lavish silks and Genoese velvets, those of his grooms and valets of humble wool; and as a further embellishment, he bought everyone gilt or silver collars.

In Milan, the duke, nicknamed the Count of Virtues, grew to be a friend with whom he was to correspond for many years. In the same city he also met the future Pope Alexander V who seventeen years later was to remember him with 'esteem and singular affection' on account of his 'singular virtues'. From all sides he won golden opinions. Lucia Visconti, a young cousin of the duke's, was so taken with him that six years later, aged twenty-one, she would refuse to marry the bridegroom chosen by her family, on the grounds that she had vowed to marry no one but Henry of Derby, and would wait for him for ever even if she had to die three days after the wedding. It is interesting to note that Lucia's story is unmixed with scandal, from which we may presume that Henry responded to the fifteen-year-old Italian girl's passion with the same mixture of virtue and courtesy shown by the hero of the poem, *Sir Gawayne and the Grene Knight*, written some twenty years earlier. Sexual continence was a characteristic that set him apart from his relatives, his own father, his grandfather, King Edward III, and his uncle, the Black Prince, all of whom, unlike Henry, begot illegitimate children. But Henry was faithful to his wife; there was to be no shadow to dim the lustre of his still more shining reputation when he arrived back in England at the end of June.

Richard, while his cousin's thoughts had been on these pleasant and idealistic pursuits abroad, battled with more practical considerations, the far less glamorous, persistent problem of lack of money, which threatened to put a stop to his new policies. For although the war with France was in abeyance and no longer emptied his coffers, he needed funds to pay for his increasingly magnificent court, the golden image that he was bent on creating for the monarchy. In the two years from September 1392 to September 1394 the expenditure of the great wardrobe was to double from £8,000 to £16,000, of which £6,203 was spent on fabrics (mercery) alone,

£4,431 on hangings, £2,219 on furs, and £387 on harness. He dared not ask parliament to grant taxes to pay for these luxuries. So how was he to finance them? The solution he found was in just over seven years' time to have fatal repercussions for him in his final confrontation with Henry.

Alluringly within sight of Richard's most frequented palaces of Westminster and Eltham, was another source of income, its church spires and towers jutting into the sky. The London of William Dunbar's well known poem was in all essentials the same tempting picture that the hard-up Richard saw a century earlier:

> Soveraign of cities, seemliest in sight,
> Of high renown, riches and royaltie;
> Of lordis, barons and many a goodly knyght;
> Of most delectable lusty ladies bright;
> Of famous prelates, in habitis clericall;
> Of merchauntis full of substance and of myght;
> ....
> Pryncesse of townes of pleasure and of joy,
> A richer restith under no Christen roy (king).

Richard was determined to have a share of those riches from his capital which had so disloyally taken the appellants' side in 1387 and 1388, and ever since denied him the facilities accorded in Edward III's reign and during Richard's own minority when it had been the custom for the city of London to lend money to the monarch. Since March 1388, when London had agreed to lend him £5,000, he had been unable to raise even a small loan there. His request for one in 1389 had met with the irritating excuse that most of the citizens were 'neither merchants nor powerful men' and when in February 1392 Richard had tried another method to raise money he failed. On ordering the sheriffs to search out citizens with an income qualifying them for knighthood - the king was entitled to a fee for each man who became a knight - he was informed that there was no one who could count on receiving the necessary income every year. Since the qualifying sum was only £40, it was an unlikely story, but one that Richard had no means of proving untrue. Nevertheless, he was resourceful and the royal power, cleverly used, was very great.

By the summer he had devised another means to grab some of the London 'merchantis' substaunce'. He would take advantage of a law passed in 1354 which made the civic authorities liable to large fines should they fail to keep order. Disorder was endemic in a walled city crammed with bands of retainers, rival craft gilds, unemployed soldiers, travellers bringing back new heretical ideas from abroad, hot-blooded young apprentices and students of logic practising their art in public disputations, and no less turbulence than usual had distinguished this place of churches, abbeys, great houses, hovels, markets and shops in Richard's reign. On the contrary, in 1391 there had been so many armed felonies and crimes that in November and December the mayor had declared an 8 p.m. curfew, policed by an armed watch.

So the king had not long to wait for the particular excuse he sought. It came one winter's day in the shape of a disgraceful affray in Fleet Street. A servant of the bishop of Salisbury, treasurer of England, snatched a 'horse loaf' from a baker's roundsman and when the roundsman very naturally objected, the servant struck him. Onlookers gave chase and the chief ran into his master's inn nearby, where his fellow retainers fastened the gates to protect him. The frustrated crowd, bent on punishing the man themselves, roared angrily: hand over the miscreant or they would burn the place down. Fortunately just before this threat was put into practice, the mayor and sheriffs arrived and ordered the crowd to disperse.

The incident was tailor-made for Richard's purpose, since after such an unruly scene it could reasonably be claimed that the Londoners were failing in their duty to govern themselves.

In May 1392 the royal wrath burst upon the unsuspecting citizens. Richard decreed that the chief organs of government, the court of common pleas, the chancery and the exchequer should be moved from Westminster to York. No longer would hosts of officials, lawyers, clerks and petitioners pour money into the neighbouring city, frequenting her taverns, buying goods from her little shops, and market stalls in Cheap, and employing the skills of her goldsmiths, tailors, cordwainers and myriad other craftsmen. Without the usual activities at Westminster London's purse would be pinched indeed.

But she was yet to suffer worse. The city had long held the right to elect her own dignitaries. Richard summoned to appear before him and his council at Nottingham on 25 June the mayor, John Hende, and his two sheriffs under pain of forfeiture of life and limb, and when these men nervously stood before him, the king declared that 'notable and evident defaults' had been found 'in the governance and rule of the city'. He therefore arbitrarily deprived all three of their offices, and sent them to prison, then appointed a royal councillor and king's knight, Sir Edward Dalyngridge, to rule London in Hende's place, and also himself selected two new sheriffs. London had lost her most cherished privilege, but Richard had not finished punishing her even now.

He issued a commission of 'oyer and terminer' to enquire into the 'defaults' in the government of the city, and the commissioners pronouncing John Hende, his sheriffs and aldermen guilty of negligence, declared that the previous mayor, William Venour, his sheriffs and aldermen were also to blame. Upon this verdict both sets of civic authorities were together ordered to pay fines totalling 3,000 marks, while on the city itself the enormous fine of £100,000 was laid, a sum then impossible to raise. Yet the king's demands were legal. As the citizens desperately lamented their predicament a solution was proposed to them: the king might be prepared to relent if they would pay £10,000 for their pardon and stage at their expense a suitable ceremony of reconciliation in which the king could star.

They had no choice; they prepared swiftly and spent lavishly the money they had sworn to the sheriffs in February that they did not possess, putting on a show so magnificent that Gaunt's confessor, Richard of Maidstone, was inspired to write a Latin poem in praise of it.

Arriving with his queen one late August day on the south side of London Bridge, King Richard was welcomed by the warden, aldermen and craft gilds in their brilliant liveries, and solemnly presented with the sword and the keys of the city, the emblems of independent government. To the sound of cymbals, lyres, cytherns and viols, he and Anne then rode over the bridge through the city and down Cheap, which in his honour had been adorned with hangings of gold and silver tissue and of tapestry. Here they were showered with rich presents: a gold crown each, gold cups, gold images of the Trinity and St. Anne, and a crystal chest and ewer inlaid with gold, also a pair of white horses, trapped in the royal red and white, their harness glittering with gold and silver and tinkling with silver bells. And an extra special bit of flattery awaited them above the gate at Temple Bar: a tableau depicting one of Richard's patron saints, John the Baptist, surrounded by dragons and other beasts in a painted desert with a forest in the background. As a gentle hint St. John was pointing to an *agnus dei*, lamb of God, symbol of Christ's mercy.

Richard had undoubtedly been warned of the happy surprise now in store for him, because he stopped to admire the little scene, thus providing the opportunity for an 'angel' to 'fly' down and present him with 'a tablet studded with gems, fit for any altar, with the crucifixion embossed thereon'.

That day's ceremonial was yet another of the king's beloved charades, for throughout it he pretended, contrary to the truth, that no hard bargain had already been struck and that the city's fate still hung in the balance. With artistry he acted the part of the wronged monarch finally driven to magnanimous mercy at the pleas of his stricken subjects. At Temple Bar, taking the tablet offered by the angel in his hand, he said loudly, 'Peace to this city! For the sake of Christ, his mother and my patron, St. John, I forgive every offence.' However, positive proof of this forgiveness was carefully withheld until the end of the day when in Westminster Hall

Queen Anne fell on her knees before him also to plead on behalf of the city, addressing him in Maidstone's words as, 'My king, my husband, my light, my life! Sweet love, without whose life mine would be but death,' phrases suggesting that with Richard she lived in a passionately emotional world. Then, at last, having raised her to sit beside him on the throne, the king handed back to the warden the symbolic sword and keys.

It was the climax of the day and soon afterwards he graciously pardoned the civic authorities, remitting their fines and those of the city; the court of common pleas, the chancery and exchequer were authorized to return to Westminster from York, and London was once again allowed to elect her own mayor and sheriffs. And in February 1393 Richard graciously acknowledged receipt of the city's £10,000 fine.

Just like Henry, wending his leisurely way back from Jerusalem, Richard had scored a triumph. He had replenished his coffers quite legally without having to raise unpopular taxes. And in case he ever needed to raise money again from an unwilling London he had retained a hold over it; the letters patent restoring her liberties stated that they did so only conditionally 'until the king shall otherwise ordain'. In other words they could be withdrawn at any time the king wished.

No longer a tiresomely intransigent, independent minded place, his capital was cowed, and the Londoners were eager to appease and honour him in every way possible. That Christmas he and Anne kept at Eltham. The citizens sent mummers to entertain them and presents of two expensive and curious jewels, 'a dromedary with a boy seated on its back for the king and a bird with a wide throat for the queen'.

At their own expense the following summer the citizens made another conciliatory gesture, erecting two freestone statues, one of the king, one of the queen, above the stone gate on London Bridge, and to make the coloured robes and gilded sceptres appear still more brilliant, they whitened the stone wall outside the gate with plaster. These statues loomed over the main entrance to London, their heads sheltered by canopies of estate, their shields of arms beside them. Significantly, there was also a third shield bearing the arms of Edward the Confessor, which for the rest of Richard's reign were to be displayed in close proximity with the royal arms. It was a symbol of what was to come. So, in shining majesty and an aura of saintliness Richard intended to dominate England.

He was unaware that in thus milking and humiliating London he had lost the hearts of its citizens for ever, and that this was to prove a fatal mistake.

X   THE MASK OF THE KING

'The same kyng is wont ... to be so
variable and ffeynyng ... that almost ther
was no levyng man ... myht trust in hym.'
Charge against King Richard, Julius B
11, *Chronicles of London*

In 1393 while Henry was still on his pilgrimage to Jerusalem, Richard appeared to be overcoming his enormous difficulties at home. He had tamed his unruly capital city and at the same time found a way to raise money without parliament's consent, so that he was no longer entirely subject to its dictates. More important still, he had tamed his turbulent barons, transforming the five lords who had once threatened to depose him into his good liegemen, faithful and obedient.

Almost miraculously it seemed, the leader of the rebel appellants, Thomas of Woodstock, duke of Gloucester, had come round to supporting the policy of peace with France, although this went against his very nature. But Richard had bribed and threatened him into acquiesence, on the one hand dangling before him the prospect of acquiring rich lands for himself in Aquitaine, and on the other forcing him to make recognizances into chancery for £ ,000 marks. Gloucester had finally discovered where his best interests lay. Richard was now certain enough of the support of his bellicose youngest uncle to send him on embassy to France in March, 1393. With his elder brother Gaunt to keep an eye on him, the now conciliatory duke set sail to pursue the peace talks, camping for the purpose outside Calais in a splendid tent. The dukes' temporary abode, the author of the *Annales* tells us with chauvinistic glee, far outshone any of the pavilions of the French, being of unbelievable size and richness, 'for he had erected, not just magnificently but miraculously, a huge hall ... and a campanile which tolled the hours of the day and night, a chapel, rooms, a cloister, and various courtyards for entertaining the rest of his people, in which every day there were markets, stalls for merchandise and court cases'. In these opulent surroundings the terms of a treaty were drawn up, and Gloucester's part in this success set the seal on the new feeling of accord between him and his nephew.

Henceforward the king was often to be seen walking arm in arm with his youngest uncle through the tapestried halls and the gardens at court just as he did with the long trusted Gaunt. Never had they appeared so friendly before. The king regularly chose Gloucester as a member of the royal council, showered upon him lucrative gifts and appointed him justice of Cheshire and North Wales for life.

With the earl of Arundel, Gloucester's chief ally among the appellants during their uprising in 1387, and another one-time thorn in the king's flesh, Richard's relationship was cooler, but still cordial. Arundel also frequently attended the council and in 1395 the king presented him with a fine diamond, for although, unlike Gloucester, he still opposed peace with France, at least ever since the rebellion he had refrained from the rude verbal attacks on the king in public which had so infuriated Richard in earlier years. Aged forty-seven, Arundel appeared mellowed by a combination of middle age and marriage to his new young wife, Philippa Hastings, the duke of Clarence's grand-daughter, on whom he apparently doted.

In her honour his castle of Shrawardine, in Shropshire, was rechristened Castle Phelip and decked out with hangings of blue embroidered with red roses and the arms of his three sons-in-law, the earl of Nottingham, Lord Charlton of Powis and Sir William Beauchamp. The earl also showered on her head-dresses 'of pearls as of other attire'. While providing us with a glimpse into the couple's private life, the earl's will stipulates that she should inherit the silver candelabra that they used while eating supper together in winter.

The third member of the 'indivisible trio', and the most genial and attractive, Thomas Beauchamp, earl of Warwick, had more or less faded from the political scene. In his mid fifties, an old man by fourteenth century standards, he spent much of his time at Warwick Castle, surrounded by his tapestries of the golden bear and silver staff, of the adventures of Guy of Warwick, and of the stories of Alexander, and John the Baptist. It was at this period in his life that he completed Guy's Tower, which balances Caesar's Tower on the other side of the gatehouse on the north east front of the castle to this day.

As for the last two appellants, Henry, with his splendid prospects in Aquitaine, was a staunch royal supporter, while Mowbray had become again apparently one of the king's most cherished companions. Neglecting his own estates so that he could be constantly at court, he was to be used by Richard on those diplomatic missions nearest to the royal heart (he sailed to France to negotiate Richard's second marriage in 1396 and in 1397 journeyed to Frankfurt in an attempt to further Richard's grandiose ambition to be elected Holy Roman Emperor). Mowbray was a more frequent member of the council than either Gloucester or Arundel and in 1394 Richard underlined their friendship by paying £200 to celebrate the marriage of the earl of Nottingham's son to the daughter of Richard's half brother, John Holland, earl of Huntingdon.

The rebellion that broke out that spring was inspired not by the appellants, or indeed by any of the barons; it arose from the common people, the inhabitants of the king's own palatinate and earldom of Cheshire. A poor county which had come to rely on war with France as a source of livelihood, Cheshire was full of men whose only trade was the sword, the lance, the pike, the bow and shooting flights of arrows into French cavalry. They were men whose fathers and grandfathers had fought and won at Crécy and Poitiers, returning home laden with precious spoils.

For them, the years of truce had spelt disaster. The piratical ways, that had won them praise from their commanders in France, won them only punishment in England, and for their habitual unruly behaviour the king had imposed on them in 1390 an enormous fine of 3,000 marks, to be paid in instalments in exchange for a charter confirming their liberties. But the men of Cheshire would not tolerate it; after handing over the first instalment they simply refused to pay more, and the sheriffs' attempt to raise the next 2,000 marks they resisted by force.

Into this cauldron bubbling with discontent in the spring of 1393 there fell the news that two of the royal dukes, Gaunt and Gloucester, were in France negotiating, not simply another truce, but perpetual peace which meant perpetual unemployment for Cheshire's sons. To infuriate them still more, they heard that Aquitaine, for which they had fought so hard and many of their companions had died, was to be given away by the king.

The descendants of the men of Crécy and Poitiers did not hesitate to act in the way they understood best. They attacked the ambassadors who were negotiating this obnoxious deal and anyone who stood to gain from the alienation of the duchy. Overnight, nailed to the door of every parish church in the county, there appeared a manifesto telling the people that the dukes of Lancaster and Gloucester and the earl of Derby meant to give away their liege lord's kingdom in France and also to deprive Cheshire of its liberties.

Once more, the men of Cheshire armed themselves for war, taking down from their cottage walls pikes and swords, bows and arrows, until some twenty thousand of them were riding and marching ominously about the countryside, shouting death to Gaunt, Gloucester and Derby. To make the problem worse, this area of rebellion bordered on another where disorder had been rampant since 1387, when Gaunt's estates in Yorkshire became plagued by a band of outlaws, criminals whose actions if not their motives resembled Robin Hood's. It had begun with a man named William

Beckwith, who believed he had been denied his hereditary right to be Gaunt's master forester, and had set up camp in the forest, from which he led raids of revenge against the duke's castles. Beckwith himself was now dead, but the dogs of war he had unleashed ran on. His raids and murders had led to a blood feud that nothing seemed able to stop. And although the disturbances in Cheshire and Yorkshire proceeded from very different causes, together they added up to a substantial part of England in open revolt. It was in vain that the king sent his half brother, John Holland, the earl of Huntingdon, and Sir John Stanley to restore order. The mobs continued to riot and he was finally forced to recall Gaunt from the precious peace talks in France, a fact that shows he regarded his eldest uncle as still the ablest of his ministers.

Except in so far as they once again revealed the all too easily inflammable nature of Richard's subjects, the revolts themselves proved to be not too serious. Showing tact and statesmanship typical of his middle-age, Gaunt pacified the counties with almost no bloodshed. He succeeded mainly by providing work, recruiting able-bodied men into the army he himself intended to take with him to Aquitaine in 1395 to claim his right to the duchy. By the time Henry, returning from pilgrimage, had reached Calais on 28 June with his souvenirs, his leopard, his ostrich and his Turkish convert named Henry, order had been restored both in Cheshire and Yorkshire.

But the end of the revolts was not the end of trouble, for the uprisings had uncovered a seam of distrust that ran beneath the smooth, calm surface of the years following the Appellants' Revolt, a distrust that was to damage the new royal image. Incredibly, the king was suspected of prompting the Cheshire men to murder the three magnates, Gaunt, Gloucester and Henry, earl of Derby.

To appreciate the shock of this suspicion it must be remembered that in the eyes of their contemporaries the lords involved were much more than three rich, powerful men, they were also representatives of the government of the realm. For, as the modern historian Galbraith put it, 'the necessity of ruling in co-operation with the great nobles was the unwritten law of medieval kingship', and should the king plot against them he would be breaking that law, as well as betraying those who had paid him homage, to whom he owed good lordship in exchange for military service and support.

Suspicion of Richard was based on his relationship with Sir Thomas Talbot, leader of the Cheshire rebels. Talbot was a king's knight, one of that small specially chosen handful of men attending on the king in his bed-chamber. The story went that Talbot had been encouraged by Richard who, beneath his affectionate gestures to Gaunt and Gloucester, his kindness to Derby, secretly wanted to see all three killed. It reawakened disturbing memories of the attempt on Gaunt's life in 1385, a plot in which Richard was alleged to have been involved. If the story was true the foundation of society was endangered.

Such a rumour could destroy the picture of the just king which Richard had been at such pains to paint in the years since the Appellants' Revolt, and he felt compelled to deny it. He published in May a proclamation addressed to the dukes of Lancaster and Gloucester, as well as to the sheriffs of Shropshire, Staffordshire, Derbyshire, Leicestershire and Warwickshire, in which he informed them that he was innocent of any attempt to 'destroy the great ones of the realm', an ill judged announcement. One can imagine the effect of hearing such extraordinary words uttered by the town crier. On the grounds that there is no smoke without a fire, the proclamation could only encourage the damaging rumour of Richard's bad faith, especially in view of the leniency with which he treated Talbot.

Gaunt himself had pardoned many of the rebels, but Talbot he had reserved for the king's justice, expecting that the rebels' leader at least would suffer the accustomed punishment for such crimes: to be hanged and quartered, his head spiked above London Bridge as a deterrent to anyone who felt like following his unruly example. But Talbot's punishment was a mockery. Although to Henry, earl of Derby - who on his return to England helped his father by examining the prisoners - the knight confessed that he had indeed attempted the lives of the three lords, he nevertheless suffered nothing worse than brief imprisonment in the Tower of London, imprisonment from which he soon escaped, probably with the connivance of his captors. And if that was not leniency enough, less than three years later in April 1397 Richard actually pardoned him for his 'felonies, murders, rapes and treasons', then in November 1397 re-employed him as a king's knight with a retainer for life of 100 marks a year.

All this occurred despite repeated protests by Gaunt and Gloucester. Richard's handling of the aftermath of the Cheshire revolt was one of a series of events that helped to discredit him in the eyes of his subjects, eventually made his government appear inadequate and paved the way for Henry's attempt on the crown.

Not that Richard seemed in any danger in 1393; on the contrary, he appeared more powerful than ever, the leading lords being so divided among themselves that they no longer posed a threat to him. He knew that the revolt of the appellants had only succeeded because they presented a united front, symbolized by their linked arms as they entered the Merciless Parliament. Now some of the great ones were at each other's throats, none more fiercely so opposed than Gaunt and Arundel.

Between these two a deep hostility had grown by 1393, the fault it seems mainly of the earl, who hated the peace policy advocated by Gaunt and was shocked at the idea of royal Aquitaine being turned into a hereditary duchy of the House of Lancaster. He was also probably jealous of Gaunt's dominating role in government. Quick to anger, the duke was an easy man to make an enemy of; and the Cheshire revolt caused this enmity to explode, for Gaunt had grounds for believing that Arundel, who had estates on the borders of Cheshire and Shropshire, had encouraged it. The earl had himself been residing in Lion Castle, at Holt, on the River Dee, when the revolt began, and he had under his command a large retinue of armed men. But he had done nothing to quell the disturbances. Why? Gaunt had a ready answer. Because the earl supported the rebels. He, too, wanted Gaunt, Gloucester and the earl of Derby killed.

Given the proud nature of the two men a public quarrel was inevitable, and it came in the January parliament of 1394, which Henry attended. Parliament opened with its usual dignity in the White Hall of Westminster Palace, Richard occupying his throne, crowned and in heavily embroidered robes, the bishops on his right, the barons on his left and the chancellor seated on the woolsack before him. But no sooner were the formalities over, the receivers and triers of petitions appointed, and the opening speech of the chancellor made, than Arundel rose abruptly to his feet. Forgetting his recently acquired veneer of tact, he declared brusquely that, 'there were certain matters lying so close to his heart that he could in no way in conscience conceal them for the honour and profit of the king and kingdom'. He indicted Gaunt on the following five counts: it was against their lord the king's honour that he should often walk with Gaunt hand-in-hand and arm-in-arm, and that royal retainers should wear collars of Gaunt's livery; the duke often spoke so arrogantly in parliament and council that he, Arundel, and other members of the Lords and Commons often dared not speak out their full intent; it was greatly against the king's interest that he had given the duke the duchy of Aquitaine; Gaunt had wasted the kingdom's money on his adventures in Castile. And lastly Arundel thundered that the peace treaty Gaunt was negotiating with France was against the interests of the kingdom.

As the earl knew well, these accusations added up to the capital offence of treason, and the fact that Richard made no attempt to make use of this charge against Gaunt suggests that he was indeed innocent of any intention to destroy his minister and eldest uncle at this moment. He was too concerned with Arundel's impertinence. It seems the earl's words reminded Richard of all those infuriating occasions when the overbearing earl had lectured him in the past.

Crowned and anointed as a child, Richard II felt set apart from other men. He bore on his body the sacred marks of kingship.

Jousting. Henry of Bolingbroke won renown for his prowess in this dangerous, knightly sport, as well as on the field of battle. Unlike his cousin Richard.

Thomas Arundel preaches to the English people and exhorts them to follow Henry of Bolingbroke in his revolt against King Richard.

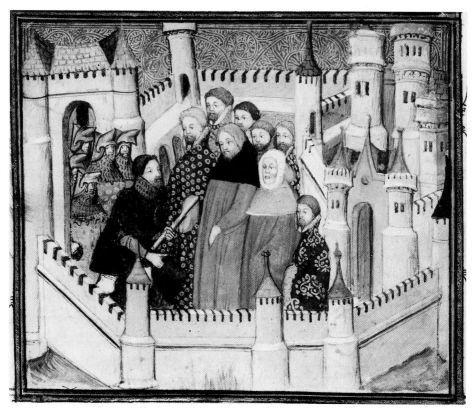

Enemies meet at Flint Castle. Although Henry shows the respect proper from a subject to his lord and king, both are aware that Richard is really Henry's prisoner.

Henry of Bolingbroke delivers Richard II to the citizens of London.

Richard has been unkinged. Henry of Bolingbroke, in tall black hat, is about to step forward and claim the vacant throne.

A hundred torch bearers in black surrounded Richard's funeral carriage as it travelled slowly south from Pontefract to London. There is was met by thirty torch bearers in white. It was important people knew the deposed king was dead.

Effigy of Henry IV, the usurper king. His hands were broken by Cromwell's troops in the seventeenth century.

He was twenty-seven, a divinely appointed king, yet Arundel dared to criticize him! He rose majestically to his own and Gaunt's defence. It was not only with the duke of Lancaster that he walked arm-in-arm and hand-in-hand, he declared, he behaved in exactly the same way with his other uncles, too. Gaunt had not imposed the SS collar on him, he himself had taken the collar from round Gaunt's neck and he wore it 'en signe de bon amour d'entier entre eux', as a sign of wholehearted love between them, just as he also sometimes wore his other uncles' liveries. It was by his command that his own retainers wore the SS collar. Arundel and everyone else could perfectly well speak out as they wished, for all that he personally had ever heard Gaunt say in council or parliament. And as for the grant of the duchy of Aquitaine, it had been made by assent of the estates in full parliament, which had also consented to the subsidizing of the Spanish campaign. Gaunt had not paid back that subsidy because it was owed to him for other military services. In the matter of the peace treaty the duke had done nothing of any kind which had not been by order of the king and the assent of the king and his council.

Richard's overbearing tone dared anyone to disagree. Not even Arundel had the temerity to argue against such a tirade, and his restraint appears to have mitigated the royal wrath, because when in his turn Gaunt accused Arundel of secretly helping the Cheshire revolt, the accusation fell on deaf ears. No drastic action was taken against the earl. The king did no more than order him to quit parliament and the council until he should be recalled, and to apologize. We still have the earl's clumsy attempt to obey this humiliating order before he strode from the hall. It was uttered not in polite French but in simple English:

> Sire, sith that hit seemeth to the kyng and to the other lordes, and eke that yhe ben so mychel greved and displeisid be my wordes, hit forthynketh me, and byseche yowe of your gode lordship to remyt me your mautalent.

> (Sire, since it seems so to the king and to the other lords, and also that you are so much grieved and displeased by my words, I repent and I beseech you of your good lordship to remove from me your displeasure.)

Such a grudging apology did nothing to cure the ill-feeling between the two lords, which spread to include Henry. It was never to subside. But far more disturbing to Gaunt than his quarrel with Arundel was the question of the king's true feelings towards himself. Richard's leniency to Talbot had cast these in doubt. Beneath his show of trust and friendship did the king perhaps harbour a secret animosity towards him? Even by the king's defence of him in parliament, Gaunt was not completely reassured. He was still worried enough by the Talbot business and Arundel's accusation to write to the king in a letter translated from the original French by Galbraith:

> I dare to call God to witness and all loyal men that never have I imagined, or tried to do, anything against your most honourable estate, nor otherwise than a true subject should, in everything to show loyalty towards my most sovereign liege lord.

Gaunt's distrust of the royal good faith had spread to his opponent. If the king's chief minister could not feel himself safe how much more uncertain was Arundel's situation. And when he considered Richard's recent tirade against him in parliament the earl, too, was nervous. To protect himself, however, he characteristically resorted to a far more high-handed approach than Gaunt's humble declaration of loyalty, attempting to armour himself in the law against anything Richard might intend against him in the future. He demanded and received from the king a new pardon 'for the treasons and insurrections which he had committed with the commons and for those which others had committed at his instigation'. Already he had been pardoned for his share in the Appellants' Revolt. With this new pardon his safety seemed doubly assured, despite the gulf between him and two of the king's most powerful allies, the duke of Lancaster and the earl of Derby.

If this gulf was largely accidental the same cannot be said for that which lay between Gloucester and Mowbray, which had been deliberately created by Richard. For after the recent revolt the king had given Mowbray Gloucester's office as justice of Chester and North Wales, thus driving a wedge of jealousy between them. And there also existed by this date a cause of dispute between Mowbray and the earl of Warwick over the lordship of Gower. By the summer of 1393 the former unity of the five appellants had splintered into pieces, putting each lord at the mercy of the king should that monarch choose to destroy him, and a fear had arisen that just such violent intentions might already lurk beneath Richard's mild semblance.

Nevertheless it would be wrong to suggest that for Henry the year 1393 was spoilt by such anxiety; danger was no more than a momentary glimpse beneath the even tenor of his own and his father's relations with the king, soon put out of mind. He enjoyed his life. That much is clear from his accounts. With his glitteringly hopeful prospects in Aquitaine, his energy, optimism and wealth, he led a brilliant existence, dividing his time between his own and his father's castles and manors on the one hand, especially Peterborough and Hertford, and the king's palaces of Westminster, Sheen, Windsor and Eltham on the other.

So renowned was he now that foreign potentates and poets courted his favour. He exchanged letters with Sigismund, king of Hungary, as well as with Gian Galeazzo Visconti, duke of Milan, his host on his journey back from the Holy Land, whom Henry called by his nickname 'Comes Virtutum', Count of Virtues. Henry sent him presents of greyhounds, greyhound collars, horses and three large silver-gilt hunting horns, in return for which Galeazzo sent gold and red Milanese velvet. Even his future liege lord, the king of France, ordered his own jester to Henry in England to enliven his Christmas of 1393.

As a further mark of the earl of Derby's prestige, the popular and elegant poet, John Gower, who had been until now a protege of the king's, in 1393 joined Henry's household instead, accepting his livery of an SS collar, and presenting him with a new version of the *Confessio Amantis*. At the beginning of this manuscript, in place of the original dedication to the king, Gower had written:

I send unto myn oghne lord
Which of Lancastre is Henry named

His desertion of the king for Henry was indeed a compliment for it was not a question of money. This poet, already in his sixties, was a man of substance, with his own coat of arms and the means to dress with some splendour. The painted effigy on his tomb was to depict him clad with quaint grandeur, 'on his head a chaplet like a coronet of four roses, a habit of purple damasked to his feet, a collar of esses gold about his neck'. Such a man, described by his friend Geoffrey Chaucer as 'moral Gower' was able to write for the patron he preferred, and he chose Henry rather than Richard.

Chaucer's situation was different. He depended on the king for royal gifts and grants, but he also enjoyed Henry's company. In 1392 both had borrowed money from the same London banker, Gilbert Mawfield, and in 1395 Henry gave Chaucer a scarlet gown lined with 101 civet skins, costing £8. 8s. 4d. So, with his romantic foreign adventures, his powerful and cultured friends, his rank and his money, the earl of Derby was a dazzling figure. On the best of terms with his father, he spent Christmas 1393 with him at Hertford Castle before moving on to Westminster to exchange presents with the king and queen, Gloucester and Mowbray, and of course, to compete in the New Year tournament. He rode into the lists carrying a shield painted black-and-white, striped with gold forget-me-nots.

If his wife and children were there to watch his victorious performance they would have added still further to his prestige, for Henry and Mary now had five healthy children - Henry, Thomas, John, Humphrey and Blanche - while Mary was pregnant yet again, a startling contrast with Richard's childless state.

After twelve years of marriage Richard still had no son to inherit his crown, and though less complimentary reasons have been suggested for his lack of offspring, the most likely cause is that Anne was barren. If so, Richard did not bear her a grudge. She was one of the few close friends of his youth left to him by the Merciless Parliament and Richard adored his plain, sweet high spirited queen who provided peace and refuge from the stresses and strains of a king's life.

Although, unlike his cousin, Henry did not make a theatrical display of his emotions in public he probably felt no less love for Mary, who gave him a child every year and shared as well his passion for music. But with painful suddenness in 1394 both Richard and Henry were to lose their wives.

Plague, cholera and typhoid being then endemic in England, and medical knowledge rudimentary, death when young was all too frequent, but that year the House of Plantagenet was to be more than usually unfortunate: no less than three of their ladies died. First, the duchess of Lancaster, whom a mysterious illness killed on 24 March 1394. Gaunt had never loved her, though he owed her much. Through her his daughter sat on the throne of Castile and he himself received annually coffers full of gold florins sent on mule-back over the Pyrenees. She had never created embarrassing scenes over his relationship with his mistress. It was thanks to this forbearance that he had been able to take Katherine Swynford, mother of his four Beaufort children, with him everywhere, even to Windsor on St. George's Day, on which anniversary ever since 1387 she had been among the few ladies issued with the robes of the Garter, a very special honour not accorded to Mary de Bohun, countess of Derby, until the following year. To make things even easier for the lovers, latterly Constance had withdrawn from Gaunt's company, living apart with her own household. And now by dying while still so young, she had performed her final unselfish service for him. Perhaps in gratitude the duke spent the grand sum of £584. 5s. 9^1/$_2$d. on her obsequies and a marble tomb in the collegiate church of Our Lady in the Newark at Leicester, the family burial place of the House of Lancaster. And in his will he instructed that a chantry should be built in the same church to pray for his soul and that of his 'dear companion, Dame Constance', her obit to be celebrated annually there for ever.

But if this first death was a blessing in disguise for the husband concerned, that was far from being the case with the two deaths that followed; they were heavy blows. When Richard's beloved queen died on 7 June the whole kingdom was left in no doubt of the extent of his sorrow. Anne of Bohemia's death came suddenly within a few hours of her being taken ill at Sheen, probably with plague. For the rest of June and most of the following month she lay embalmed in state in the island palace while the king sent for vast quantities of special wax from Flanders to illuminate her last journey, and when on 29 July the funeral procession set out, first for St. Paul's and then for Westminster, her bier was lit by a forest of corpse candles.

Determined to see her escorted with the greatest possible honour, Richard had sent orders to the peers to attend her funeral procession 'setting aside all excuses', and every lord had obeyed except one. With cruel tactlessness and no sense of self-preservation, the earl of Arundel had chosen this moment to show pique for the humbling apology Richard had forced him to make in the January parliament. In the procession that wound slowly and solemnly through the summer countryside he alone was missing. He compounded this rudeness by arriving late for the final obsequies in Westminster Abbey and then immediately demanding from Richard licence to withdraw on urgent business.

Heart-broken over Anne's death, deeply offended by the irreverence and disobedience of the earl, who had nearly deposed him in the past and had gallingly criticized him so many times, Richard allowed to slip the mask of forgiveness he had worn ever since the Appellants' Revolt. Seizing a rod from a royal officer, he struck Arundel on the head with such force that he fell bleeding to the pavement and the king would have struck again had he not been forcibly restrained. Shocked and bruised, the earl was then sent to the Tower to be left in prison for a week. Then, since it had been desecrated by this violence, the church had to be reconsecrated by bishops before the funeral service could proceed. It was deep night before Anne of Bohemia was finally buried.

Afterwards Richard lamented her loss with an extravagantly spectacular funeral pyre. He ordered that the entire palace of Sheen where she had died should be burnt to the ground, not only the island sanctuary of La Neyt that he had had especially built for her, but also the moated manor and the buildings outside the moat. It was an alarmingly impractical act for a king always impecunious, but Richard was so crazed with grief that only a sacrifice of this magnitude could begin to assuage his feelings.

To commemorate his queen he had commissioned a double tomb in which one day he too would lie. And to adorn it, two crowned effigies in gilded copper and bronze, their outer hands holding sceptres, the inner hands linked in love.

Anne's death was followed in less than a month by that of Mary de Bohun. Aged twenty-four, Henry's wife died on 4 July just after having dutifully given birth at Leicester Castle to her sixth child and second daughter, Philippa, future queen of Denmark. Henry gave the expected instructions. Like Constance, Mary was buried in a marble tomb in Our Lady's at Leicester, and her funeral ceremonies lasted two days. To commemorate her, Henry made provision for twenty-four poor men, the number of years Mary had lived, to receive gowns made of black cloth, and he donated a hundred marks to the dean and canons of the church for repairs and new buildings, all conventional arrangements that do little to reveal his true feelings. These, unlike his cousin Richard, he kept to himself, but we may gauge his deep distress by the effect of Mary's death on his life. The happy menage in the manor at Peterborough that had welcomed him when he chose to return from his travels was no more, his family home was broken up, his sons and daughters scattered.

The children were cared for in turn by different people in different places. Quaintly dressed in black straw hats, scarlet caps and gowns of green russet and white plunket furred with bysse and popil, they were shuttled from Mary's mother, the cruel, characterful countess of Hereford, at Bytham Castle in Lincolnshire, to family retainers at Eton and the castle of Tutbury in Staffordshire, thence to the countess of Norfolk, Thomas Mowbray's mother, at Framlingham Castle, Norfolk.

XI OVER-MIGHTY SUBJECT

'Ther mey no grettir perell growe to a
prince, than haue a subgett equepolent
to hym selff.' Sir John Fortescue, *The
Governance of England*

Henry's prospects had at first glittered with promise in the spring of 1394.
Parliament opened at Westminster in January with the chancellor reading
the terms of the peace treaty drafted the previous year by the dukes of
Lancaster and Gloucester, Burgundy and Berry in the silken pavilions
outside Calais. It included the proposal that 'the duke of Lancaster and his
heirs should be for ever lord and inheritor of the whole country of
Aquitaine'.

As such, Henry would step into the magnificent shoes of the Black
Prince, who had reigned here 'seven years in joy ... with jousts and with
revels from Bordeaux to Angoulême', providing dinner in hall every day
for no less than 'fourscore knights and full four times as many esquires'.
Here, in the walled city on the River Garonne with streams of money from
wine and pilgrims, bound to and from the shrine of St. James of
Compostela, cockle-shell badges in their hats, he too would hold his court
and rule over this beautiful and historic area of France. He would be a
great potentate, for as rulers of Aquitaine Gaunt and his descendants could
hold or alter the balance of power between England and France as they
pleased.

From the English king's viewpoint it would be dangerous power for
one of his subjects to possess. But when Richard wanted something enough
he rarely counted the cost, and he desperately wanted peace with France,
both to save money otherwise squandered on military expeditions, and for
a larger, more idealistic purpose: he believed that such a peace could usher
in a new and wonderful era in poor trouble-torn Europe, a dream shared
in his periods of sanity by King Charles VI of France. Once the war was
over they planned to work in unison to heal Europe's two grievous ills, first
the 'great schism' which for sixteen years had divided the Church between
rival pontiffs, one in Rome and one in Avignon, each urging 'crusades', not

against the Turk, but against the 'heretics and schismatics' in the other pope's camp.

Popes Boniface and Benedict, so shabbily squabbling over St. Peter's keys, were amusingly dubbed Maleface and Maledict by irreverent punsters, but it was a jibe that did nothing to cure the nightmare uncertainty that the schism had brought to the lives of most pious fourteenth-century people. Once peace was made between France and England, the situation could at last be resolved, because the brother kings would force both Maleface and Maledict to resign, then have elected in their place a new universally recognized and respected pope.

Having put an end to the schism, they would then be free to deal with Europe's second ill, the advancing Turkish hordes which in the two years from 1387 to 1389 had conquered Thessalonika, Bulgaria and Serbia. Now they pressed against the borders of the Holy Roman Empire and their sultan Bayezid I, ominously nicknamed Ilderim - lightning - had sworn to over-run the rest of Europe, boasting alarmingly that he would feed his horse off the altar of St. Peter's in Rome on his way to France. Unless measures were taken against this looming threat Christian civilization was itself in peril. Together, French and English knights would, in Richard's mind, mount a crusade to rescue Europe from the Turk's clutches and send him reeling back. Then they would march on to Palestine and rescue the holy places from infidel hands and spread Christianity throughout the world.

It is true that there were obstacles. Among Richard's subjects there was enormous opposition to the proposal for Aquitaine, not only from more ordinary men, but also from his lords and knights. These as a whole were in favour of a permanent peace with France, but unwilling to pay the price of the necessary preliminary deal. The proposal that the crown should give up Aquitaine filled them with indignation. Had not the Plantagenets as clear a right to this duchy as to England? As it was, France had already swallowed a large part of Eleanor of Aquitaine's dowry, including the twelfth-century abbey of Fontevrault in the valley near the Loire, where two English kings, Henry II and Richard I, lay buried.

The earl of Arundel was not alone in objecting when the terms of the treaty were read out in parliament. There were roars of 'great prejudice to the crown' and 'ruinous disinheritance of the King of England in perpetuity'. These hostile remarks were directed at Gaunt, who stood to gain most from the deal, and had of course been its chief English negotiator. Reporting the scene, the Monk of Westminster adds his own shocked and angry comment to give us a measure of parliament's feelings. 'Truly if ordinary men had done this they would have incurred, not unmerited, the stigma of treason.'

Fortunately for Gaunt, he was no ordinary man, he was armoured in the king's favour, so these barbs left him untouched. Richard was determined to bestow Aquitaine where he pleased and he had learnt to handle awkward parliaments. To help him in this session he had a capable ally in both the Lords and the Commons. Gloucester, in the Lords, still loyal at this time, spoke in support of the treaty, his heavy personality bullying more timid men into silence. While in the Commons Richard's policy had a most eloquent advocate in the speaker, Sir John Bushy, henceforth to be one of the king's most useful supporters. The arguments of these royal spokesmen finally convinced men already softened into a grudgingly receptive state by the theme of the chancellor's opening speech: to renew the war meant more taxation. So, although reluctantly and 'with great deliberation', parliament agreed to the terms of the treaty and the formal investiture of Gaunt as hereditary duke of Aquitaine. Both Richard's peace and Henry's grand inheritance seemed assured. For the moment the tension and rivalry between them that had been inexorably mounting towards snapping point was in abeyance; there was no reason for anything but harmony and friendship. As heir to the duchy of Aquitaine, Henry's ambition would be satisfied and the cousins could peacefully co-exist.

However, they had all made the great mistake of reckoning without the peculiar temperament and obstinacy of the Gascons. It is one of the extraordinary facts of history that whole kingdoms and parts of kingdoms have been handed over from one ruler to another in marriage and peace settlements without noticeable protest from their inhabitants. But the Gascons who lived in this small corner of Europe between the Garonne and the Pyrenees, all that was left of Aquitaine, were less obliging. Among these people in recent years there had grown up a very different point of view from that which had made so many of the duchy's subjects 'turn French', in Froissart's phrase, soon after the resumption of the Hundred Years War in 1370, with whole towns and lordships falling one after the other like dominoes to the French king. The Gascons were motivated entirely by practical considerations. Possessing no special feeling of loyalty to Richard, they nevertheless believed their prosperity depended on their relationship with the English crown, and they were astute enough to realise that, should Aquitaine become a hereditary dukedom of the House of Lancaster, they would eventually find themselves linked more closely with France than with England.

On 6 April some forty apprehensive and angry Gascon prelates, barons and town representatives gathered in Bordeaux Cathedral to hear the official proclamation from England read by Sir Peter Arnold of Bearn. The duchy had been granted to John of Gaunt 'purely and absolutely to him and his heirs in perpetuity'. And they were commanded to obey the duke and render him homage as their sovereign lord in place of the king.

There and then, amid the Romanesque rounded arches and embedded pillars of the church where Richard had been christened, the Gascon notables formed themselves into a defensive organization called 'the union', and swore an oath to stand together, then they sent a message to Richard: they refused to accept Gaunt and his heirs as their hereditary dukes. They stood by their right, recognized by Edward III, to be ruled by the English king, or his eldest son only. They would no longer obey Gaunt's officers, and begged Richard to make alternative arrangements for their government. Meanwhile, they asked for safe conducts for the ambassadors that they wished to send him to plead their cause.

It was the beginning of an angry exchange of messages that sailed backwards and forwards across the Channel throughout the summer. Refusing both the Gascon requests, Richard summoned their representatives to appear before him at Waterford on 22 June when, as he threateningly expressed it, 'he would put an end to the debates and dissensions in Aquitaine'. There were no dissensions among them, retorted the Gascons; on the contrary, they were all in agreement, 'determined to be ruled only by the king himself and in this resolve they would live and die'.

Richard tried to over-ride them. In September he loftily announced that he had reaffirmed his grant of their lands to Gaunt and his heirs. And in November, Gaunt himself set sail to make good his claim with an army of fifteen thousand men, enough to impose his will by force.

The Gascons refused to be intimidated, to recognize his authority or even simply to allow him to enter his own capital city of Bordeaux. And in the end, with the whole population against him, Gaunt decided to try bribery rather than force. Compelled to reside outside the walls in Saint Seurin, he issued lavish grants, but in vain; the Gascons refused to be moved by these either. Only when he had confirmed their rights, liberties and privileges, which included keeping their special link with the English monarch, did they finally agree to recognize him as their duke, and allow him to enter Bordeaux.

It was a blow to the hopes of both Richard and Henry: Richard's lofty vision of an Aquitaine freed from the domination of the English crown to become wholly a part of France, a necessary first step to perpetual peace; and Henry's dream of a splendid Lancastrian empire across the Channel.

His family's prospects in the duchy, recently so brilliant, were never to recover.

The winter of 1394-95 was mortifying in other ways for the House of Lancaster, too, for in England Henry also had lost face. While Gaunt had been preparing to set sail to enforce his claim in Aquitaine, Richard had been impressing ships for a journey in another direction, across the Irish Sea, Ireland as usual being in a state of grave disorder. Even the Pale, the area between the coast and Dublin that was traditionally the home of English government, had been over-run by the 'wild Irish', as the original inhabitants of the country were termed. And the 'Anglo-Irish', descendants of those families sent to quell them, had become almost as unruly, intermarrying with the natives and adopting their customs, fighting with double-headed axes, riding with bare legs and no saddles and, worst of all, joining in their tribal feuds. Richard planned to re-impose his rule at least in the Pale, that part of Ireland in which English law had been acknowledged since the conquest of King Henry II. But surprisingly, although he was one of the few younger barons with any military experience, Henry was not included among those selected for this expedition.

A few weeks before Gaunt sailed for Aquitaine Richard left Haverfordwest to sail to Ireland, still 'clad with his train in weeds of mourning' for Anne, flying streamers of St. Edward the Confessor's arms and equipped with 'two large ironbound wooden chests containing £1,600 of gold and silver'. Humiliatingly, Henry was left behind in England with the regent, his uncle, Edmund, duke of York, and the disgraced earl of Arundel.

In place of the hero of the siege of Vilna, Richard took with him a group of new favourites, his nephew, Thomas Holland, Sir John Beaumont, Sir Thomas Percy and Sir William Lescrope, as well as Roger Mortimer, earl of March, largest landowner in Ireland. The highest command went to the untrustworthy Edward, earl of Rutland, Richard's closest friend these days. He was appointed captain of Ireland and created earl of Cork by the king, although he had seen no military action at all. Of Henry's fellow appellants, Richard took with him no less than two, Thomas Mowbray and the duke of Gloucester. Even Sir Thomas Talbot who had led the Cheshire revolt was chosen in preference to Henry. The earl of Derby's deliberate exclusion suggests that Richard was jealously determined not to add to his cousin's military fame.

In the event, Henry missed little fighting. Mowbray led a raid against Art MacMurrough, the legendary, self-styled King of Leinster, but most of the chiefs came to heel and quickly and meekly accepted Richard's very disadvantageous terms. Aware that the English army would soon return to England and leave them again to their own devices, they agreed to exchange their lands in the Pale for others elsewhere in Ireland if these could be conquered from their present rulers. To crown this surprisingly easy success, no less than three Irish 'kings' accepted knighthood at

Richard's hands and humbly agreed to be taught 'civilised' manners; they promised to wear breeches and to seat their household at dinner in hall according to the formal English fashion of separate tables for different ranks, a change indeed from the Irish custom of casually seating everyone from kings to scullions all together at one huge, communal board. With surprisingly little effort on Richard's part, it seemed that the 'wild Irish' were becoming tamed.

Meanwhile, as affairs were thus re-ordered in Ireland, Henry and his uncle had to deal with a revolt in England of a different nature: the heretical Lollards chose the occasion of the king's absence to show the strength of their following for the first time. They displayed it in the most prominent way, choosing a moment when as many as possible of the most influential people in England were gathered in one locality. To raise more money for the Irish expedition, Parliament had been summoned to meet in January 1395, and riding in to London and Westminster from the far corners of the kingdom, the Lords and Commons were faced with a challenging sight. Two of the most conspicuous places, the walls of Westminster Palace and the door of St. Paul's Cathedral, were covered with screeds of Lollard literature, the twelve conclusions of the Lollard faith, criticizing all aspects of the Catholic Church, its power, riches and ritual, and accusing it of idolatry.

Ever since John Wyclif's death in 1384, his revolutionary ideas had been carried across the country from village to village by the 'hooded men' in long russet robes. Their doctrine had attracted rich and poor alike, including one of Richard's own knights, Sir Richard Stury, who was rumoured to have such disrespect for the sacrament of communion that he had once spat the sacred bread into his hand to take home to eat with his oysters.

Because the Lollards had seemed harmless the king had turned a blind eye to their activities, until in the winter light of January 1395 they revealed themselves abruptly as a menace to society, of which the established Church was a fundamental part. Informed of this development by the council, of which Henry was a member, Richard threatened the Lollards and their protectors with death 'unless they recovered their senses', and returning to England in May, rounded on Stury in a scene colourfully described by Walsingham. He forced Stury to promise on the gospels to give up his heretical beliefs, then took the book into his own hands and swore to make the knight die the most shameful death should he ever violate his oath. After this, Walsingham tells us, the Lollards retired into their shells like tortoises, but only for a short time. It was left to his successor to stamp out the problem with a law requiring heretics to be burned to death. Richard, too, might have acted more positively against the Lollards had he not been still so preoccupied at this date with negotiations for his treaty with France, fated now to failure.

His chance of achieving a permanent peace, and Henry's of acquiring a French dukedom, ended in a July heat-wave at Eltham Palace where a great council meeting had been called to hear a delegation from the Gascon rebels. Its deliberations are known to us through Jean Froissart who, visiting the palace at the time to offer the king a collection of his love poems, a gift gorgeously 'bound in crimson velvet, with ten silver-gilt studs, and roses of the same in the middle, with two large clasps of silver-gilt, richly worked with roses in the centre', kept his ears open. Exactly what had happened at the council meeting he learned from the Lollard knight, Sir Richard Stury, who retailed it to him as they strolled through pleasant, vine-shaded walks.

The Gascons had claimed that the grant of Aquitaine to Gaunt was not consistent with their special relationship with the English crown, and surprisingly Richard's legal officers had agreed with them. Most of the lords - they had consented to the creation of a hereditary dukedom only reluctantly in the parliament of 1394 - followed suit. It was in vain that Gloucester and Henry spoke in favour of the grant, the duke maintaining that it was against the king's honour to give in to Gascon pressure, the earl that the arguments for the grant should be re-examined.

No one was on their side. And as the council meeting began to break up the two disgruntled lords left their fellows still talking, 'issued out of the chamber ... and came into the hall at Eltham and made a cloth to be laid on a table, and so sat down to dinner', neither having any heart for the usual communal repast.

For Henry, it must have been a grave disappointment, for through this council meeting he had seen his whole empire vanish away. The proposal that could have given France and England peace instead of so many more blood-stained years of war, that could have prevented Joan of Arc and Agincourt, also deprived the young earl of an outlet for his restless energies and abilities, one that might eventually have stopped him aiming at Richard's crown. Although the council made no conclusive statement on the matter it was tacitly understood that the Gascons had won acceptance of their case, and that Richard would now compromise by making a long-term truce instead of a permanent peace.

Greatly disappointed also, Richard treated Gaunt on his return to England as though the failure in Gascony was his fault. When just after Christmas the duke finally sailed in from Aquitaine and reported to Richard at King's Langley, the duke was received, Froissart tells us, with civility but no love.

Henry's loss of dominion over Aquitaine was followed startlingly by the loss of his unique position in England, for Gaunt's return heralded changes in the family situation. Eighteen months having passed since Constance's death, Gaunt would pay lip service to convention no longer. Leaving King's Langley after his chilling reception by the king, he rode north to Lincoln and Katherine Swynford's warmer welcome. At the beginning of January and 'to the amazement of all' he married her, a mere knight's widow without a drop of royal blood in her veins, provoking the great ladies of England, according to Froissart, to declare that they would not enter a room while she was there. But authority proved more tolerant. In September Pope Boniface IX obligingly issued a bull confirming the duke of Lancaster's marriage to his mistress and declaring legitimate their four children, John, Henry, Thomas and Joan Beaufort.

Although still the heir, instead of being Gaunt's only legitimate son, Henry suddenly found himself the eldest of four. Despite his past good relations with his half brothers, it was a change that he strongly resented, revealing his bitter feelings in the alteration that he himself later added to the act Richard passed legitimising them; in this document he was to make it illegal for any of the Beaufort brood ever to inherit the throne.

Almost simultaneously, Henry's chances of ever succeeding to the throne himself seemed to slip away, too. They had been faint, but they had existed during the lifetime of the childless Anne of Bohemia, as we can see from the *Whalley Abbey Chronicle* story of Richard's brief deposition. The claim of the heirs of the duke of Clarence was not inviolable. Since William the Conqueror no one as distantly related to the king as the earl of March had succeeded to the throne and the custom of primogeniture had not always been followed. King John's accession in the lifetime of Arthur, son of John's elder brother, could be used for a precedent, as could Henry I's accession in the lifetime of his brother Robert. Should Roger Mortimer, earl of March, die, leaving only a child heir, England might yet change her habit. She had only to copy France, to introduce a Salic law, making illegal any claim passed through a female, and all the duke of Clarence's descendants would be disinherited. With that branch of the family eliminated, Gaunt and his son would then be closest to the throne after Richard himself. So while Anne had been queen the crown was an interesting if distant glimmer on Henry's horizon.

In 1396 this light too vanished from the earl of Derby's life, for Richard remarried.

Anne being dead, it was the king's duty to take a new wife, and he wasted no time in fulfilling it, choosing as his bride the little daughter of his 'brother' of France, eight-year-old Princess Isabel, a choice that would enable him to secure at least a really long-lasting truce with France. Henry was among the English lords who crossed the Channel with Richard to take part in the final proceedings in the now usual sumptuous encampment outside Calais. In the royal retinue, all garbed like the king himself in long red velvet gowns, decorated with Anne of Bohemia's heraldic white bend - a touchingly nostalgic if untimely tribute to the dead queen - he escorted Richard to his first meeting with Charles. The French were also all dressed in red velvet gowns, but shorter, reaching only to the knees, with a black and white heraldic bend and red and white shoes.

Although before the meeting it had been thought necessary for both kings to swear on the gospels to keep the peace, and to forbid their escorts to wear sword, dagger or even staff, everything went smoothly. As a special compliment to Richard, Charles wore a brooch of his livery of the white hart, while not to be outdone in courtesy, Richard wore a circlet of precious stones that had been given to him by the French king.

Four days later, negotiations completed, Richard, in a robe of blood-red cloth of gold, was presented to his tiny bride, her immature little body clothed in a close-fitting tunic of red velvet, powdered with fleurs de lis, a miniature crown on her head. Between a man of twenty-nine and a small child this marriage could easily have been disastrous, as Charles seemed suddenly to realise, handing over his daughter with these impassioned words: 'Dear Son, I commend to you this creature loved by me above all creatures of the world except our son and our wife'.

But the unlikely couple were oddly well matched, as Henry was able to observe, with what feelings of frustrated disappointment we can imagine. From the beginning Richard treated Isabel with tender flattery. When she was presented to him, he took her by the hand, thanking the King of France 'for such an honourable and beloved gift'.

Thenceforward, he pretended that she was the grown-up heroine of a courtly romance and he her humble and adoring knight, a piece of make-believe that would have sickened many children, but delighted Isabel. He allowed her to take with her from France an unusually large number of attendants, so many ladies and 'damoiselles' that twelve chariots were needed to carry them. And on the celebration of their marriage in Calais he showered her with presents, including a frontlet of great rubies, sapphires and large pearls.

When finally she reached England after a crossing so stormy that Richard's silken tents and most of his household furniture were swept away in the Channel, she found more enchanting presents awaiting her at Eltham Palace.

Soon the king nearing thirty and the little princess were devoted to each other, and there was no reason to doubt that in a few years' time they would have children. The terms of the marriage treaty took their fruitfulness for granted, specifying what lands in France each child was to inherit.

It is interesting to see that in the list of splendid wedding presents made by the English lords to Isabel, although Mowbray gave her three, including a belt of pearls and Grecian gold, and Rutland gave her the same number, among them a mirror shaped like a marguerite, there is only one small gift from Henry; just a gold greyhound, one of his own badges, adorned with a ruby and a large pearl hanging from its neck. Perhaps it was a sign of his disappointment at seeing yet another ambition dimmed.

The previous two years had been disastrous for Henry's ambitions because in that short time he had lost both the duchy of Aquitaine which he had been promised and also the remote possibility of some day inheriting the English crown. The only way he could now acquire it would be through taking the matter into his own hands and seizing it by force, already perhaps a temptation.

After such visions of vanished empire, the Lancastrian inheritance in England which was all that he was now heir to must have seemed a mere bagatelle. But his claim to this, too, was about to be threatened.

XII   RICHARD'S REVENGE

'Let the fox with the tail beware, while
the lark sings, Lest he be captured at the
same time as the seizer of the cattle and
the horse.' Prophecy, *Annales Ricardi
Secundi*, trans. Duls

Though he had so long pretended amity towards them, Richard had never
forgotten the injury done to him by the appellants in the Merciless
Parliament. And although he was not to make his final dramatic move
against them until nine years later in July 1397, before that time there had
been signs that he was increasingly haunted by his friends' fate. Those
whom flight had saved from execution still suffered. Robert de Vere,
Michael de la Pole and the banished Alexander Neville lived an almost
penniless life in exile, a wretched existence soon ended for the former
chancellor by death. De la Pole had died in Paris in 1389, and de Vere had
then left that city to join his other companion in misfortune, the once great
archbishop of York, who worked humbly as a parish priest in Louvain in
the duchy of Brabant. There the proud Robert de Vere was soon
surrounded by creditors. To make matters worse for Richard, he had the
pain of knowing that he had himself consented to their punishment,
although it had been against his will.

The Monk of Westminster has a revealing incident to relate. In 1390
when Gaunt pleaded pardon for a protégé, John of Northampton, the king
replied that he was powerless to help. And Gaunt, staunch believer in royal
absolutism, replied, 'This and greater things than this are in your power to
do.' Richard seized desperately on the idea. 'If I can do that', he declared,
'there are others that suffer great misery. And so I know now what I may
do for my friends in parts across the sea'.

Two years later he had attempted to have them recalled, a move
which sickeningly only aggravated their misery. Not only did his council
vehemently object to the suggested recall, it also insisted that he banish
them for ever, and Richard felt compelled to agree to his friends' new
sentence, an experience made none the less traumatic by the fact that both
men followed de la Pole to the grave within the year, de Vere dying

mysteriously of an injury received at a boar hunt.

Death did not stop Richard's mind from dwelling on them, especially on de Vere. He paid for the body of the 'king's kinsman' to be embalmed in balsam like royalty, coffined in Cyprus wood and three years later brought home. In September 1395 at Colne Priory in Essex, the family burial place of the earls of Oxford, he staged a macabre funeral before a small gathering of bishops and relations. (All the lords whom he had invited in an attempt to do his friend the greatest possible honour had indignantly though unwisely refused to come). Before the tomb engulfed the coffin Richard had it opened so that he could look once more on his beloved friend's face and clasp his hands; then, in what was presumably a conscience-stricken attempt to make amends for those penurious years in exile, he covered de Vere's fingers with precious gold rings.

This moment of history that allows us to look back across the centuries into the king's most deeply felt inner self, also held a presage of the future for his contemporaries. De Vere's funeral was not only an intensely personal occasion but a political statement as well, spelling danger to the appellants. For with this splendid burial Richard was proclaiming his view that de Vere was not the traitor he had been declared by the Merciless Parliament; that his condemnation had been against the royal will, and that the king's power had at that time been usurped, a crime punishable by death. The message of de Vere's funeral was one that the appellants would have done well to heed, just as it would have paid them to note another indication of the way Richard's mind was working, a sign of his increasing belief in his own link with the divinity.

By 1397 he no longer used Edward the Confessor's arms simply in proximity with his own, he impaled them so that the 'cross patence or on a field gules with four doves argent' shared the shield with his royal leopards and lilies. It was yet another indication of his growing belief in his kinship with the Almighty, and that 252 years before King Charles I was to die for that conviction, Richard II believed in the divine right of kings. It followed that anyone who in Richard's estimation compelled such a sacred being against his will committed an unforgivable crime. Not without cause did the observant Sir John Bushy, speaker of the Commons, who treated Richard with 'not human, but divine honours' rise suddenly in the royal favour.

There were two reasons why Richard at last felt able to take his revenge on the appellants in 1397. First and foremost was his faith in the Cheshire archers. He had mustered them for the expedition to Ireland and paid them regularly (a rare luxury for medieval soldiers, often paid after the fighting was over and sometimes not even then); and they had become attached to him by a special feeling of loyalty. In these soldiers who proudly wore his white hart badge on their doublets he felt he at last had the basis of his own army.

Secondly, he was unlikely any longer to be at the mercy of a hostile parliament. For thanks to peace with France and decreased taxation, England was prosperous. And the Commons, skilfully manipulated by Sir John Bushy, who had continued to be their speaker ever since 1394, were behind him. He also had plenty of carefully nurtured supporters among the Lords. As well as Gaunt, the duke of York, and ostensibly Henry, earl of Derby, he had his set of very special friends: Thomas Mowbray, now completely Richard's man, the Hollands, his half-brother John, earl of Huntingdon, and nephew Thomas, earl of Kent. John Montague, heir to the earl of Salisbury; Lord Despenser, and Richard's latest and greatest royal favourite since de Vere, young Edward, earl of Rutland. In legitimising Gaunt's children by Katherine Swynford and creating John Beaufort, the eldest, earl of Somerset, Richard clearly hoped to add yet another new young lord to his cause.

The humble and obedient parliament that met in January 1397 at Westminster bore little resemblance to its turbulent predecessors of the 1370s and '80s. This parliament was actually to help Richard to take a significant step on the road to his goal of absolute monarchy. The means has become known as Haxey's bill.

Presented among the usual jumble of petitions, it appeared so conveniently that historians have suggested it may have been prompted by the king himself, but, if so, Richard acted his indignation at its contents most convincingly. Drafted by Thomas Haxey, a king's clerk, keeper of the writs and rolls of the common bench, the bill had the temerity to criticize the royal household. Complaining of Richard's extravagance in providing hospitality for an unnecessary number of bishops and ladies at court, it was a disturbing echo of the past.

Similar criticisms of the royal household in 1376, 1381 and 1386 had been the prelude to baronial intrusion and controls, and consequent loss of freedom by the king. But now Richard was in a much stronger position. He would not only defend himself against this new criticism, but use it as an excuse for an attack that would stop interference in the royal household for all time. He would seize this opportunity to put an end for ever to the humiliating pattern of dictation by parliament to the English crown.

Richard's protest, in French, sent to the Commons and preserved in the parliament rolls, was a revolutionary document.

> The king takes it greatly to grief and offence that the Commons who are his lieges should usurp or presume upon themselves any ordering or governance of the person of the king or of his household or of any

persons of rank that he pleases to have in his company. And it seems to the king that the Commons commit in this great offence and an offence against his regality and his royal majesty and the liberty of him and his honourable progenitors which he is bound and wills to maintain and sustain through God's aid.

The Commons rightly interpreted 'great offence' as meaning 'treason'. It was a new definition of this most serious of all crimes. In thus denying parliament the right to criticize his household Richard was claiming for the monarchy a whole new status of untouchability in a most crucial area, for the king's household and the government were interdependent, and if the king spent too much on his household, parliament would have to impose on the people the burden of increased taxation. One might have expected parliament would leap to its own defence, but nothing of the sort happened.

The sequel shows how brilliantly successful Richard's policies had been since the disasters he had suffered at the hands of the appellants in 1388. Far from objecting to this tyrannical measure, on receiving the royal protest the Commons apologized. 'Making great dolour', a deputation of them trooped into his presence in the White Hall. They vowed they had never meant 'to do anything that might offend or displease the royal majesty of the king ...' And as 'for this matter of his demesne and the ordering of his household or of the gentlemen and ladies in his company ... they knew that such things did not concern them but only the king himself.' They suggested that 'the lords should pray the king to consider his honourable estate and to do in this matter as he wished', and a final abject touch, they 'submitted themselves to the grace and will of the king, humbly praying to his royal majesty graciously to excuse them ...'

The Lords, including those who had risen in arms when the king redefined this crime in 1387, behaved with similar docility. For criticizing the royal household they meekly agreed that Haxey was a traitor, worthy of a traitor's death, a fate from which he was only rescued by the Church, in the shape of a delegation of bishops. Led by the archbishop of Canterbury - that same Thomas Arundel who in 1386 had threatened to depose the king if he did not do parliament's bidding - they came before the king, and in the most obsequious way, pleaded for Haxey's life. Declaring that it was their 'whole and full intention and always would be to save and guard without blemish the royal estate and regality' they begged him 'of his grace to have pity and mercy on Thomas', respectfully adding that they did so 'through no right or due that belonged to them ... but only of the king's special grace'.

The humble clerk had been the means to an extraordinary gain, helping Richard to erect an almost impenetrable new hedge of defence around the crown; and to make the king's victory more complete, it had been achieved without a murmur of opposition, proof that at last he was perfectly in control of his kingdom. In the circumstances Richard could afford to be generous and to follow his natural instinct for clemency, to reprieve Haxey and hand him over to the custody of the archbishop.

At last, Richard felt powerful enough to please himself. Soon after Haxey's condemnation a ship set sail from Ireland bearing men who had never expected to see England again, the justices who, for setting their seals to the new definition of treason in 1387, had been divided from their families and exiled to Ireland for life. This parliament had agreed to their recall. Then, having rescued his friends, Richard turned his attention to his enemies.

This was to be Richard's year of triumph, the year when, in the words of the chronicler Adam of Usk, he appeared 'glorious as Ahasuerus', the omnipotent Persian ruler, and as ruthless.

In the spring of 1397 the duke of Gloucester was the one man who cast a shadow over the royal effulgence. For many years now he had curbed his critical tongue and actively supported Richard's policies, the pattern of a loyal subject. But all that had been abruptly changed by the French truce which had accompanied Richard's marriage to Isabel. Its terms had reawakened all Gloucester's earlier mistrust of his nephew's judgement, for in his opinion they were not nearly favourable enough to England. Unlike the conditions of the peace which he himself had helped to negotiate in 1393 these did not guarantee or even mention the restoration of the boundaries of Aquitaine. And to make the situation even more galling, the truce was to last for twenty-eight years. So for over a quarter of a century, and perhaps for ever, Aquitaine would continue to be a mere coastal strip from Bordeaux to Bayonne.

The duchy which it had fought to gain and defend was being thrown away, and it seemed to him that Richard had compounded this terrible error with another, further dismembering the English empire: he had agreed meekly to hand over the fortresses of Cherbourg and Brest, barbicans of the realm, easily supplied from the sea. In 1394 Cherbourg had been returned to the king of Navarre. Now Brest as well was to be handed over to the duke of Brittany. It was too much to be borne. To Gloucester, it made no difference that in returning these fortresses - lent in exchange for a large sum of money and for the duration of the war - England was merely honouring an agreement. For although the money had been repaid who could be sure that the war was really over? And why had Richard not consulted more with the lords before parting with these assets?

All Gloucester's long buried scorn for his nephew had surfaced again. Where was it all going to end? Richard was unworthy to hold the throne or to fight any but the 'wild Irish', the most primitive of soldiers. Grumbles of the sort had been voiced by the disgusted duke to his friends throughout the spring, acid words that were bound to reach and sting the king's sensitive ears. But despite presumably mounting irritation he took no action until in the summer of 1397 the duke insulted him in public.

This incident, recorded by the author of the *Traison et Mort* who is thought to have been an eye-witness, took place in Westminster Hall at one of those medieval banquets open to all comers. The duke was sitting near the king at the high table when, numbered among many guests near the end of the room, he caught sight of some soldiers newly returned from the redeemed fortress of Brest. It was after the last course of wine and spiced cakes had blunted his caution that the duke aggressively drew the king's attention to them. '... your people who have come from Brest, who have faithfully served you, but have been badly paid and know not what to take to'.

The words reached Richard in mellow mood and he protested mildly, saying that they would be paid in full and that four good villages near London would be given up to them so that they might live there at his expense until they received their due.

Again Gloucester attacked, hectoring and rude. 'Sire you ought first to hazard your life in capturing a city from your enemies, by feat of arms or by force, before you think of giving up or selling any city which your ancestors, the kings of England, have gained or conquered'. It was a criticism Richard had suffered throughout his reign, that he had never taken part in a siege or a full-scale battle, and it touched a sensitive place.

Hardly able to believe what he heard, Richard made his uncle repeat the remark, then replied 'very scornfully':

> Do you think that I am a merchant or a traitor that I wish to sell my land? By St. John the Baptist, no, no; but it is a fact that our cousin of Brittany has restored, and well and truly paid us the sum which our ancestors had lent him on the city of Brest; and since he has honestly paid us, it is only just he should have his pledge back again.

Beneath the apparent composure of this speech Gloucester's barb had found its mark and the wound festered, for after this confrontation the Chronicler tells us, although 'they parted politely' and 'continued to give each other civil reception' when they met, they did so 'with a bad will'. Shortly afterwards Gloucester found it politic to leave court and retire to Pleshy Castle, in Essex.

As far as we can see, across the centuries, Richard had every reason to hate Gloucester and none, apart from family loyalty, for liking him, but what finally spurred him into taking action against his youngest uncle that summer was fear, as much as revenge. He had in truth never fully recovered from the trauma of the Appellants' Revolt and the experience of being deposed and held helpless in the Tower for three days, then forced to do their will. Behind the smiling faces and humble reverences of his courtiers in their wasp-waisted, high collared doublets and billowing wide-sleeved gowns, he sensed secret hostility and plotting. Already far gone in the suspicion that looks up at us from his effigy in Westminster Abbey, he had no faith in the surface of things. He even employed an astrologer to distinguish his friends from his enemies.

Ironically, it was in this moment of his success after the Haxey bill affair that he knew himself to be in most danger, for although his lords had agreed to the new definition of treason with humble words, who knew whether they had accepted it in their hearts? He could not forget that a similarly novel definition of treason had spurred the appellants into taking up arms in 1387.

While the king was in this uneasy state of mind the original leaders of that rebellion, the 'indivisible trio', made their gravest mistake: the three of them met together over dinner in Arundel Castle. According to the *Traison et Mort*, Mowbray and Henry were there too, and afterwards Mowbray told the king all that had passed. Exactly what was said on this occasion has ever since been clothed in mystery and rumour, but we must presume that in such company the conversation turned to criticism of royal policies. Since no proof was ever to be publicly produced, we may discount the *Traison et Mort's* account of an actual plot against the king. But even without such evidence, it is easy to see just how suspect the gathering in itself would have seemed to Richard and how easily any words of criticism would have taken on an alarming colour. For with all the appellants together again - what else could it mean but treason?

This time, Richard would not be taken by surprise, he would attack first, fiercely and finally. Constantly at the royal elbow was his new young favourite, Edward, earl of Rutland, egging him on with the oft repeated advice that he would never enjoy full regal power until the 'indivisible trio' were dead. Richard listened to him, in no mood for half measures.

Inevitably, in the tiny aristocratic society of the day, the three lords were forewarned, and when the king invited them to a royal feast only the earl of Warwick ventured to accept. Gloucester pleaded illness, while

Arundel, with his usual gracelessness, simply failed to appear, remaining instead in his fortified castle at Reigate. Their fears were realised, for having wined and dined him, as a novel form of desert Richard had Warwick arrested and taken to prison.

However, he meant no harm, he assured Thomas Arundel. It was all a charade. He was merely displaying his power to impress some German ambassadors then in England. The archbishop should pass the reassuring news to his brother. Cheered by this message, as the king intended, the earl of Arundel, Thomas's brother, was enticed in all innocence to court where he at once suffered the same fate as Warwick.

Richard could not rest until his uncle also was safely behind bars; he could not wait for Gloucester, too, to come to the lure. On the evening of Arundel's arrest, with a large number of men-at-arms and archers, he himself took horse for Essex, riding all through the night. From his battlemented walls at dawn Gloucester saw the shadowy group appear and realised that his only hope lay in submission. He emerged from the castle in a procession of priests and clerics, and knelt before the king in a show of humility that came too late. Richard put a hand on his shoulder and personally arrested him.

After his prisoner's chapel had celebrated Mass for him and his prisoner's kitchens provided him with a generous breakfast the king rode away, leaving further crude details to his nephew, Thomas Holland, earl of Kent, and Sir Thomas Percy, steward of the royal household and seneschal of England. As these lords, turned gaolers, set off with Gloucester on the journey that led to his death, the duke managed a bitter joke: should he or one of them lead the way?

The famous trio was no longer indivisible. Richard took care of that, sending each in a different direction, Warwick to Tintagel Castle in Cornwall, Arundel first to the Tower and then to Carisbrooke Castle in the Isle of Wight (he travelled in Mowbray's custody), and Gloucester across the narrow sea to Calais, this last being a necessary precaution. For Richard could not tell what he had stirred up.

The country was plunged into shock by the lords' arrests, the duke's in particular exciting a wave of sympathy among the commons, who had regarded him as their champion ever since the Appellants' Revolt. On hearing of his fate they expressed their feelings in dramatic form. Through the summer countryside there moved stark processions clad in mourning black for the duke's misfortune. Richard put an end to these with a simple threat. He proclaimed that the arrests had been 'for the peace of the people and to save them harmless' and forbade any man 'under pain of forfeiting life and limb and of being reckoned a traitor to the king ... to make or procure assemblies'. But, had Gloucester been in England, some kind of revolt in his favour would have been a distinct possibility, for the arrests seriously damaged Richard's popularity.

Suddenly his subjects saw a sinister new Richard, the true face of the king who had been hiding all these years behind a mask of reason and appeasement, a king who had only pretended to pardon and forgive the appellants, who had smiled with them, dined with them, walked through his gardens with them arm-in-arm, while all the time harbouring thoughts of revenge.

In a second proclamation made on 15 July Richard tried to alter this picture and to justify the arrests. He stated that the lords had been imprisoned not for their part in the events of 1387-88 but for new crimes, 'for great number of extortions, oppressions, grievances etc. committed against the king and people and for other offences against the king's majesty which shall be declared in the next parliament'.It was a promise never to be fulfilled, for there were no 'new crimes'. The prisoners were to be tried and condemned for their part in the Appellants' Revolt through a procedure deliberately designed to mock and echo that of the Merciless Parliament.

With the help of king and council in Nottingham Castle charges against the three lords were prepared by eight new appellants: the turncoat Thomas Mowbray, earl of Nottingham, Edward, earl of Rutland, John Beaufort, earl of Somerset, John Holland, earl of Huntingdon, Thomas Holland, earl of Kent, John Montague, earl of Salisbury, Thomas, Lord Despenser and Sir William Lescrope.

To hear the appeal, parliament was summoned to assemble at Westminster on 17 September. Even before it met arrangements were made to divide the three lords' property among Richard's friends. And there were other ominous signs of his intentions towards them as well. He had recruited in Chester two thousand archers and men-at-arms who were ordered to meet him at Kingston-on-Thames on 15 September, escort him to the capital and remain there throughout the trials. To provide additional military strength, eleven magnates - the eight new appellants, Henry and two other lords - were each ordered to bring with them to Westminster strong retinues of armed retainers. All in all this was an army - an army to guard and protect the king while parliament came to the decision he wanted. So that the approaching proceedings could be constantly under armed surveillance, Richard had built an open-sided pavilion in the middle of the palace yard for them.

As they pondered on the meaning of these disturbing preparations and waited for the day of the new parliament, it is easy to imagine the trepidation that Henry and Mowbray would have felt. Of the original five appellants they alone now remained out of prison. True, Richard still extended his favour to them, but had he not also smiled benignly on Gloucester and Arundel? If we accept that Henry and Mowbray had indeed been at the dinner party at the castle, then their fate looked shakingly uncertain. Any day the guards might come to take them away in chains. Mowbray had perhaps saved himself by acting as Richard's spy and afterwards becoming one of the new appellants, but Henry's situation was altogether more perilous.

A few days before parliament opened there came news from Calais to frighten the two young lords still further: the duke of Gloucester was dead. Of natural causes, the report said, but unofficial reports told a different story, that Gloucester had been murdered, smothered with pillows in his bed.

Despite their disputes over the de Bohun inheritance Henry's relations with his youngest uncle had been good in recent years, and he grieved at his death, but this was no moment to show his sorrow. When such a thing could happen to a peer of the realm it was clearly time to throw overboard all principles and adopt instead the morality of *sauve qui peut*. There must be no hint of mourning.

Henry adopted a mask of cheerfulness, on the eve of parliament giving a most magnificent banquet in his Fleet Street mansion. The menu included thirteen curlews, thirteen doves and thirteen parrots, intricately designed by the king's painter, John Prince 'with silver and gold and other colours', subtleties which took one man four days to mould in sugar and paste, and another eight men two days to decorate. Probably the king himself was a guest. In his fear for his own safety Henry could not do too much to assure Richard of his loyalty, and further to prove this feeling he had his state barge newly covered with forty ells (50 yds.) of canvas in the royal red and white. Although, unlike Mowbray, he was not among the new appellants and did not act as a gaoler to any of his former colleagues, he had arrived for the parliament as commanded, with a large armed retinue to be put completely at Richard's disposal.

For this support the king had promised a new pardon superseding all others to Henry and Mowbray. But the royal promises had lately meant very little, and it must have been in great anxiety that on 17 September the two earls took their parliamentary seats with other peers in the strange, open-sided building surrounded by archers standing prepared to shoot. Within a short while their anxiety spread to everyone present.

The chancellor's opening address began with a statement of the king's determination to be the most powerful man in the country. Edmund Stafford, bishop of Exeter, had chosen as his text a quotation from Ezekiel, 'one king shall be king to them all', and from this he proceeded to list three essentials for good government: first, that the king should be strong enough to govern; second, that the laws by which he governed should be guarded and executed justly; third, that his subjects should obey the king and his laws.

Stafford went on to state some of Richard's most deeply felt beliefs, that in order to govern, kings had many privileges given them in their coronation ceremony which they were obliged to guard and sustain, and these they could not legally alienate or translate.

From general principles, his argument then focused on the purpose of this particular parliament. It was for this reason, he said, that the king had assembled the estates: to discover from them if any of these rights had been *suistretz* or *amenusez*, withdrawn or diminished, and if so to seek a remedy so that he could enjoy the same liberty as his forbears. Those who usurped these rights were worthy of the penalty of the law.

At last the accusation was out in the open and it was terrifyingly all-embracing. In effect, it meant that anyone who had interfered with the king's prerogative, or had persuaded him to do anything against his will was a traitor, not only everyone who had taken part in the Appellants' Revolt, but also all those who had consented to the acts of the Merciless Parliament.

Richard wished to suspend in the same state of apprehension as Henry and Mowbray as many as possible of his subjects. The chancellor made that clear in his next statement. The king proclaimed his grace 'to all who might be among the aforesaid offenders, only excepting fifty persons and some others to be impeached in this parliament'. Fifty only were to be accused. It was not many, but who could be sure he was not among the unlucky fifty? Having discovered that fear created obedience, Richard refused all requests to reveal their identity. To those who nagged at him to reveal the names he gave a threatening answer when parliament met on Wednesday:

Forasmuch as many ask me to disclose those fifty persons who are excepted in the general pardon, I simply will not, and whosoever asks it is worthy of death.

Not surprisingly, the requests stopped. Before that, however, on Tuesday, one of the names had been divulged. Many of the charges against the accused were to be made in the form of petitions ostensibly from the Commons and presented by their speaker, Sir John Bushy, one of Richard's most trusted ministers. At eight o'clock on Tuesday morning he presented himself before the lords and set the tone of the new monarchy. He addressed the king 'devising adulatory and unusual words incongruous to mortal men, so that whenever he spoke to the king, sitting on the throne, he adored him with extended arms, supplicating hands, begging his, as it were, eminent, high, to-be-adored majesty that he would deign to grant this or that'.

One favour that he begged the king to grant was to consider the conviction for treason, not only of the duke of Gloucester and the earl of Arundel, but also of the earl's brother, Thomas, archbishop of Canterbury. In the opinion of the Commons these were the three men, he said, who had 'principally transgressed against your majesty and royalty', since they had been largely responsible for forcing him to grant the commission that had governed the kingdom from 1386 to 1389.

If even an archbishop could be accused of treachery no one was safe. And Thomas Arundel was not even to have the chance to answer the charge against him, for when he rose indignantly to reply, the king indicated that he should be seated with an abrupt, 'Tomorrow'. That tomorrow was never to come, for the following day he was refused leave to enter parliament.

It is not surprising that none of the lords objected to the proposals Bushy now made. That same day they agreed to annul the commission and all its acts and to recall the general pardon issued after the Merciless Parliament and the special pardon more recently granted to the earl of Arundel. Just for a moment, when the proposal was put that any man convicted of acting against the government should be punished as a traitor, it looked as though they might object, as Adam of Usk recounts. 'There was ... some bustle', and commotion, soon ended by the sight of the king's archers, 'who to the number of 4,000 surrounded the parliament house ... bending their bows, they drew their arrows to the ear, to the great terror of all who were there; but the king quieted them.'

What happened on Thursday is a gauge of the tension Richard had generated among the peers. It was on that day that Bushy brought in more specific charges, describing the commission of 1386-89 as having usurped the royal authority and 'traitorously done to death' Sir Simon Burley and Sir James Berners. For several terrible moments everyone who had been involved in the commission felt the approaching shadow of the hangman's rope and the headsman's axe.

Then the king spoke. Apart from the two Arundels and Gloucester, he regarded all others who had been joined in the commission to be faithful, loyal and free from treason, 'and especially Alexander Neville, late archbishop of York'.

Thus abruptly released from terror of their lives, Adam of Usk tells us, 'my lord Edmund of Langley, duke of York, the king's uncle, and my lord William of Wykeham, bishop of Winchester, who had been of the commission, shedding tears, fell on their knees and thanked the king for so great favour'.

Henry and Mowbray would have to wait until the Saturday before they too were fully absolved from blame. Bushy then declared that, though named in the commission, they were 'innocent of malice', a statement warmly espoused by the king, who declared that he personally bore witness to their 'loyalty and good fame'.

By such means Richard had his lords well under control before the actual trials began. Throughout, they were to be putty in his hands. Gaunt and York were to besmirch the memory of their dead brother. Even Henry was to do just as Richard wished.

On Friday 21 September there appeared before parliament the eight new appellants, including Mowbray, dressed alike in 'red robes of silk, banded with white silk and powdered with letters of gold'. Pronouncing the duke of Gloucester, the earls of Arundel and Warwick traitors, they informed the king that the accused 'would have deposed you from your royal estate and majesty and taken your crown into their keeping ... had they not been prevented by Henry of Lancaster, earl of Derby, and Thomas Mowbray, earl of Nottingham'.

Immediately after the appeal against him had been read the earl of Arundel was brought to the bar. Clad in 'a robe of red', he was, to symbolise his guilt, roughly stripped of his knight's belt and his scarlet hood, so that his robe billowed ridiculously around him and his head was humbly bare. Yet he retained his dignity before his accusers. Refusing to take the only course that might possibly have saved him, to beg the king's mercy, he obstinately and furiously rebutted the accusations and insisted that his pardon remained valid.

Like a bear baited by dogs he stood at bay, while accused by his enemies, Henry, Gaunt and Bushy. We must presume that Henry's pardon had been partly bought by his turning king's evidence against the earl, but it must be admitted regrettably that it was a role he played with unedifying gusto. He had never forgiven Arundel for accusing Gaunt of treason in 1394. Back and forth snapped the arguments. He was no traitor, Arundel insisted. If he was no traitor why had he asked for a special pardon? demanded Gaunt as high steward.

'To close the mouths of my foes of whom thou art one,' retorted Arundel. His pardon had been recalled 'by the king, the Lords and us his faithful Commons,' declared Bushy.

'Where be those faithful Commons?' scornfully declared the earl. 'The faithful Commons are not here. They, I know, are sore grieved for me, and I know that thou hast ever been false.'

The king joined Henry in delivering the coup de grace which is re-enacted in all its drama in the pages of Adam of Usk.

Then rose up the earl of Derby and said to him: 'Didst thou not say to me at Huntingdon, where first we were gathered to revolt, that it would be better first of all to seize the king?' The earl replied: 'Thou, earl of Derby, thou liest at thy peril! Never had I thought concerning our lord the king, save what was to his welfare and honour'. Then said the king to him: 'Didst thou not say to me, at the time of thy parliament, in the bath behind the White Hall, that Sir Simon Burley, my knight, was, for many reasons, worthy of death? And I answered thee that I knew no cause of death in him. And then thou and thy fellows did traitorously slay him.'

The king had clearly waited a long time for this moment when he could avenge his murdered friends. With the mention of Richard's old tutor, marched sick and fainting to his execution, Arundel too was doomed. Sentence of death having been passed on him by the high steward, he was immediately led to Tower Hill by John and Thomas Holland and others of his 'foes' with a guard of Cheshire archers. On the same spot where Burley had suffered he was summarily beheaded; a life had paid for a life.

Henry's special task was now done. When his uncle's alleged crimes were read out he did no more than go along with his fear-driven fellow peers, listening in silence to the confession so conveniently extracted before Gloucester's alleged natural death, in which the duke admitted that he had agreed to the temporary deposition of the king in 1387, repented of it and then pathetically pleaded for mercy in these words:

> ... I was in place ther it was communed and spoken in manere of deposyl of my liege loord, trewly I knowlech wele that we were assented thereto for two dayes or three, and than we for to have done our homage and our oothes, and putt him as heyly in hys estate as ever he was. Bot forsothe ther I knowlech that I dede untrewely and unkyndely as to hym that is my lyege loord and hath bene so gode and kynde loord to me. Wherefor I besech to hym naghtwythstondyng myn unkyndenesse, I beseche hym evermore of his mercy and of his grace as lowly as any creature may beseche it unto his lyege loord.

> (I was there where the deposing of my liege lord was discussed, truly I admit that we were agreed on it for two or three days and then we performed our homage and our oaths and set him in his high estate as before. But I admit that I acted falsely and unnaturally to him who is my liege lord and has been such a good and kind lord to me. Therefore I beg him despite my disloyalty, I beg him evermore to

show me mercy and grace as humbly as any man may beg it of his liege lord.)

But even after his death no mercy was to be granted to the duke. With his fellow peers Henry agreed that this 'lowly creature', already murdered, should be declared posthumously a traitor.

The third member of the once 'indivisible trio' was more fortunate. When the earl of Warwick was brought to the bar the lords at last shook off their shackles of fear and dared to protest. Warwick was now an old man, he could no longer be a danger. He spent most of time away from court at Warwick Castle. Surely he at least could be allowed to live. Henry probably joined in the general attempt to save him from the block, 'all, as it were lamenting and seeking the royal favour', a plea that was successful.

For Richard's desire for revenge was now satisfied. He agreed merely to banish the earl for life to the Isle of Man, depriving him of all his property. And with this sentence the main business of parliament came to an end.

It remained only for Richard to reward his supporters, beginning with the loyal archers. The county of their origin, Cheshire, was proclaimed a duchy and enlarged by the gift of Arundel's confiscated lands on its borders. And then it was the turn of the lords, who between them received ten new titles. Henry, earl of Derby, was created duke of Hereford; Edward, earl of Rutland, became duke of Aumerle; Thomas Holland, earl of Kent, became duke of Surrey; John Holland, earl of Huntingdon, became duke of Exeter; Thomas Mowbray, earl of Nottingham, became duke of Norfolk; and John Beaufort, earl of Somerset, became marquess of Dorset. Thomas Despenser became earl of Gloucester, William Lescrope, earl of Wiltshire, and Sir Thomas Percy, earl of Worcester. Ralph, Lord Neville, became earl of Westmorland. As an extra mark of the royal favour the new dukes were licensed to use the arms of Edward the Confessor 'either alone or impaled' like the king.

We know that Henry hastened to show his appreciation of this last honour publicly. His accounts list payment to Peter Swan of 13s. 4d. for 'embroidering nine labels with feathers on a cotearm, with arms of St. Edward', so that as he thundered down the lists, the confessor's arms emblazoned on the surcoat he wore over his armour, his pledge of good faith would be clear for all to see. Henry also paid 36s. 9d. for a silver seal bearing the arms of St. Edward quartered with those of Hereford and England.

His best hope of survival, he was aware, lay in thus giving this new and terrible Richard such tangible assurances of his loyalty.

XIII   THE KING IN GLORY

'Leaping in arms upon the mountains
and passing over the hills, he has tossed
about the clouds and the sun and has
brought out the light of the sun more
clearly.' *Kirkstall Chronicle*, trans. Duls

The autumn of 1397 was the summit of Richard's achievement in his struggle to recover his 'dignyte, Regalye and honourable estate'. His star was at last in the ascendant, a blaze of power outshining all lesser luminaries, an image Richard himself adopted. It was no accident that he chose in this year to use for the first time, as well as his own white hart which he had adapted from his mother's emblem of the white hind, his father's badge of the rising sun; and others besides Richard recognized its significance. The *Kirkstall Chronicle* described with ungrudging approval Richard's actions in that momentous parliament: 'With admirable and long-lasting patience becoming a king, a certain sun was formerly covered with a cloud, that is, the regal majesty (was obscured) by the might of another; but now, leaping in arms upon the mountains and passing over the hills, he (the king) has tossed about the clouds and the sun and has brought out the light of the sun more clearly'.

The chronicler, a Cistercian white monk, was delighted with the autocratic way Richard had disposed of the duke of Gloucester and the earls of Arundel and Warwick, who in his opinion had deserved their fate. But England was soon to discover that it was not only rebel barons who were to be tossed about like clouds in that new phase of Richard's reign which had been ushered in by the autumn parliament, but a great many quite ordinary, innocent subjects as well. The sun, brilliant and terrible, was an apt symbol for the beginning of that extraordinary period of Richard II's reign when he ruled his kingdom through fear and made all his subjects obedient by a similar method to the one he had used to control his Lords and Commons.

The cancelling of the general pardons of 1388 affected not only the leaders of the Appellants' Revolt but everyone who had rallied to their banners and Gloucester's fox's brush nine years before, which was most of the inhabitants of south-east England. Just how ruthless Richard would be in imposing this new policy, it took his subjects some time to realize. Nervously, after the Westminster parliament dispersed, many of them had rushed to the palace to sue for new pardons, but by January the demand had fallen off, people assuming that by now surely the king would have tired of paying off old scores.

They were sharply disillusioned by a royal proclamation when the sheriffs announced that everyone who had ridden against the king in 1387 must sue for pardon, and not later than 24 June 1398. No one who had joined with the appellants was too humble to need a pardon; whether knight, merchant or man-at-arms, he was to appear before a committee of the king's council and pay whatever fine was demanded. Consisting of the chancellor, treasurer, keeper of the privy seal and the king's most trusted trio of servants, Sir John Bushy, Sir William Bagot and Sir Henry Green (known to the public irreverently as the 'bush', the 'bag' and the 'green') the committee soon acquired a sinister reputation. Paying over his allotted fine to these high officers of the crown in the belief that that was the end of it, the donor would observe with alarm his precious coins clinking into a secret leather bag with no clerk recording the transaction, nothing being done to show he had paid, so he might be fined again for the same offence. Bushy, Bagot and Green, who had also taken part in the 'ridings' and had themselves to sue for pardon, were among the lucky few allowed to have their pardons enrolled. Not surprisingly the members of the committee, especially the treasurer, William Lescrope, earl of Wiltshire, and the 'bush', the 'bag' and the 'green', became some of the most hated men in England.

There was another version of Richard's sword of Damocles which was used at the same time to intimidate his subjects, the infamous 'blank charter', so called not because it was empty of words - far too much was written on it for many a victim's liking - but because it gave Richard carte blanche to do more or less as he wished with the property of the unfortunate person whose name appeared on it. A man suspected of having ridden against Richard was forced to set his seal on a document admitting offences against the king, declaring himself a traitor and thus making all his possessions liable to forfeiture at any time Richard cared to claim them. The sealed document was then taken away and locked up in a chest with a store of similar charters.

Obviously, since there was a limit to how many of these blank charters his black-gowned clerks could write with only quill and parchment to help them, Richard soon resorted to another method of intimidation, one that would suspend his Damocles sword of fear not simply over individuals but whole counties, thus helping to fill the ever needy royal coffers. In December 1397 £2,000 was demanded from the men of Essex and Hertfordshire in exchange for a pardon for all their treasonable activities before 1 October. Should anyone refuse to contribute, his name was to be given to the king. Since no one cared to have the royal attention thus unfavourably drawn to him, the threat worked so well that in the end the two counties actually gave Richard more than he had asked for.

According to the *Annales* similar treatment was meted out to London and the sixteen adjacent counties from which had come most of the supporters of the 1387 revolt; in exchange for a pardon they were forced to pay a large fine called 'Le Plesaunce', the king's pleasure. And by the late summer of 1398 proctors for the same counties had set their seals to letters in which the inhabitants all admitted their guilt and swore to uphold the acts of the recent parliament. It is a measure of Richard's triumph that many of those same people who had seized up staves and billhooks and marched angrily on London rather than pay the poll tax of 1381 now meekly agreed to pay these more plainly unjust levies.

But, as Richard understood, this enforced meekness could easily explode into rebellion should his subjects decide that his financial exactions and his treatment of the barons made him a tyrant. As the months passed the prospect of such a rebellion increasingly haunted him. To forestall conspiracy he tried to control men's tongues, and even their pens, in private letters. By January 1398 sheriffs were being made to swear to imprison at once anyone whom they heard speak ill of the king, and in March of the same year he attempted to censor correspondence with other countries. A writ to the mayor and sheriffs of the ports forbade any but business and official communications to leave England without a royal licence, and declared that all letters from foreign parts addressed to lords and great men of the realm were to be sent to the council for examination.

Richard's nights began to be troubled by bad dreams, out of which he would start in terror. He dreamt repeatedly of the earl of Arundel, executed on Tower Hill and buried in the church of the Austin Friars in Broad Street, London. There were stories of miracles at his grave, chief and most disturbing among them was the rumoured report that the decapitated head and body had joined together. Pilgrims began to visit the grave as though the earl was a holy martyr, and when Richard heard the news he fell into one of his recurrent uncontrollable rages, for such a cult could become the seed of revolution. The *Annales* gives a ghoulish account of how he tackled the political problem and tried at the same time to set his mind at rest.

At his order on a dark night a group of his most trusted servants, including the dukes of Lancaster, Aumerle, Surrey and Norfolk and the earl of Northumberland, rode to the church and ordered the terrified friars to open the grave. On discovering that the head and body were indeed joined, by human not divine means, sewn together by some intrepid spirit with thread, the lords commanded that they should be separated a second time and that a friar should walk between head and drunk to prove that the separation was complete. Afterwards, the corpse should be interred in an unmarked grave under the pavement. Seven of the friars who had been involved in fostering the cult were banished from the kingdom.

We can presume that the macabre ceremony and operation did the trick, for we hear no more of pilgrimages to the earl of Arundel's grave. Nevertheless Richard's sleep remained broken, troubled by fears of a sudden attack in the night, while even by day he felt unsafe, surrounding himself with guards to an extent that was quite contrary to custom. It is after the parliament of 1397 that we first find him retaining a large permanent bodyguard of the Cheshire archers, sporting on their doublets silver brooches of the livery of the white hart, 311 highly paid and well organized guards who were divided into seven squadrons of forty-four to forty-six men under seven leaders, called his 'masters of the watches'. These archers 'whithersoever the king went, night and day, as if at war, kept watch in arms around him', a chronicler reported, 'so that as he thought he was under their secure and peaceful protection everywhere he breathed'.

Humbly born though most of these guards were, he trusted them far more than anyone else in his entourage and they were permitted to treat him with great familiarity, even addressing him by an affectionate diminutive, and one kind, rough fellow was heard to say, 'Dycun, slep sicury quile we wake, and dred nouzt quile we lyve sestow' (Dick, sleep safely while we remain awake and fear not while we live, seest thou), words whose intimacy offended the courtiers who were at the time treated ever more formally.

It is to this period that the chilling description belongs of Richard's strange new attitude to some of the grandest among his subjects:

> Aftir this, the kyng in solenne dies and grete festis, in the which he werid his croune and went in his rial aray (royal attire), he leet ordeyne and make (had ordered and made) in his chambir, a trone (throne), wherynne he was wont to sitte fro oftir mete (supper) unto evensong tyme, spekynge to no man, but overlooking alle menn; and yf he loked on eny mann, what astat or degre that evir he were of, he moste knele.

To men used to walking arm-in-arm with the king this sudden distancing would have been deeply offensive, especially in comparison with the informal manners between him and the Cheshire archers.

For these privileged guards no licence was too great. Authorized to dispense with court etiquette, they were also allowed to transgress the laws of the land. A wild bunch, puffed up with pride of their position, they robbed and killed with impunity, and if brought before a court 'argued with their swords' and intimidated the jury. At a time when all armed retainers had a bad reputation the Cheshire archers behaved even worse, it appears from the contemporary poem, *Mum and the Sothsegger*, which describes how they took advantage of the royal badges they wore on their doublets.

For tho that had hertis on hie on her brestis,
For the more partie I may well avowe,
They bare hem the bolder for her gay broches,
And bushid with her brestis and bare adoun the pouere
(For those that had heart badges up on their chests
For the most part I may well declare,
They bore themselves the bolder because of their showy brooches,
And puffed out their chests boastfully and oppressed the poor)

Richard's Cheshire archers were to become as unpopular as his financial exactions and his infamous trio of advisers, the 'bush', the 'bag' and the 'green', adding to the fast-growing enmity towards him among both nobles and commons alike.

The king's dread of revolt was bound to touch on its potential leaders. Pre-eminent among these of course was Henry, who possessed the military experience, the status and the popularity to persuade others to join him, a man moreover, who on Gaunt's death would command the House of Lancaster's great wealth and formidable army of retainers.

To Richard's wariness of Henry there is a colourful reference in the Lambeth manuscript of the *Brut*. A court astrologer had warned Richard that he should beware of toads, for a toad would destroy him, this chronicle relates. And as the king 'thouhte and mervayled in his mynde how that shulde be', he gave a Christmas feast which the lords attended 'in the gayest desgysing (fancy dress) that they could devyse'. Henry came in a gown 'broderyd (embroidered) al abowte with toadys'. Ever afterwards the king 'had this Herry, earl of Derby, yn Ielwsy (jealousy) and mystruste, supposying that yt shulde be he that shulde destroy hym ...'

That Henry wore a gown patterned with toads is quite possible at a time when rich men's gowns were embroidered with a strange assortment of devices especially during the season of Christmas and New Year festivities. And the story itself can be interpreted in different ways: as a bit of apocryphal hindsight inserted into the chronicle to please the popular taste for prophesy, or as an inspired guess by someone peculiarly sensitive to the conflicting forces at court. But whether true or false it suggests that rumours abounded of Richard's fear of his cousin.

An even more puzzling story comes to us from the *Traison et Mort*, according to which Richard claimed in 1399 that he had twice or thrice been advised by the duke of Lancaster to put Henry to death and had once ridden all through the night to prevent Gaunt himself from putting his own son to death. One of these strange incidents, as has already been suggested, could have occurred at the time of Gaunt's return from Spain after the Appellants' Revolt. Did another occur now at the time of Richard's revenge on the appellants? Did Gaunt throw out a wild, murderous suggestion, as he may have done in the former hour of peril, in the secret hope that once again it would help to protect rather than destroy his son? It is a fair speculation if we remember that Gaunt, who had long possessed a room at court, was experienced not only in politics but also in that strange country, the king's nature. Since Richard was ten its vagaries had been known to him, its capriciousness, its murderous rages that blew over as suddenly as they arose and great spurts of energy that fizzled out as quickly. He probably recognized in Richard as well a residual loyalty and affection for the cousin he at the same time hated and feared. Had Richard contemplated Henry's death after the dinner at Arundel Castle, Gaunt may have known of it. Did he then advise it, counting on Richard's considering it, rejecting it and then turning away from the idea in revulsion, his hostility purged? If so, it would have been a desperate gamble that paid off at a time when desperate measures were called for.

But by whatever method he achieved it, Gaunt's success in protecting Henry from Richard's holocaust of revenge in the autumn of 1397 was probably a triumph of political skill, a skill that was to be tested again in the last month of that same year when an incident occurred that burst the king's fragile sense of security like a bubble and made Henry in his turn suspect the king of the most sinister machinations against himself.

Shortly before Christmas the new duke of Hereford was riding from Brentford to London with the court, when his only surviving fellow appellant, Thomas Mowbray, now duke of Norfolk, caught up with him and casually began to talk of different matters. Suddenly he blurted out a warning, 'We are about to be undone'. The king had not forgiven them for their part in the battle of Radcot Bridge; Henry and Gaunt were to be killed when they came to Windsor after the parliament in the New Year, he rushed on. The king's special friends, the duke of Surrey, and the earls of Wiltshire, Salisbury and Gloucester were all in the plot against them and there was a move afoot to reverse the judgement on Thomas of Lancaster, which would disinherit both them and many others.

Today it seems probable that for once the turncoat Mowbray was telling the truth, for we have evidence of a definite plot of this date against the lives of Henry, his father and other members of the House of Lancaster, by William Bagot, who was later made to enter into two highly suspicious recognizances. On 1 March 1399 he made a recognizance of £1,000 to be levied from him should he 'in time to come make suit for disherison (the disinheritance) of John duke of Lancaster, his wife or any of his children'. And two days later he made a recognizance and bond 'that if John duke of Guyenne and Lancastre, his wife or any of his children shall in time to come be by him slain, upon proof thereof he shall be put to death without other judgement or process'. As Bagot was Richard's creature it seems all too probable that he was made a scapegoat for the king after the inconvenient truth leaked out.

But Henry would not yet have had this evidence and he dared not trust a man who had been actively instrumental in the destruction of all the other leaders of the Appellants' Revolt to date. He would have borne in mind that Mowbray had told Richard of the dinner party at Arundel Castle which had precipitated the arrests in the summer and, as constable of Calais, Mowbray must have facilitated the duke of Gloucester's murder. He had besides acted as custodian of the earl of Arundel on his way to prison and joined in the appeal against all three appellants in the autumn parliament. He had willingly aided and abetted Richard's revenge. Was he now looking for a fourth victim? Henry was bound to wonder. Had his own turn for betrayal come? Instantly on his guard at Mowbray's words, and aware that every word he uttered himself would probably be reported to the king, he replied very carefully, expressing amazement at the suggestion of a royal plot.

Oblivious to Henry's suspicions, Mowbray, whose nature was fatally impetuous and rash, plunged on, giving details of the plot and laughing to scorn Richard's promise to pardon them.

On reaching London Henry hastened to take counsel with his father, who seems to have agreed that Mowbray's warning was probably a trick, an attempt to convict Henry of treasonable words, and that his only chance of escaping the trap set for him was to reach the king first with his version of the conversation.

So Henry did as Gaunt advised but it did not rescue him from danger, for the newly nervous Richard smelt disaffection somewhere in the business. (If the king himself had a hand in Bagot's plot he had double reason to be nervous.) One of the two men, either Henry or Mowbray had treasonable thoughts. But which? Richard had no means of knowing and, unable to choose between them, decided to solve his problem simply. He would destroy both, and thus rid himself of the last of the appellants who had so hurt and humiliated him ten years before. This seems the only possible construction to put on Richard's actions, when one considers how little damaging were Mowbray's actual words, and how easily the whole affair at this stage could have then been shrugged aside. As Froissart suggests:

> He shulde rather whan he herde the wordes fyrste have sayde to them bothe, 'Ye are two lordes of my blode and lygnage, (lineage) wherfore I commaunde you bothe to be in peace and lette nouther hate nor rancoure engendre (breed) bytwene you, but be frendes, lovers and cosyns togyther ...' If the kynge had sayde those wordes and apeased these lordes thus he had done wysely.

But instead of this, which Froissart tells us would have had the approval of the French as well as the English lords, Richard enlarged what was a trivial matter into an affair of state. He had it brought up in the parliament, which reassembled on 3 January 1398 at Shrewsbury. On 30 January Henry was arraigned before both Lords and Commons at Richard's command where he read a report of the conversation in question, a report which, couched in the most skilfully diplomatic terms, is still preserved in the parliament rolls. As one reads it the scene comes alive again, time rolls back and one can picture the duke with his sturdy frame, forked red beard and seemingly open, candid manner as he spoke the words that he hoped would save him from whatever dire fate the king contemplated:

> Sire, in the month of December in the twenty-first year of your reign as I rode between Brentford and London the duke of Norfolk came up to me at great speed and talked to me of diverse matters among which he said to me, 'We are on the point of being undone.' And I said, Why? And he replied, 'Because of Radcot Bridge.' And I said, how could that be, because he had made us grace and declared for us in parliament, saying that we have been good and loyal towards him? And the duke of Norfolk replied that regardless of that he would have done with us as he had done with others before, because he wished to annul that record.

Cunningly, Henry alluded only most vaguely to the events of the Merciless Parliament and passed on to the royal pardon he had received and the signs of favour the king had shown him. In their light, he hinted delicately, any plot such as Mowbray mentioned was surely impossible, for the king was kind and good, not a monster of perjury.

159

And I said that would be a great marvel, after the king had said it before the people and after that he would have it annulled. And the duke of Norfolk said that it was a marvellous world, and a false. I know well said he that ... your father of Lancaster and you would have been taken to death when you came to Windsor after the parliament. And that the malice of this deed was in the duke of Surrey, the earl of Wiltshire and the earl of Salisbury. And that they had sworn to undo six lords, that is, the dukes of Lancaster and Hereford, of Aumale (Aumerle) and Exeter, the marquis (John Beaufort) and him. And also the duke of Norfolk said that they purposed to reverse the judgement of earl Thomas of Lancaster, and this would cause disinheritance to us and to many others.

One can imagine the expression of incredulous innocence over Henry's face as he continued.

And I said, 'God forbid, for it would be a great marvel if the king would assent to that. For he has made me, as it seemed to me, such good cheer and promised to be good lord to me and to all the others. And the said Duke of Norfolk replied, saying that so he had done many times to him swearing it on the body of our lord and that he should not be trusted any the more because of that.

It was a clever speech. Parliament's sympathies could not but be stirred by it. One can see the peers nodding their heads in sage approval. And at the same time as Henry had made any attempt by the king to destroy him without forfeiting parliament's good opinion very difficult indeed, he had also avoided accusing Mowbray of treason. So the quarrel between the two nobles could yet have been stilled had not Richard deliberately fanned into hatred the mistrust between them.

Himself presiding in judgement at Oswestry on 23 February, the king had Mowbray summoned there to confront Henry and commanded him to tell his version of events. Inevitably, it differed greatly from Henry's. The duke of Norfolk denied that he had spoken the alleged words and tempers flamed. The upshot of the argument is described in the *Traison et Mort*. Henry swept off the black bonnet from his head and, addressing the king, called Mowbray 'a traitor, false and recreant towards you and your royal majesty, to your crown, to the nobles and to all the people of your realm'. And Mowbray retorted that 'Henry of Lancaster, duke of Hereford, has lied in what he has said and wished to insinuate against me, like a false traitor and disloyal subject as he is'.

The matter had now become too public and gone too far to be

allowed to drop. Richard had both lords arrested. Bail was granted to Henry and sureties were given by his own father and the dukes of York, Aumerle and Surrey, while Mowbray who was unable to find such powerful friends, was first imprisoned at Windsor then taken to London and placed in the custody of the mayor under day and night guard in the King's Wardrobe.

Expressly to settle the controversy between the two lords, on the last day of parliament a committee of eighteen had been set up, a body for which Richard was later to find other sinister uses also concerned with the destruction of the dukes. It met at Bristol in March and decided that their case should go before the Court of Chivalry at Windsor on 2 April. This was a decision bound to lead to trial by battle, that extraordinary method of dispensing justice inaugurated for disputes such as this where neither party could produce a witness to his innocence. It was a drastic solution and, though legal, one very rarely used in the case of such important men, for the dukes would be expected to fight to the death.

At the hearing of the Court of Chivalry royal pleas were made to the contestants to make peace, but this was mere play-acting, part of the ritual of the occasion so graphically described in the *Traison et Mort* - from which, as ready-made theatre, it found its way into Shakespeare's *Richard II*. The king sat on a platform which had been erected in 'the square of the castle', all the lords and prelates of the kingdom with him:

> Then a herald cried on the part of the king that the duke of Hereford and the duke of Norfolk should come forward before the king, to tell each his reason why they would not make peace together. And when they were come before the king and his council, the king said to them himself, 'My lords, make matters up; it will be much better.' 'Saving your favour, my dear sovereign,' said the duke of Norfolk, 'it cannot be, my honour is too deeply concerned.' Then the king said to the duke of Hereford, 'Henry, say what it is you have to say to the duke of Norfolk or why you will not be reconciled.'

But Henry had by now thought of some new reasons, first, 'that Thomas, duke of Norfolk, has received from you eight hundred thousand nobles to pay your men-at-arms who guard your city of Calais, whom he has not paid as he ought to have done; I say this is great treason, and calculated to cause the loss of your city of Calais.'

It was a grave charge but there was a more serious accusation to come, a curiously rash one in view of Richard's own almost certain involvement in Gloucester's murder. Henry declared that Mowbray 'by his false counsel and malice, caused to be put to death my dear and beloved uncle, the duke of Gloucester, son of King Edward, whom God absolve, and who was brother of my dearly beloved father, the duke of Lancaster'.

And he offered to 'prove the truth of this by his body between any sunrise and sunset' the statutory period for trial by battle which was as much a trial of endurance as of military skill.

Mowbray replied that what Henry said was 'all falsehood, and that he has lied falsely and wickedly like a false and disloyal knight; and that he has been more false and disloyal towards you, your crown, your royal majesty, and your kingdom, than he (Mowbray) ever was in intention or in deed'. He had, he insisted, performed all his essential duties in Calais and any money he might have used was due to him for the expenses of diplomatic journeys to France and Germany which he had paid for himself. Carefully avoiding any mention of the sensitive murder charge, he ended, 'I beseech you to grant me justice and trial of battle in tournament.'

At this point the king consulted with his council and then again asked the dukes if they were willing to be reconciled, a suggestion which after all that had passed was, of course, vehemently refused. Whereupon 'the duke of Hereford threw down his pledge, which the duke of Norfolk received. Then swore the king by Saint John the Baptist that he would never more endeavour to reconcile those two; and Sir John Bushy, on the part of the king and council, announced that they should have trial of battle at Coventry, on a Monday in the month of August (in fact, September), and that there they should have their day (of combat) and their lists'.

In the eyes of the watching public it was an uplifting scene, all the participants brimming over with noble virtues, the king with generosity and love of peace, Henry and Mowbray with high courage, loyalty and honour. But beneath the surface pageantry its real meaning was grim: since God was expected to help the just, whoever succumbed in the battle was guilty of treason according to the law, and if not killed in the lists would be handed over to the executioner in a terrible and humiliating procedure whose brutality was fresh in Richard's mind. By coincidence this had been described for Richard recently in a treatise on such trials, *The Ordenaunce and Fourme of Fightyng within Listes*, written by the murdered duke of Gloucester in his capacity as constable of England. It declared that:

> He that is convicte (overcome) and discomfite (defeated), shalbe disarmed in the listes by the commandement of the conestable (constable), and a corner of the liste brokyn in the reprove of hym (to symbolise his disgrace), by the which (he) shalbe drawen oute with hors fro the same place, there he is so disarmede, thorugh the listes unto the place of justice, where he shalbe hedid (beheaded) or hanged aftir the usage of the countrey.

So, although in appearance resembling the tournaments that Henry so loved, the spirit of the duel at Coventry would be very different, its object being, not sport, but death for the weaker contestant, hence the bitterness of Gaunt's comment, reported by Froissart, 'Nowe the king suffreth that my sonne and heyre shall do batayle for a thynge of nought'.

It was a cruel return for Gaunt's long years of loyalty and unjust both to Henry and to Mowbray, who were now caught up in a lethal process from which there was no escape.

XIV BATTLE TO THE DEATH

'... their heavers down,
'Their eyes of fire sparkling through sights of steel,
'And the loud trumpet blowing them together.'
William Shakespeare, *Richard II*

When the Court of Chivalry at Windsor set a date four months ahead for
the duel between Henry and Mowbray it was due not to any kindly desire
to give the combatants a chance to arrange their affairs before facing
death, but to a quite callous reason: what was to be a form of public
execution was also an entertainment, a Roman holiday staged as a
magnificent spectacle. Time was needed for painters and embroiderers to
adorn the arena with flags, to ornament the pavilions of the contestants
with their heraldic badges (Henry's patterned all over with Lancastrian red
roses, Mowbray's perhaps with mulberries); for carpenters to build the lists,
the barriers and the spectators' stands; and for the king to name the
privileged audience. At the royal order messengers must be dispatched
with invitations to foreign nobles across the sea and summonses to all
bishops, lords and members of his council throughout England. Most
important of all, time was needed for the contestants to equip themselves
in dazzling apparel.

Since nothing, even in Henry's lavish collection of jousting gear, was
good enough for such an exceptional occasion he sent to Italy for a new
suit of armour from his old friend, the Duke Gian Galeazzo of Milan, with
whom he had corresponded ever since his pilgrimage to the Holy Land.
The Count of Virtues lived up to his name; excited by the approaching
drama, Galeazzo invited Henry's emissary to choose from the ducal
armoury himself, and sent him back to England accompanied by four
Milanese armourers to adjust the fit of the intricate pieces of steel and
leather, and to strap Henry into them on the day of the duel. Meanwhile,
Mowbray's envoys had been engaged in buying his armour in the Holy
Roman Empire, German and Italian armourers being currently reputed
the best in Christendom.

Although trial by combat had its root in the belief that God would
help the innocent to destroy the guilty, it is doubtful if many people in 1398

really believed this. Even the Monk of Westminster was sceptical of divine intervention in such matters, telling us of a trial by duel between two felons in 1391, when 'the accuser was defeated although it would seem that he had the better cause'.

Leaving supernatural forces out of the reckoning, Henry's prospects seemed the brighter of the two, if only because public opinion was on his side. As the appellant and challenger, he was generally regarded as the innocent party, in token of which he would enter the lists bearing on his shield the emblem of England, St. George's blood-red cross on a silver ground. And this blameless impression had been reinforced when three great lords, as well as his father, had stood bail for him. Quite apart from its helpful effect on public opinion, the latter gave him the added advantage that he was able to live as a free man during the four months leading up to the duel, whereas the less fortunate Mowbray was forced to spend the intervening period in prison, unable to exercise like his opponent, something which could be decisive in a day-long clash of arms.

However, these factors were not enough to make Henry certain of victory, for in military skill the dukes were well matched, while Henry had excelled in the jousts at St. Ingelvert, Mowbray had won fame at Smithfield. Challenged by the Scottish earl of Mar, who prided himself on his prowess in the sport, Mowbray had more than vanquished him, attacking so fiercely that the Scottish earl and his horse were thrown to the ground and Mar was carried home all the way up to Scotland on a litter. Then there was the matter of chance - a slip of the hand, a sudden gleam of sun in the eyes, the unexpected swerve of his horse that could be fatal. And should Henry lose there would be no mercy for, according to a story from the *Chronique de Saint Denys*, Richard had sworn to uphold the law to Gaunt himself. When one day the duke of Lancaster said to the king in a jesting manner, 'I do not doubt that the cause of your cousin is just, yet if he should succumb what will you decide to do with him?' the king replied: 'Believe me, if he should be vanquished I shall let him be taken to the gibbet; and do not wonder at it, for in a like case you yourself would be treated no better.' Indeed a jest with a sting in its tail.

To prepare for the duel, which was to occur in Gosforth Field, outside the high walls of the prosperous cloth town of Coventry, Henry moved to Kenilworth Castle nearby, bringing his children with him, determined to spend what well might be his last few days of life in their company. And, observing etiquette to the end when on Sunday 15 September, the day before the duel, Richard too arrived on the scene, staying at Baiginton Tower, belonging to Sir William Bagot, Henry went to take his leave of his liege lord. The following morning at dawn, Mowbray followed suit, then after leaving the tower and in hope of receiving divine help, he heard three masses in the Carthusian monastery of St. Anne's. For the dramatic events that followed we have what is almost certainly an eye witness report in the *Traison et Mort*.

By eight o'clock in the morning Gosforth Field bustled with activity. The stands were packed with English lords and dignitaries and 'foreigners who had come from over sea', while the officials of the Court of Chivalry busied themselves about the lists. The constable and marshal (the dukes of Aumerle and Surrey, alias Edward Plantagenet and Thomas Holland) were instructing twenty attendants, all 'well-armed' and clad for the occasion in 'a livery of red kendal cloth full of belts, in the fashion of a silver girdle', each belt bearing the motto of the Order of the Garter, 'Honniz soit cellui qui mal pense', words which rang defiantly in the atmosphere of widespread disapproval of the imminent trial.

Of the duellists, Henry, as challenger, arrived first, approaching the barrier at the east gate with six attendants mounted on 'noble coursers', while he himself, we are told, rode a 'white courser barbed with blew and grene velvet, embrowded sumpteously with swannes and antlopes of goldsmithe's worke, armed at all poyntes'. If we can believe Edward Hall's splendid description, written in the sixteenth century from sources no longer available to us, the choice of the Bohun swan badge would have been very significant. Because this had been Gloucester's favourite emblem, and wearing it would have been a reminder to everyone present of the disreputable facts of his death, facts that implicated Richard as much as Mowbray. It is an indication that, at least on this fateful day, which might be the last day of his life, Henry was no time-server.

From a spectator's point of view the occasion was a vividly theatrical mingling of the rituals of church, tournament and law court. Meeting him at the barrier, although everyone in the field knew the answers to their questions, the constable and marshal asked Henry who he was, what he wanted and for what purpose he had come thither, whereupon, raising his visor, Henry replied in a loud voice, 'I am Henry of Lancaster, duke of Hereford and I am come here to prosecute my appeal in combating Thomas Mowbray, duke of Norfolk, who is a traitor, false and recreant to God, the king, his realm and me'.

Assisted by a priest with cross, crucifix and open missal, the constable and marshal administered to him the three oaths. He swore first that his bill against Mowbray was 'sothe' (true), from beginning to end, secondly that he had no other weapon than those allowed, and no magic help, no herb, nor charm nor any other enchantment, and lastly, that he would either make his adversary 'surrender or kill him' and that he would 'depart out of the lists before sunset'. Then pushing forward his silver shield, Henry signed himself with the sign of the cross with his hand 'as lightly as if he had not been armed', and rode to his red-rose-strewn pavilion by the lists.

The proceedings having been carefully orchestrated, King Richard next arrived with his most important guest, the duke of Brittany, and with them came the first grim sign of the deadly reality that underlay all the colour, sparkle and enjoyment of the occasion. For they were accompanied by an army, light glinting from the conical, steel basinets of no less than '20,000 archers and men-at-arms in great number'. Their presence showed that Richard feared some kind of armed demonstration in favour of one or both the duelists and was making sure that there would be no escape from judgement for either of them, no last minute rescue by friends and retainers.

The king ascended to his handsomely decorated box and signalled to Sir John Bushy. The minister read from a scroll in French the traditional warnings to the audience which were then repeated and proclaimed by the duke of Brittany's herald so that all could hear.

> It is commanded by the king, by the constable and the marshal that no person, poor or rich, be so bold as to put his hand upon the lists on pain of having his hand chopped off; and that none enter within the lists save those who have been ordered by the king and council, constable and marshal, upon pain of being drawn and hanged.

Then thrice at each tribune of the lists, a herald cried, 'Oyez, behold here Henry of Lancaster, duke of Hereford, appellant, who is come to the lists to do his duty upon pain of being declared false.' It was Mowbray's cue at last to appear at the west gate, riding, in Hall's words, a horse 'barbed with crimson velvet embroidered richly with lions of silver and mulberry trees'. Pausing like Henry to take the oaths, he cried loudly, 'God speed the right!' and rode towards his pavilion, whereupon officials, having first measured the lances of the combatants, led them to their places opposite each other in the lists. The *Traison et Mort* takes up the story:

> Then the herald cried, by order of the king, the constable and the marshal, that they should take away the tents of the champions, that they should let go the chargers, and that each should perform his duty. When the duke of Hereford had proved his lance he pushed forward his shield and signed himself with the sign of the cross, then placed his lance upon his thigh and advanced seven or eight paces towards his adversary to perform his duty.

But as everyone familiar with Shakespeare's *Richard II* knows, the moment the spectators had eagerly awaited was to end in anti-climax, for

167

the king rose to his feet, cried loudly, 'Ho! Ho!' and cast down his warder into the lists to stop the battle. There was amazement on all sides, for it was a sign that he had taken the quarrel into his own hand and would himself pronounce judgement.

Officials solemnly carried the combatants' lances away and led them back to their seats - Mowbray's being 'of crimson velvet, curtained about with white and red' - where, tightly strapped in their armour and racked by new suspense, they waited for nearly two hours while king and council debated their fate.

According to the law of the duel, by 'taking the quarrel into his own hand', Richard had stated that neither contestant was guiltier than the other. The way was now open for him to punish them both.

But when the judgement came, once more read by the invaluable Bushy, then proclaimed by a herald, it caused such an uproar of protest that men could not hear each other speak.

Bushy began by praising the dukes for having 'appeared here valiantly, both ready to do their duty like brave knights', then by a step of false logic he advanced to a harsh sentence on the man most people took to be innocent, 'but because the matters are so weighty between the two lords, it is decreed by the king and council that Henry of Lancaster shall quit the realm for the term of ten years, and if he return to the country before ten years are passed he shall be hanged and lose his head'. Well might the spectators feel that justice had miscarried.

When the herald made himself heard again above the angry shouts, he pronounced on Mowbray an even harsher sentence, showing no trace of Richard's former great affection for him. 'Thomas Mowbray, duke of Norfolk shall quit the realm for the rest of his life, and shall choose whether he would dwell in Prussia, in Bohemia or in Hungary or would go right beyond the sea to the land of Saracens and unbelievers'.

Truly a savage punishment. Even though he had confessed to having misappropriated Calais funds, he had not deserved to be exiled for life in countries so alien. Hearing this verdict, Mowbray felt nothing could be worse, and was overheard to complain in desperation, 'We might as well have gone to the great parliament at Shrewsbury, for if he and I had gone there, we should both have been put to death, as the earl of Arundel was'. Seemingly he forgot that Henry had not only gone to the parliament at Shrewsbury but been arraigned before it.

The vengeful judgement turned recent enemies into fellows in misfortune, and sensing a possible future conspiracy, Richard attempted to forestall it. Before they left the field both dukes were made to swear an oath before him that in their exile they would never meet, live in the same country or correspond.

They were heavy sentences indeed, with just one redeeming feature — unlike convicted traitors, the two lords were to be allowed to keep their lands and receive some of the income. From the proceeds of Mowbray's Richard would reimburse himself for the misappropriated Calais funds, but the duke could still retain ultimate ownership of his estates which on his death would descend to his heir. Henry, more leniently treated, would again be able to enjoy his property when he returned from exile in ten years' time. And should Gaunt die in the interim he would still inherit all the power and wealth of the House of Lancaster. The patent rolls preserve a grant made at Windsor Castle on 3 October to 'the king's cousin ... Henry of Lancaster, duke of Hereford', in which Richard promised, 'that if any succession or inheritances descend or otherwise fall to him in his absence, for which he ought to do homage, he may by his attorneys sue and have livery thereof, and that his homage and fealty may be respited for reasonable fine made, until it shall please the king that he return to do them in person'. Encouraging for both dukes was the fact that, to guard his interests while he was abroad, each was allowed to appoint his own lawyers. All in all, it began to look as though for Henry at least things were not really so black.

It was soon apparent that for him there were to be more consolations. He discovered, on going to bid farewell to Richard at Eltham Palace, that his sentence had been substantially reduced and there was in the king's apologetic manner, as reported by Froissart, a suggestion of a softening attitude: '... the kynge humyled hym greatly to his cosyn of Derby and said: "As Godde helpe me, it right greatly displeaseth me the wordes that hath been bytwene you and the erle marshalle; but the sentence that I have gyven is for the beste, and for to apease therby the people who greatly murmured on this matter; wherfore, cosyn, yet to ease you somewhat of your payne, I release my judgement fro(m) tenne yere to syxe yere."'

Indeed, so malleable seemed Richard's mood, that in thanking him Henry is said boldly to have hinted that he would expect further concessions. 'Sir, I thanke your grace, and when it shall please you ye shall do me more grace.'

The same optimism inspires the French chronicler's account of a conversation between Henry's peers after the judgement at Coventry. These had foreseen only a short, comparatively painless exile. 'My Lord of Derby can go and play and fight out of the kingdom for two or three years. He is young. Let him go to Prussia, to the Holy Sepulchre, to Cairo or St. Catherine. He can take other voyages to make the time pass away, and he will know where to go. There are his sisters, the one is queen of Spain and the other of Portugal, he can very easily go and see them.'

The general opinion was apparently that Henry had little to worry about. What was more, for the brief time it lasted, his exile would be spent in comfort. He was to be allowed an annual £2,000, enough money to enable him to lead the princely life he was accustomed to, a household of two hundred retainers as well as 'all vessels of gold, gilt or of silver, all other jewels, horses, harnesses and other property of his which are needful for him'.

They were conditions very different from those of his wretched adversary, who in his lifelong exile was to be permitted a yearly allowance of a mere £1,000 and a household of only thirty people. Mowbray from this point on was a ruined man, and fated, after going on pilgrimage to Jerusalem, to die of the plague in Venice within the year. As befitted his sad prospects, he left England from Keykelerode, near Lowestoft, Suffolk, so quietly that his departure is barely mentioned in the chronicles. By contrast Henry's departure was sensational, for the duel and its outcome had made him more than ever a popular hero. He spent his final days with his father in London, and when the moment came for him, accompanied by his household and carts full of coffers and bundles, to ride for the last time through the city, the people lionised him.

The mayor rode with him and, Froissart tells us, 'a great number of the chiefe burgesses', while the streets were crowded with 'mo thanne fourtie thousande men wepyng and cryeng after hym, that it was pytie to here; and some said: "O gentyll erle of Derby, shall we thus leave you? This realme shall never be in joye tyll ye retourne agayne"'.

The sentiments of the Londoners spread through the rest of England. To his many discontented countrymen the unjust sentence of exile had made Henry their obvious leader, their focus of potential rebellion against the tyrant. Richard had forged a weapon which might all too soon be turned against himself.

XV BANISHED

'Eating the bitter bread of banishment.'
William Shakespeare, *Richard II*

Impatiently ignoring Richard's licence to spend a month in Calais followed by six weeks in the English castle of Sangatte nearby, Henry rode almost at once to Paris. There he was welcomed as if he still stood high in Richard's favour. The four royal dukes rode to meet him outside the city walls and took him at once to their king, who fortunately at the time was enjoying one of his periods of sanity that came between the new and the full moon each month. Charles VI entertained him with wine and spiced cakes in the Hotel de St. Pol and presented him with the French royal badge, a gold and jewelled collar of broom pods similar to the one given to Richard before his wedding to Princess Isabel.

Also he put at Henry's disposal in Paris the Hotel Clisson, with an allowance of 500 crowns a week for his expenses. Here Henry set up magnificent house with his two hundred retainers and all the gold and silver plate he had brought from England, while the king and the dukes diverted him with a succession of hunts, tournaments, minstrelsy and disguisings 'to the entent he shulde thynke the season the shorter bycause he was out of his owne nacion'.

According to Froissart, they found him 'a gracious knyght, curtesse, meke and tretable, (courteous, modest and agreeable), and a man good to be spoken unto', rating him so highly that the duke of Berry even suggested he should marry his twenty-three-year-old daughter Mary. Since the French dukes assumed that this ridiculous sentence of banishment on an important man who had committed no crime would soon be revoked, no honour was too great for him, not even a match with the daughter of the king's uncle.

So it was at first, until the extraordinary truth dawned on them that Henry really was in disgrace and might never again be restored to Richard's favour.

How they discovered their error must have caused acute embarrassment in the formal French court. The earl of Salisbury had been sent to Paris to reach a settlement on little Queen Isabel's dowry, the terms of which had still not been completely finalised two years after her marriage. On meeting his countryman, Henry, the new idol of French society, Salisbury ignored him, loudly declaring in front of King Charles VI that 'the earl of Derby' was a traitor who 'wolde betray his naturall soverayne lorde'. Forced by this public snub to accept that the envoy's attitude must reflect his master's, the French dukes nevertheless continued to entertain Henry but dropped the proposal that he should wed de Berry's daughter, such a dynastic pawn being too important to waste on a man whose future was so darkly shadowed. While it is unlikely that Henry had had time to become emotionally attached to the girl, the breaking off of the match was humiliating and perhaps contributed to the decision he now took to leave France for Hungary. Here he meant to join in an expedition against the Turks, forgetting his troubles in the excitement of battle. But the proposed journey was never to take place, developments at home prevented it.

Among his preparations before leaving, he had dutifully sent Sir John Dymock to England to ask Gaunt's permission for him to go, and at the same time to report on the well-being of his children left in the care of Hugh Waterton. When Dymock returned it was with deeply disturbing news. His father was mortally ill and wished Henry to remain as close as possible in France.

This exchange makes it clear that, although now in his thirties, Henry still relied on the judgement as well as on the unshakable affection of his father. News of Gaunt's approaching death would have been distressing, but there was more at stake than this sad but inevitable personal loss. In jeopardy was the Lancastrian inheritance, the vast estates that had come through his mother, the duchess Blanche and his grandfather, Henry, first duke of Lancaster; the castles that had been presented to Gaunt by Edward III, lands that covered such a large part of England and Wales that they made the duke of Lancaster the king's richest and most influential subject. Despite Richard's promise to allow Henry to claim his inheritance, now that Gaunt was dying it was wise for his heir to remain within easy reach of England and the attorneys. Besides, there was always a chance that the king might relent enough to allow Gaunt to see his beloved eldest son just once more before he died.

To the man who had done more than any other to prop up Richard's shaky throne, no such mercy was to be forthcoming, but Gaunt was nevertheless to make a handsome bequest in his will. To his 'tresredoute (dread) lord and nephew' the duke of Lancaster left his 'best covered gold cup', and his 'gold salt with the garter and a turtle dove on the lid', besides twelve lengths of cloth, red satin striped with gold, 'originally ordered to make a bed which has not yet been commenced', the 'best ermine cover' he owned and the piece of arras given to him by the duke of Burgundy.

Was this a sop to royal greed, so that the king would not try to grab more? A last attempt to protect his son? Possibly this was Gaunt's intention, but if so it was to fail wretchedly, for Richard had his eye not just on a few select items but on all his uncle's possessions, riches that could be used to reinforce the power of the crown.

On 2 February 1399 the duke finally succumbed to 'a great weakness' at Leicester Castle, and after he had lain in state here for several weeks, his coffin departed in a candlelit procession of sombre magnificence, spending the first night at St. Albans and the second at the convent of the Carmelite friars in London, before proceeding to its last resting place in St. Paul's Cathedral. Richard attended the obsequies, watching the coffin lowered into the tomb of Gaunt's first duchess, the once 'fair and bright' Blanche. Then almost immediately he acted to ruin their eldest son.

Ever since the end of the Shrewsbury parliament the previous year, he had been cultivating the perfect tool for the purpose, in the committee of eighteen which had then been formed to enquire into the dispute between Henry and Mowbray. Given wide powers, it had never been disbanded and on 18 March he used it to disinherit Henry. The committee declared that the letters patent to his attorneys allowing them to claim the Lancastrian lands in his absence had been 'granted by inadvertence and without proper advisement or deliberation'. The letters and the circumstances in which they had been granted had since been 'diligently examined', and it had been discovered that they were contrary to the judgements made at Coventry. Because after that judgement the duke of Hereford was 'no fit person to inherit'. Therefore the letters and all that belonged to them were 'revoked, annulled, broken and repealed ... and pronounced null and void for ever'. It was further decreed that Henry's exile was to last not for six years or even ten, but for life. Afterwards the members of the committee swore on the cross of Canterbury to uphold their decision.

Richard wasted no time in putting his punishment into effect, with the result that in Paris Henry received within a month of the report of his father's death the shattering news that his inheritance was already being dismembered, that some of his estates had been granted to royal favourites. The king's nephew, the duke of Surrey (Thomas Holland), received Tutbury Castle, where Henry had spent so much of his childhood, Kenilworth Castle, where he had prepared for the Coventry duel, and Leicester Castle, where his father had died. Monmouth Castle, where Henry's eldest surviving son had been born, had gone to the king's brother, the duke of Exeter (John Holland). The castle of Lincoln had gone to the duke of Aumerle (Edward Plantagenet), and so it went on. The wording of the grants, that the estates were to be retained by the recipients so long as they remained in the king's hands, carrying though they did a suggestion that they might one day be returned to Henry's family, offered a hope too faint to be of much comfort.

Richard's actions had some justification. An almost autonomous palatinate, the size of the duchy of Lancaster, in the middle of his kingdom was politically dangerous. But to disinherit Henry was even more perilous, because the injustice of it outraged public opinion and made the king seem more than ever a tyrant. It also, almost certainly for the first time, changed Henry from an uncertain friend unequivocally into an enemy, for with the unexpected forfeiture of his inheritance Richard had dealt him a crushing blow.

It left him with no prospects at all. His lands were lost not only to him but also probably by his children as well. He himself faced a fate as wretched as that of the once glamorous Robert de Vere - who had died persecuted by debts; for with his lands his income would vanish, too, and henceforward he would be destitute and dependent on the charity of the French king.

If Henry is blamed for his later treatment of Richard, the shock effect upon him of this sentence should be remembered. It was the final severance of a bond of loyalty and affection which, however fragile, had existed between them, despite the tensions and antagonisms of their adult years, ever since it had been forged by Edward III. Because of this, Henry had prevented the deposition of Richard in 1387, and Richard had finally stopped short of making Henry fight to the death at Coventry. Now the last link in this cousinly feeling was shattered because, both as Henry's blood relation and his king, Richard had broken faith. As well as his personal promise made after the Coventry duel, he had broken the oath made to the peers at his coronation.

In that ceremony he had sworn that he would 'observe the laws, customs and liberties granted unto the church and laity' by King Edward the Confessor, and that he would 'administer indifferent and upright justice', using 'discretion with mercy and verity'. And each lord in turn had knelt on one knee, placed his hands between Richard's and sworn too, 'I become your man liege of life and limb and truth, and yearly honour to you shall bear against all men that now live, so help me God and holy doom'.

This oath had been sworn by Henry twice, once on reaching the age of twenty-one, and again a few months later, after the Merciless Parliament of 1388. But the oaths of the king and his subjects were each dependent on the other and Richard had not kept his share of their feudal bargain. For the right to inherit property, unless convicted of crime, was included in the 'laws, customs and liberties' which he had sworn to uphold. That meant that Henry, too, was absolved from his promises.

For Henry, it meant the death of old illusions and the birth of new resolve. Because if royal justice had been defiled, making Richard no longer worthy of his sacred office, surely it would be justifiable to bring about his downfall. Such an attempt would have the approval of contemporary philosophy as expressed in Sir John Fortescue's *Governance of England*, which states roundly, 'When the king ruleth his realm only to his own profit and not to the good of his subjects he is a tyrant'. Through his financial exactions alone, it could be claimed that Richard deserved this name, and it was considered 'shameful and degrading for free men to live under a tyrant'. Henry would be able to claim that he had right on his side.

Others had been thinking along the same lines. Henry was still in the first shock of his disinheritance when there came to him in Paris a counsellor perfectly designed by character, ability and experience to help him execute the most desperate design. Thomas Arundel, ex-archbishop of Canterbury, ex-chancellor of England, who had been banished to France in 1397, had been watching events carefully, and decided that now was the time to act. A life of poverty and prayer in some humble cure had no appeal for this politically-minded cleric who had been for eight years chancellor of England, and nine years archbishop of York, before he was appointed to the see of Canterbury. He would fight to recover the power and the great offices he loved.

Travelling to Rome immediately after he landed in France in 1397, he had persuaded Pope Boniface IX to write asking Richard to reinstate him as archbishop of Canterbury, a request that elicited a tart reply from the English king. Arundel, he said, was a traitor; he was surprised at the pope's attempt to interfere, and would not tolerate it. The pope was welcome to provide for his protege elsewhere, but not in England. 'We cannot allow him to dip in our dish,' he added, with a telling kitchen metaphor. Having thus exhausted this legal channel of restitution, Arundel resorted to an illegal one; he would strike back through the dispossessed duke of Hereford.

Froissart tells us that the archbishop rode to Paris disguised as a monk on pilgrimage, accompanied by a party of no more than seven men. His mission must be kept secret even from the French king, for it spelt danger to Charles's daughter and son-in-law. An orator so capable and cunning that he had persuaded Richard to agree to the impeachment of de la Pole in 1386, Arundel had an easy task with the indignant, furious Henry, who was probably already more than half convinced of the desirability of bringing about his cousin's downfall. With a man of the Church beside him, it would not have been difficult to translate self-interest into a God-given mission.

So as spring greened the trees along the Seine, behind the high ornamental doors of the Hotel Clisson Henry and Arundel began to plot, soon joined in their scheming by the dead earl of Arundel's young son. Another Thomas Arundel, the youth had contrived to escape in London from the custody of Henry's brother-in-law, John Holland, duke of Exeter. To add to their advice, Henry had also his household officers and faithful retainers who had sailed with him from England. They too planned to return to their native land by the only way that was possible for them: by conquest.

At first sight, the scheme must have seemed the wildest folly, considering that the duke had no ships, that no help could be expected from the French king, since he was Richard's father-in-law; and that Henry himself had a household of only two hundred retainers. And their plot would certainly have been doomed to failure without two salient features, most important of which was the nature of the two leaders. Both were practical men whose expertise complemented each other's. Archbishop Arundel had the political skills he had acquired as chancellor, and Henry the military experience he had gained during his expedition to Prussia with the pocket-sized army he had led against the Lithuanians.

The second factor was the growing unpopularity of Richard's government, which over the past eighteen months had deliberately established a reign of terror. The king had offered pardons with one hand, withdrawn them with the other, then gone on to invent new offences for which more pardons would be needed. To the sound of a great bell and the Norman French cry of 'oyez oyez', town criers up and down the country had repeatedly proclaimed conflicting and contradictory royal announcements.

Richard's declaration in the autumn parliament of 1397 that all except fifty men would be pardoned had been contradicted when the same parliament reassembled the following January at Shrewsbury. There he had issued a general pardon but excepted from it all those who had ridden against him in 1387-88; these, he informed them, were to sue for their pardons separately. Then in February 1399 came the frightening revelation that even those who had not ridden against the king were in danger; for in a writ to the sheriffs Richard indicated that the general pardon itself was not to be permanent, but only 'extended' until Martinmas 1399. What was to happen after that?

Meanwhile, over the heads of seventeen counties and many individuals, there hung the threat of those incriminating blank charters. It was a bewildering and constantly worrying situation in which men felt they would never be finished paying, and not even the humblest of them could feel secure.

By the spring of 1399 Richard had succeeded in filling most of his subjects, from silk and satin-clad peers to frieze-gowned ploughmen and serfs, with smouldering resentment needing just two sparks to cause a conflagration, a name and a cause, and Henry could provide both. He was young, brave, nobly born and deeply wronged; everyone who owned any property whatsoever could sympathize with him over the injustice of his disinheritance. Long beloved by the Londoners, through the threatened duel and the vindictive judgement at Coventry, he had captured the imagination of England. He was the deliverer Richard's oppressed subjects craved and believed in, for had it not been so stated by the prophet?

Today it is hard to credit the importance that the Middle Ages attached to prophecies, at that time taken so seriously that King Henry VII was to declare them against the law on the grounds of political danger. In the fourteenth century so popular were the obscure ramblings of John of Bridlington and the two Merlins (Merlin Ambrosius and Merlin Sylvestris who were reputed to have lived respectively in the conveniently distant times of Vortigern and Arthur) that, like the Bible, the manuscripts were chained to desks in the libraries of abbeys and priories.

In 1399 dissatisfied men and women eagerly searched these sources for a prediction that would rescue them from tyranny, and they found it in the *Prophetia Aquilae*, the Prophecy of the Eagle, which in many manuscripts accompanied the prophecies of Merlin. It foretold a period of terrible calamities ended by the arrival of a godlike figure from over the sea:

> Thereafter it shall be said throughout Britain: he is king and is not king. Thereafter he shall raise his head and show himself to be king, at the cost of much destruction, and nothing repaired. Thereafter shall come the time of the kites, and whatever anyone takes he shall keep for his own; and this shall last seven years. There shall be plunder and bloodshed, and many churches shall be committed to the flames, and what one man sows another shall reap, and death shall be preferred to a wretched life, and few men's love shall remain beyond reproach, and what is pledged in the evening shall be repudiated in the morning. Then the eaglet shall come from the south, with the sun, on wooden horses over the sea's foaming flood, sailing to Britain; and as soon as he lands he shall desire another eagle's nest, very soon shall he desire another.

To fourteenth century Englishmen accustomed to interpret the signs of heraldic bird and beast, the identity of the eaglet presented no problem.

The eagle was the emblem of St. John. John was the name of John of Gaunt. Thus Gaunt's son Henry was the eaglet about to sail to their rescue and to reclaim his inheritance.

Aware that, from France, Henry might attempt to create trouble for him, Richard tried to put an even thicker blanket of silence around the country, and the day after Henry's disinheritance he issued a writ insisting that all letters sent abroad must actually be shown to the king, council or chancellor. Even with the royal licence, no communication could henceforth be sent unread, and aliens bringing in forbidden letters would do so under pain of forfeiting life and limb.

But while Richard could censor letters, he could not censor word of mouth, and among the throng of royal envoys, merchants, mercenary soldiers, pilgrims, friars, scholars and minstrels constantly crossing the 'narrow sea' there were people happy to keep Henry informed of developments in England and to tell him of his new, resplendent role in the public imagination.

Indeed, so opportune was this prophecy for Henry's plans, so perfectly did it prepare the ground for invasion, that one suspects his supporters may have had a hand in its promotion. For now, if once he could but contrive to cross the Channel, his fellow countrymen would flock to his standard and themselves provide the army that Henry lacked.

As easily as news flowed out of the country to Henry did his secret messages filter in to potential rebels. Soon, he was in communication with such influential men as the now aged William of Wykeham, bishop of Winchester, and Henry's half brother, John Beaufort, marquis of Dorset, as well, we suspect, as the earl of Northumberland and Richard's current favourite, the duke of Aumerle; and, equally important, the many Lancastrian retainers thickly dotted all over the country on what had been Gaunt's estates, men who were deeply loyal to the family they had long served and who would eagerly form the nucleus of a new army when Henry eventually landed. As spring changed to summer so the conspiracy spread like a hidden virus through the whole of England.

It seems incredible that Richard chose this moment to leave the country. And not only to leave it, while he himself led an army into Ireland, but to leave it under the regency of his ineffectual uncle, the duke of York. The most likely explanation of this disastrous decision seems to be a natural belief that a man who possessed no ships and no army could not effectively invade England; so it would be safe enough to spend a few weeks restoring order in the Irish Pale. Of this there was grave need. Infuriatingly, since his last expedition, only four years ago, Ireland had reverted again to being 'a land of wars'. Three of the kings of the 'wild Irish' who had then meekly accepted knighthood at his hands had rebelled against English rule.

MacMurrough, O'Brien and O'Neill had united with the earl of Desmond to attack the earl of Ormond; and Richard's lieutenant and deputy, young Roger Mortimer, earl of March, potential heir to the throne of England, had been killed in an ambush. Sent over to Ireland to replace him, the duke of Surrey had failed to stamp out the rebellion and Richard felt he had no option but to go himself to complete what he had begun.

To be fair, he did not leave England with an entirely easy mind. The *Annales* says that, asked one day what he was sighing, 'he replied that not only was he nervous about the outcome of the Irish war, but he was nervous about an exasperated populace at home: "Do you wonder then that I sigh, I who am fated to so many unavoidable evils."'

To keep the evils in check in his absence, he had endeavoured to bind his people to him with oaths of loyalty. In the autumn of 1398 Dru Barentyn, the new mayor of London, had been required to swear on behalf of the citizens, 'not only to uphold the acts of the Westminster and Shrewsbury parliaments, but also the judgements and ordinances made at Coventry', and in January 1399 every county, city and borough of the realm was forced to take a similar oath; while on 8 February it was the turn of the Church. Each bishop, abbot, prior, dean and archdeacon was required to swear an oath and affix his seal to a register of oaths to be returned to the king. He ignored the fact that, while his contemporaries abhorred the sin of perjury, they regularly found some pretext to commit it, just as Richard had done himself, breaking the oaths he had made during and directly after the Merciless Parliament.

Having thus, as he hoped, shackled rebellion at home, Richard turned his mind to the Irish expedition, still unaware of what was going on in France; it is one of the puzzling features of this dramatic summer that while Henry's information about England was excellent, Richard's knowledge of his enemy's preparations was either non-existent or disastrously misleading and inaccurate.

So while at the Hotel Clisson in Paris Henry prepared to cross the Channel, in England Richard got ready to leave the country in what was truly a triumph of royal mismanagement. Instead of organizing an army of defence facing towards France, he was making ready to turn his back on the enemy and cross the Irish sea. The royal summons went out to 'all yeomen who take the livery of the crown' to 'draw speedily towards the city of London ...'. And Royal officials swarmed over the countryside, employing the ancient and hated right of royal purveyance to seize without the owner's leave whatever was needed for the expedition. From the ports of Colchester, Orwell and all ports and places on the sea coast northward as far as Newcastle upon Tyne, they sailed away all ships of twenty-five tons and over.

In addition, they drove away riding horses, teams of harness horses and wagons. They seized bread, wine and salt meat, herded off cows and calves, and also impressed humble men for sailors, both freemen and serfs, the small payments that would eventually be made for these goods and services being well below market price. Meanwhile, men whose gentle birth enabled them to escape the miseries and humiliation of being press-ganged, were not exempt from service. It was their duty to organize and supply their retinues with horses, lances, swords and armour, and set off towards the rallying point and port of embarkation. By May 1399, under a flutter of pennons and banners bright with armorial insignia, they were streaming into the little port of Milford Haven.

Among this colourful throng rode two young Frenchmen to whom posterity owes a substantial debt, an anonymous knight and his squire, Jean Créton, who like Chaucer's squire in *The Canterbury Tales* could please the ear with a pretty tune - Créton's instrument was the harp - and write verse. The real-life drama in which he was about to find himself would inspire him to write a long narrative history, part poem, part prose, which, entitled *Histoire du roy d'Angleterre Richart*, is one of our best sources for the events of July and August 1399.

As yet there had been no premonition of disaster among Richard's friends. All was festivity and excitement. As Créton tells us, he and his knight had joined the army in search of adventure. They had 'quitted Paris, each full of joy, travelling late and early without stopping' till they reached London, where, arriving on a Wednesday 'at the hour of dinner', they saw already 'many a knight taking his departure from the city'. Following on to Milford Haven, they found the town resounding to the music of minstrels and trumpeters that continued day and night until the morning of 29 May, when there blew a favourable north wind. On that fine breezy morning, laden with archers, men-at-arms, horses and provisions, Richard's big bellied wooden ships triumphantly raised their sails, painted with his badge of the sun, and set off merrily for Ireland. They left England defended only by an army of promises and the incompetent duke of York.

Meanwhile, in France, Henry's preparations were almost complete. Somehow, so secretly that we still do not know who provided them, he had found ships. The most likely source is the duke of Orleans, with whom he made a mysterious treaty of friendship on 17 June, each vowing to share the same friends and the same enemies, and to protect the other's life and honour. Since an exile like Henry had no business making a treaty at all, we need not take too seriously its proviso that the promises held good only if they did not conflict with each man's loyalty to his king. But the duke of

Berry may have been privy to the plot as well, since, according to the Monk of St. Denys, he advised Henry to visit the royal abbey on his way to England.

Soon after signing the treaty Henry left Paris, giving out that he was going to stay with his sister in Spain, an explanation that would account for his large escort, except that once outside the gates he turned his horse's head towards the north coast, stopping only a few miles from the city to visit, as advised, the royal abbey of St. Denis.

This visit had a significance to which attention has hardly been drawn, a significance that removes all doubt as to the nature of Henry's intentions on setting sail again for England. For the abbey housed not only the tombs of French kings and the official chronicles of their reigns, but another precious object besides, which had a special meaning for Henry at this crucial moment in his life: it was here in time of peace that the sacred oriflamme was kept. And here at the start of each war that the kings of France came to receive from the hand of the abbot the little cleft crimson silk banner that was the symbol of their strength and led their forces into battle.

On arrival, Henry made the abbot a promise: he would restore to the abbey the revenues of Deerhurst Priory in Gloucestershire which Richard had placed in the custody of one of his clerks. As both men knew well, this was an act only the English king could perform. It seems clear therefore that Henry came to the abbey of St. Denis in imitation of French kings, to secure the abbot's blessing on the start of a major military campaign, a campaign that had as its object an achievement no less magnificent than theirs.

Although it would have been disastrously imprudent to admit it at this stage, and Henry would not do so for many weeks, he had already set his sights on the crown of England.

XVI   THE RETURN

'Then the eaglet shall come from the south, with the sun, on wooden horses over the sea's foaming flood.' *Prophetia Aquilae*

About three weeks after Richard sailed with his fleet of two hundred ships for Ireland the coast waters of England were crossed by Henry's tiny flotilla of not more than ten small vessels - ridiculous by comparison with Richard's. Its passengers contrasted too; unlike Richard's large army of archers and men-at-arms, crammed into the deep wooden bellies of his ships aflutter with bright, heraldic streamers, Henry's force, including the members of his household and some disaffected merchants, consisted of no more than 300 men, many unarmed. Even by medieval standards when armies were small indeed, it was little more than a token force. But this apparent disadvantage was to prove in reality an advantage, misleading the duke of York, regent in Richard's absence, into taking effective measures for defence much too late.

The duke of York was by now expecting a great invasion. While Henry was still in France there had come to England a very exaggerated report of his military strength. York had heard that 'divers enemies of the king with great number of armed men and others were gathered together in Picardy, some to besiege Calais and some to attack and invade the realm in the absence of the king', and he had dutifully and correctly sent writs to the sheriffs of England to muster what forces they could and come to him in the south. But not until 7 July did he summon the lords whose multitude of retainers formed such a vital part of a medieval army. There seemed to be no great urgency to speed up defence preparations when Henry's little flotilla was sighted, for York believed the bulk of the force had been left behind, and he delayed taking the essential next step in defence of the realm. Seemingly it did not occur to him that the ten ships in the Channel could possibly be his nephew's entire armada.

On the surface of it, Henry's squadron looked hardly more formidable than the French raiders who had sacked Rye and Winchelsea and attacked the Isle of Wight in 1377. But this tiny flotilla contained sparks that once falling on land could set the entire country aflame. In justice it must be said that York was not alone in failing to recognize this danger and so act promptly against it. Equally at fault were his counsellors, the hated William Lescrope, earl of Wiltshire, Sir John Bushy, Sir William Bagot and Sir Henry Green who, blinded perhaps by the court's dazzling atmosphere of royal triumph ever since the autumn parliament of 1397, emblemed in the king's new badge of the sun, omitted to give the needed advice in time. They were no more sensitive than was York to the swell of feeling against the government in the kingdom.

In this as in everything else during that extraordinarily swift summer campaign of 1399, Henry was far better informed than his adversary, and with Thomas Arundel's help he was able to make use of the dreams and hopes of Englishmen for freedom from Richard's oppressive rule. Indeed the movements of his ships seem to have been cunningly designed not only to keep the government guessing as to his real destination, but also to work on the imagination of the people. Instead of sailing straight across the Channel and landing in some southern port, he dodged about 'appearing as though about to land, now in one part of the kingdom, now in another'. A fraction of his party actually did land in Sussex and anchored there long enough for John Pelham - easily distinguishable by the pelicans on his shield - to capture Katherine Swynford's castle at Pevensey and reinforce the regent's belief that the south of England was the invader's destination. Issuing a commission for the castle to be besieged, the duke of York added that he had 'information that certain enemies of the king in no small number, armed and unarmed, have assembled in parts beyond the sea to invade the realm'.

Meanwhile the enemies of the king, who far from being still in France were already in the Channel, sailed on eastwards, bobbing in and out of the horizon as they went, the sight of the heraldic badge on Henry's sails exciting eager watchers on the shore. With their own eyes they could see John of Bridlington's prophecy coming true: the son of the eagle on wooden horses sailing miraculously to their rescue over the sea to put an end to all their ills.

What they believed these to be we know from a song written by an anonymous poet in Latin as he too waited longingly for those tantalising sails to draw closer and for their champion to land. Crystallising the feelings of that time, his verse complains that Richard's ministers 'tax everyone to death', they are 'puffed up and blinded by money, wish to be rich and to walk on jewels'. It paints them as 'wolves glowing with evil and no glory, seeking more the gold of the earth than the treasures of heaven ... faithless in their words, dealing out sharpness of death', and it blames them for the execution of good men whose 'blood cries for vengeance'. Finally praying for the coming of the deliverer, 'our light and glory, Henry of Lancaster, our friend', it ends with a flourish of optimism.

> The eagle, our duke, will save us, coming from the
>   perfumed south
> May Christ grant that his coming be joyful

Having rounded the south-east corner of England, the eagle continued his way north, keeping always his puzzling, 'crooked course', while that incalculable factor that could destroy a naval expedition in the Middle Ages, the weather, remained mercifully fine. Apparently it had occurred to the duke of York that the invasion might occur in this area for he improved the defences of two castles, Rochester with its grey towers at the mouth of the river Medway in Kent and Queensborough, built by King Edward III on the Isle of Sheppey to command one of the main sea routes to the Thames. But he made no preparations to defend the coast much further north, and this too was a serious mistake, for Henry's plan all along had been to land in Yorkshire where the bulk of his family estates were situated and where he could assume greatest support.

Across this county strode four strongly fortified Lancastrian castles, leading to other Lancastrian fortresses south and south-west through England and into Wales, a series of conveniently spaced military bases, still largely staffed by Lancastrian retainers loyal to the heir of their dead lord; and many of these retainers were already in the secret of Henry's coming.

As a destination Yorkshire had another advantage: the less frequented inlets of its coastline would have been well known to Henry's crew and companions. It was on the beach of a partly ruined town, Ravenspur, lying just inside the mouth and on the north side of the River Humber, that he landed on 4 July in a historic moment recaptured by the *Traison et Mort*. This chronicle tells us that the duke:

> sent a small boat ashore - with some people who planted his banner on the land and left it there - and then returned to the ship. A fisherman (presently) came running up to the banner and had great marvel for what reason it was planted there, for he knew nothing about the matter, yet he beheld the ships at sea. The duke ordered his people to tell the man to acquaint the people of the town of his arrival; upon which the man went down to the town, crying out, "Our lord the duke of Lancaster is come to take possession of his rightful inheritance".

It is interesting that even the simple Yorkshire fisherman is reputed to have used the term 'our lord', although it had been proclaimed throughout the kingdom that Henry was banished and disinherited and therefore lord of nothing. Other more sophisticated men were waiting for their cue, supplied by Henry's confident message, and now there hastened to meet him his receiver general, John Leventhorpe, with Robert Waterton.

Chief forester of the castle of Knaresborough, Robert had brought two hundred foresters trained in the use of arms, a force which was almost at once augmented by the arrival of another thirty-seven Lancastrian retainers, knights and esquires at the head of companies of archers and men-at-arms. Thus protected, and without encountering any opposition, Henry marched to his castle of Pickering, about fifty miles away, a stronghold perched above the Vale of Pick, overlooking vast acres of woodland, which had been the scene of many a royal hunt in the past and now provided useful cover for an approaching army. Although the castle had been given by Richard to his unpopular treasurer, Lescrope, it surrendered to Gaunt's heir without a struggle.

So far all had gone well. Henry had survived that most dangerous period for any invader of the sea-girt isle: he had landed safely, secured a military base and more than doubled his armed force. But even as we picture him receiving the ecstatic welcome of servants who had known him from childhood, it is worth remembering just how precarious at this stage Henry's toehold in England still was; how frightening remained the odds against his success. Had the other side used only a little political sense the invasion could easily have ended in disaster. Had Richard learnt in time of the situation in England and returned at once from Ireland, or the duke of York only launched a swift attack, the rebellion might have been crushed in embryo. Henry's head might then have decorated London Bridge and the Lancastrian dynasty been destroyed before it had even begun. But Richard was not informed of the invasion and in the south of England the mustering of men proceeded at a leisurely pace, luck and the elements being on Henry's side.

Never has fortune smiled more kindly on an invader than she did on Henry in that first crucial week of July 1399; for no sooner was his tiny, vulnerable invading force on land than the weather changed. The gentle wind which had wafted his sails safely up to the north-east coast, allowing him to choose his cunning route, turned into a violent gale. While sheltered inland, Henry was able to proceed with his plan to march south-west from Pickering to his second castle of Knaresborough, which he captured after a short fight, the sea became an impassable barrier to all news of what was happening. No plea for help could reach Richard. A vital week at least was to pass before any ship dared leave harbour to inform him of the threat to his kingdom, a week in which Henry was able greatly to strengthen his position.

So, as the invader continued his march unopposed, on the other side of the raging sea, all unaware of the disastrous events in England, the king and his army lost precious time in Waterford, relaxing after a fruitless campaign in which they had pursued the rebel, Art MacMurrough, King of Leinster, through the bogs, woods and mountains of Ireland without ever catching him. (The most they had achieved was a parley at which he had made a sensational entrance, galloping bareback down a precipitous hill, clutching a dart in each hand.) In happy ignorance they ate, drank and made merry while from Knaresborough Henry moved swiftly on to the largest and best fortified of his castles in Yorkshire, the vast, many turreted stronghold of Pontefract, where he arrived on 11 or 12 July. It was here that his forces began to expand into a formidable army.

Meanwhile, in the south of England, attended by Richard's hated ministers, Lescrope, Bushy, Bagot and Green, the duke of York bestirred himself. Sensing that London was hostile, he moved to St. Albans instead and there began to try to recruit as many as possible of both lords and commons, but with disappointing results. Of the lords only the bishop of Norwich, Robert Lord Ferrers, earl of Suffolk, and John Beaufort, marquis of Dorset, who was playing a double game, rallied to the royal standard. And from the commons alarmingly few recruits came forward, although a desperate Lescrope offered to pay them in advance at double the usual rates from the royal purse.

Composing his chronicle in the scriptorium of the abbey of St Albans that overlooked the market town, the monk Thomas Walsingham gives the reason why people refused this tempting lure: they believed that Henry had only come to claim what was rightfully his own property, and regarded any suggestion that they should fight against him 'almost as a joke'. The duke of York himself had mixed loyalties. Even as he dutifully tried to collect a royal army he admitted that he thought Henry was in the right. Because of all these factors he was able to muster no more than three thousand men.

The picture was very different in Yorkshire where word of Henry's coming had spread. In place of a reluctant trickle of volunteers, there was enthusiasm. There came to Henry at Pontefract clattering across the drawbridge and under the gateway 'a great multitude of gentlemen, knights and esquires with their men', armed with lances, swords, axes, daggers, bows and arrows. They came 'some of their own free will and others for fear of future events', wrote the hostile Kirkstall chronicler, his comment revealing that Henry's cause already had the sweet smell of success that attracts time-servers.

Marching on to Doncaster, his army snow-balled again; he was met by a brilliant cluster of banners and shields, including two that must have been especially welcome since they bore the insignia of the biggest, most influential land-owners in the north, that of Henry Percy, earl of Northumberland - *or, a lyon rampant azure*, quartered with the *gules and argent* Lucy arms - and of Ralph Neville, earl of Westmorland - *gules, a saltire argent* - the most important lords left in England after the duke of York. (Westmorland's effigy can still be seen in Staindrop church in Durham, wearing a hip-belted tunic over his armour and a Lancastrian collar of SS, clad much as he would have appeared on that summer day in 1399 when he rode with Northumberland to join Henry.) With them rode Northumberland's famous son, Henry Hotspur, and William, Lord Willoughby, from Lincolnshire, who had accompanied Henry on both expeditions to Prussia; each lord being followed by a large retinue of well armed retainers.

With these welcome additions Henry now commanded a fairly large army for the time and had a good chance of achieving his objects by force. But what precisely were these objects? the more thoughtful among his men were beginning to ask. If Henry had come to reform the government they would follow him in thousands. If he had come to claim his inheritance as he had stated on first landing, they would support him too, but if he had come to usurp the crown he would forfeit the people's sympathy, for the king was their rightful head, their stability. Many were still loyal to Richard if not to his policies at this stage and they feared Henry's motives. Although it meant telling a quiverful of falsehoods it was essential to set at rest their fears, while at the same time preparing them to accept Richard's eventual deposition. A tricky piece of propaganda which, with the ex-archbishop, Thomas Arundel, beside him, Henry was to accomplish brilliantly.

The *Traison et Mort* tells us that, from Pontefract to the castles and chief towns, lords and commons, he had already sent letters explaining his own actions in terms of the king's iniquities, a catalogue of crimes that played on the anxieties of the people. These missives claimed that Richard had planned to sell all the remaining English possessions in France to the French, that he had laid secret plans to 'domineer more greatly and mightily over the kingdom of England than any of his predecessors ... had ever done', that he planned to do this with the aid of foreign allies, and 'that he would keep the villeins of England in harder bondage than any Christian king had ever held his subjects'. Furthermore, Henry declared, Richard would cause to be put to death all the chief magistrates of the cities of England because they had so often in his reign sided with the commons against him, he would have apprehended the great burgesses and merchants of all the cities of England 'and would then impose such subsidies, tallages and imposts as he should please'.

The falsehoods in Henry's letters were cunningly mixed with strong probability for who can doubt that had Richard continued to reign over England he would have become more and more autocratic, that he would have continued to punish those who had ridden against him in 1387 or imposed on him the commission of 1386? And that he would, if necessary, have used the French alliance to help him?

It was because of Richard's wicked schemes that he personally had returned, Henry stated in his letters, and at the end of the catalogue of alleged royal crimes, he wrote:

> Wherefore, my friends and good people, when the aforesaid matters came to my knowledge, I came over as soon as I could to inform, succour, and comfort you to the utmost of my power; for I am one of the nearest to the crown of England, and am beholden to love and support the realm as much, or more than any man alive, for thus have my predecessors done. And so, my friends, may God preserve you. Be well advised and ponder well that which I write to you. Your good and faithful friend, Henry of Lancaster.

But clever though the letters were, they still left the most vital question unanswered: what were Henry's intentions towards the crown?

On reaching Doncaster he felt obliged to assuage people's doubts with a public denial, the oath which more than any of his other acts was to tarnish his hitherto shining reputation. Before Northumberland, Westmorland and the army he swore on the sacraments that he intended only to claim his inheritance and that of his wife, Mary de Bohun, and that King Richard should reign to the end of his life governed by a good council of lords spiritual and temporal. His followers believed what they had wished to hear.

Henry was not alone in deceiving them. Besides the ex-archbishop, Thomas Arundel, almost certainly privy to all Henry's plans, we now have evidence that the earl of Northumberland (head of the powerful Percy family, who in 1403 were so self-righteously to accuse Henry of perjury) was also in the secret of the invader's true intentions. On 2 August, between two and three weeks after Henry's oath at Doncaster, the earl was to accept from him, under seal of the duchy of Lancaster, the wardenship of the West March, a grant which could only properly be made by the king. Northumberland was as guilty as Henry of putting into operation the cynical *necessitas non habet legem*, necessity has no law, one of the favourite maxims of the period and most evocative of its moral values.

It was an act that probably burdened Henry's tender conscience, but not to have made the oath would have jeopardised the whole invasion, which now took on new strength just as Richard finally learned of his danger.

Down south a ship bearing Sir William Bagot had at last contrived to break out of harbour and sail across to Ireland with a message urgently begging the king to return, while Edmund, duke of York, and the council frantically changed their plans to meet the ever growing threat. Since by itself their army of three thousand men was no longer large enough to tackle the invader's force, it was decided they had no choice but to wait and join up with Richard's army the moment it landed in the west; Richard, they thought, would embark for England as soon as he heard the news from Bagot. Having placed the little queen for safety in Wallingford Castle, the hated Lescrope, Bushy and Green fled straight to Bristol while York stopped briefly at Oxford to reveal yet again how little in touch with actual events he was.

Still expecting those non existent forces of invasion from France, on 16 July he issued a writ to Richard's archbishop of Canterbury in Kent, 'to raise, assemble and array all men at arms, archers and others of that county capable of defending it, and put them in readiness along the coast and elsewhere to resist the invaders'. Then, having perpetrated this last foolishness, he too rode to Bristol.

In contrast to his uncle, Henry knew exactly what was in the enemy's mind and, being determined to prevent it, turned his army south-west in the direction of Bristol also. Still unopposed, he crossed England, proceeding by way of his own castles of Derby, Leicester and Kenilworth, the last already recaptured for him by his own retainers, where he could raid his own armouries for extra weapons. Henry's letters had fuelled the people's hatred of the king's three favourite ministers, and he marched in an atmosphere of blood lust; as they went, it was spontaneously distilled into a poem by an anonymous versifier, depicting him in the guise of a heron, his companions symbolised by other birds and beasts, hopefully pursuing the loathsome trio to their deaths:

> A eron is up, and toke his flyt;
> In the noth contre he is lizt; (has alighted)
> thus here ze alle men saye.
> The stede (horse) colt* with hym he brynges;
> These buth wonder and y thinges,
> to se hem thus to playe.

Upon the busch the eron wolle reste,
Of alle places it liketh hym beste,
to loke aftur his pray.
He wolle falle upon the grene;
There he falleth, hit wille be sene,
they wille not welle away.

The bag is ful of roton corne,
So long ykep, hit is forlorne,
hit wille stonde no stalle. (remain in no stall)
The pecokes** and the ges alleso,
And odor fowles mony on mo,
schuld be fed withalle.

---

*   young Arundel
**   badge of the Nevilles

The note of triumph in the song was premature, for had Richard returned to England at once when he received Bagot's message he might have turned the tables on his cousin even now. Instead, on the advice of Edward, duke of Aumerle, he made the fatal decision to delay his departure for several days. While the bulk of the army remained with him in Waterford, he sent ahead a small force under the earl of Salisbury to North Wales. Landing in the little slate-roofed town of Conway, with its castle rising above the sea, Salisbury began to try to recruit a third royal army, but lacking the inspiration of the king's own presence, his efforts were to end in disaster.

Unlike his cousin, wasting no time, Henry continued his swoop down the Severn valley towards Bristol. Since York was also making for the same city the routes of uncle and nephew crossed at Berkeley Castle on the estuary on 27 July. For what happened there our best source is the Monk of Evesham, whose abbey on the river Avon in Worcestershire was near enough to receive reliable information. He relates that on hearing of Henry's approach York had considered launching a full scale attack, until he found there was no one in his army willing to shoot a single arrow against the duke or his followers, so he had no choice but to come to terms. After just one brief affray between a few men of either side, uncle and nephew made peace, York's sympathies having been divided all along, although he had tried his best to be a loyal regent. Shakespeare's portrait in *Richard II* of the bumbling, well-intentioned duke unhappily trying to choose between duty and inclination and in the end taking the only course available to him appears to be remarkably accurate.

In the church outside the castle walls, they made a formal agreement, though not without nearly bringing disaster on one of Henry's most powerful allies, John Beaufort, marquis of Dorset, who had been for some time secretly on the invader's side. So zealous in Henry's cause were the earls of Northumberland and Westmorland that they were on the point of having Beaufort executed as a member of York's army when Henry dramatically came to the rescue. The *Traison et Mort* tells us that he: 'pulled out a letter from his pouch of blue velvet and said, "I beseech you do him no harm, for he is my brother and has always been my friend; see the letter he sent to me in France." The duke and the marquis then embraced.'

Incompetent though he was, as the most important lord in England, the last of King Edward III's sons and still officially Richard's regent, York's adherence gave the invader an authority he had not possessed before. And Richard had still not landed to give this authority the lie. When the two armies together marched on, reaching Bristol the following day, there was no need for a long, expensive siege, all that was necessary was a proclamation read outside the city's gates. Made by Northumberland, it declared that, those who came out and surrendered would be pardoned but anyone who remained inside would lose his head. The citizens of Bristol were not prepared to sacrifice themselves for such unpopular ministers as Lescrope, Bushy and Green, and they surrendered pellmell, scrambling for their lives through doors and windows and down ropes from walls. With more dignity but probably similar sentiments, the constable of Bristol Castle, Sir Peter Courtenay, also surrendered and the gates were opened. Like the rest of England and the proverbial ripe plum, this key city had fallen into Henry's hand.

The poetic vision of the heron and his company of birds alighting on Richard's hated counsellors was about to be fulfilled. To inaugurate a new era free from financial exactions, on 29 July Bushy, Green and Lescrope were executed and their heads placed in white baskets. These ghastly objects were then displayed in prominent places: Lescrope's above London Bridge, Bushy's above York's gates and Green's above the gates of Bristol. Luckily for Bagot he was still out of harm's way in Ireland. At about the same time that the three ministers met their end, Henry learnt that Richard had finally landed at Milford Haven in Pembrokeshire.

The king had chosen an area where, as formerly Prince of Wales, he believed he could count on people's sympathy, but further disasters awaited him. Tragically, he had arrived too late, when all faith had been lost in his ability to defeat the invader, and his own men were now eager to desert him while they still had the chance. On his very first night ashore, the king lost his nerve. Suspecting treachery among the soldiers, he disguised himself in the grey habit of a Minorite friar, and with only a few followers, stole secretly away on horseback through the darkness. Intending to meet the earl of Salisbury's army and put himself at its head, he rode swiftly up through Wales, only to find on reaching the huddle of houses beneath Edward I's formidable castle at Conway that the forces Salisbury had recruited no longer existed; when the king failed to come and lead them the men, believing rumours that he was dead, had simply gone home.

It was too late now also for Richard to ride south again and rejoin his Irish army, for that too had disbanded. The duke of Aumerle and Thomas Percy, Richard's steward and brother of the earl of Northumberland had renounced their allegiance by breaking their staffs of office. The soldiers had looted Richard's treasures, stealing his gold plate, jewelled collars, rings, owches, gem-embroidered hats, gowns and doublets, and had run off with them into the mountains. Up here, in what was to them wild, unfamiliar territory, many in their turn were robbed by Welshmen who stripped them of everything, including cloaks and shoes, sending them on their way shivering and barefoot.

However all was not yet lost for Richard. He still had his life and liberty, and might yet have kept his throne had he behaved wisely. After these misfortunes his most sensible course would have been to retreat to France or Ireland. Instead, he chose to stay in Conway Castle and sent his brother and nephew, John and Thomas Holland, dukes of Exeter and Surrey, to discuss terms with his enemies who had now arrived at Chester. For on hearing of Richard's landing, Henry had left Bristol, marching rapidly through Gloucester, Ross, Hereford, Leominster, Ludlow and Shrewsbury to the chief castle in the royal earldom. In this fortress he waited while he himself sent the earl of Northumberland and Thomas Arundel, ex-archbishop of Canterbury, with a message for the king. Richard's and Henry's envoys may have passed each other on the road, but here similarity between them ended. On arrival at their destination Richard's emissaries were promptly arrested: Henry's were better treated.

Seeing Northumberland and Arundel ride up to Conway Castle with a mere handful of men, Richard ordered them admitted over the drawbridge, and on hearing Henry's terms, he was surprised to find that they were remarkably reasonable. All the duke of Hereford wanted, they stated, was the return of his lands and that Richard should call a parliament where five of his ministers would be put on trial. Henry also wished the king to come and speak to him immediately at Flint Castle, after which he would be free to make his own way to London for the parliament. Humiliating though it was to be dictated to, and threatening though the future looked for his ministers, the conditions were much easier than Richard had expected. Créton describes how, discussing them with his friends the king's mood swung from despair to wild optimism. Had he not survived an even worse situation in 1387, later to recapture his royal power? Why should that not happen again? And he propounded a cunning scheme to his devoted audience. After meeting Henry at Flint and before proceeding to London, he would go off into the mountains and collect a new army of Welshmen; and, thus reinforced he would have his revenge. 'There are some of them I will flay alive,' he vowed; he would put Henry 'to a bitter death'. Cheered by this prospect, he formally accepted the envoys' terms in the castle chapel. Northumberland and Arundel swore to them on the body of the Host at an altar before an eastern window (still to be seen today) and afterwards both sides heard Mass together to sanctify the deal.

Full of his secret plan, Richard watched Northumberland and Arundel ride away from the fortress ostensibly to prepare Rhuddlan Castle for his coming; here, so they said, he was to spend the first night on his journey to Flint. He himself left Conway to follow them a little later, escorted by about twenty men. With no intention of keeping his own side of the agreement, he yet naively trusted in Henry's good faith.

But Richard had gone only a little distance along the road when a fearful sight met his eyes: behind a rock a great body of armed men assembled and, floating ominously above, the unmistakable crescent banner of the earl of Northumberland.

The king had been taken prisoner.

XVII   THE USURPER

'Heaven knows ...
'By what by-paths and indirect crook'd
ways,
'I met this crown'
William Shakespeare, *Henry IV*, part II

The falsehoods that paved Henry's way to the throne probably did more than anything else to make him unpopular with posterity, and the official records conceal the facts even today. The parliament rolls tell us that Richard agreed in Conway Castle to abdicate, but they omit all mention of Northumberland's and Arundel's monumental perjury, their promise on the Host that Richard would remain king, and that treacherous ambush on the road to Flint.

The official line was followed by most of the monastic chroniclers who could see where their abbey's advantage lay, and this whitewashed version might still have passed for truth had it not been for the two young Frenchmen who, having joined the Irish expedition for a bit of adventure, suddenly found themselves in real danger caught up in the threatened entourage of a captive king. In Ireland they had attached themselves to the earl of Salisbury and returned with him to Wales, where they were to witness Richard's captivity and accompany him from Flint Castle to London. Jean Créton's description of Richard's downfall was completed by the year 1406, illustrated under his direction in gold and jewel colours, then presented to Charles of Anjou, count of Maine and Mortagne and governor of Languedoc.

Since he so passionately sympathised with Richard, the French squire's interpretation is suspect but most of the key facts he relates are not. For they are substantiated by a recently discovered chronicle written early in the fifteenth century in the Cistercian abbey of Dieulacres, a house which, since it owned property in both Cheshire and Staffordshire, was near enough to receive accurate news and far enough from Westminster and other royal haunts to dare to record it. The story of Northumberland's perjury at Conway and the ambush occurs in both accounts.

Although he may not have instructed his envoys to commit perjury in so many words, Henry promptly took advantage of their action. He was at least an accessory after the fact, and we cannot absolve him from blame for these dishonourable dealings. However they should not make us forget that, as with the perjury at Doncaster, he saw them as a means to a wholly laudable end: to rescue the people from injustice and tyranny; his perjuries and falsehoods should not blind us to his idealism. At thirty-three he was still the same knight who in his twenties had jousted and crusaded and gone on pilgrimage to Jerusalem, and he probably shared the romantic view held by Richard's discontented subjects, that he was their long awaited saviour.

He is not the first man in whom ideals and ambition have dovetailed neatly. Doubtless he coveted the crown for himself; at the same time he knew that the only way to reform the government of the country was under a new monarch, since King Richard could not be trusted to keep any agreement. Henry, who in 1387 had saved Richard from being deposed, would not make the same mistake again.

But he was not a man to decide lightly to depose a king - an act that was to haunt him for the rest of his life. For whatever Richard had done, he was still the Lord's anointed, he was still Henry's cousin, and once the decision was made to depose him, it was bound to set in motion a whole train of sufferings.

Through Créton's pages we see the melancholy process begin, at the start very slowly, then accelerate. Between the ambush and the meeting with Henry two nights passed, on the first of which Richard banqueted in luxury at Rhuddlan Castle, as arranged when he was free; the second, he spent less comfortably in the keep at Flint, anxiously awaiting Henry's coming next day. Créton paints his agony of mind as from the battlements he saw in the far distance, 'the duke of Lancaster as he came along the seashore with all his host', armour shining in the morning sun and minstrels playing. 'It was marvellously great,' Créton tells us bitterly of this army, 'and showed such joy and satisfaction that the sound and bruit of their (musical) instruments, horns, buisines and trumpets, were heard even as far as the castle'. Gone was all Richard's optimism as he watched the army approach, he had no illusions now as to the likely end that fate had in store for him. Through Créton's poem, deeply involved as he was in the king's predicament, we see Richard weep in the company of his four remaining friends, the earl of Salisbury, the bishop of Carlisle, Sir Stephen Lescrope and Sir William Feriby, and we hear him lament:

Alas! now see I plainly that the end of my days draweth nigh, since I must needs be delivered into the hands of mine enemies, who mortally hate me that have never deserved it. Surely, earl of Northumberland, thou shouldst have great fear and dread of heart, lest our Lord God take vengeance upon the sin which thou didst commit when thou swaredst so foully by him to draw us forth from Conway, where we were right secure. Now for this may God reward thee.

But Richard had not long to spend in such lamentations. As Henry's army drew nearer 'a great number of persons quit the host, pricking their horses hard towards the castle to know what King Richard was doing'.

Seemingly Henry could not contain his impatience, he wanted news of his captive. Among those who thus spurred ahead to the castle were Henry Percy (Hotspur) and, a bitter sight for Richard, also the duke of Aumerle, who had advised him to stay those fatal extra days in Ireland. Like the ex-archbishop of Canterbury, Thomas Arundel, he had already exchanged Richard's livery of the white hart for Henry's collar of SS.

For the king, one humiliation followed another. Henry had sent a reassuring message, telling him, 'not to be alarmed and that no harm should happen to his person', politely refraining from coming himself to the castle until after Richard had dined, but the king cannot have been much cheered by such courtesies, for soon the approaching army completely surrounded the castle. Some of Henry's soldiers then burst into the room while Richard was at table and shouted that all his companions were to be beheaded, and it was not at all certain if the king himself would live. The soldiers, part of the horde of volunteers who had joined the invader as he crossed England, had probably acted on their own initiative, their actions unknown to Henry, but it was still alarming.

So disheartened was Richard, that after making a pretence of finishing a meal he had no appetite for, he descended the stairs of the keep to meet Henry of Bolingbroke instead of insisting on his royal right that Henry should ascend to the royal apartments. Riding into the courtyard, Henry wore armour, in defiance of custom and etiquette, the insulting effect of which he had tried to soften by replacing his basinet with the high black hat that identifies him in Créton's illuminations.

This hat he removed, bowing twice as Richard descended the stairs, then respectfully waited for the king to speak. Their ensuing meeting Créton describes in prose, giving as his reason that it is easier to record accurately in that medium than in poetry, so we almost certainly have a true report of this confrontation between the cousins, that marks the high point in the drama of their relationship. Unfortunately, as so often with the major crises of men's lives, the appropriate words were not forthcoming.

The interview was conducted in full view of Henry's victorious mail-clad troops and Richard's wilting, indignant courtiers, an audience that may have had a restraining effect. Because in Créton's chronicle the speech between the cousins is banal, so we must look behind the words for the intensity of feeling, Richard's hatred and Henry's triumph, which would have shown in their tone of voice. Throughout this scene Henry appears on the defensive while Richard responds with steely politeness.

As he reaches the bottom of the stairs Richard in his turn takes off his hood, still that of a Minorite friar, and speaks a travesty of a conventional greeting, 'Fair cousin of Lancaster you be right welcome.'

And, following royal etiquette, Henry bows a third time. 'My lord, I am come sooner than you sent for me, the reason whereof I will tell you. The common report of your people is such that you have for the space of two and twenty years governed them very badly and very rigorously and in so much that they are not contented therewith. But if it please our Lord I will help you to govern them better than they have been governed in time past.'

But both are aware that Richard will not be allowed to govern at all, and the king gives his bitterly resigned reply, 'Fair cousin, since it pleases you, it pleaseth us well.'

Through Créton, we sense the king's pain, but the French metrical history's accusation that Henry deliberately humiliated him is hard to accept. Before his own arrival at the castle Henry had sent a message of reassurance, and he used the weapon of fear on one of the king's companions only, the earl of Salisbury, who had snubbed Henry in France and thwarted his marriage to the daughter of the duke of Berry. To each of the other lords in Richard's company Henry had spoken a few reassuring words, but to Salisbury he sent a knight with a curt message, 'Earl of Salisbury, be assured that no more than you deigned to speak to my lord of Lancaster, when he and you were in Paris at Christmas last past, will he speak unto you.'

However, the precautions Henry was forced to take to prevent Richard's rescue were deeply distressing to him. Somehow, the valuable captive had to be transported to London through the royal earldom and palatinate of Chester, a terrain thick with his supporters. Its inhabitants had already shown where their hearts lay by offering Henry's troops poisoned wine and ale as they marched north, so on this journey it was essential to make the king look as inconspicuous as possible. To have allowed him to appear in his silken, jewel-embroidered clothes, or to ride a large and expensive horse glittering with gold and silver harness, would have made him the immediate target for a rescue attempt. When Henry ordered that Richard was to travel in his friar's grey corded gown, on a little pony to match such a person's humble status, it was simply a useful disguise, although Créton interpreted it as a form of mockery. 'Duke Henry called aloud with a stern and savage voice, "Bring out the king's horses," and then they brought him two little horses that were not worth forty franks: the king mounted one, and the earl of Salisbury the other. Everyone got on horseback, and we set out from the said castle of Flint, about two hours after mid-day.'

The cavalcade rode first to Chester, their coming announced by the 'loud bruit' (noise) of 'horns, buisines and trumpets, in so much that they made all the seashore resound with them'. Thence on a journey that took twelve days they rode through Nantwich, Newcastle-under-Lyne, Stafford, Lichfield, Coventry, Daventry, Northampton and St. Albans to London. For Richard, as the journey progressed the indignities and mortifications mounted. There was the extraordinary business of the king's greyhound, Math, which had already transferred itself to Henry on his march north. According to Adam of Usk's story this uncanny and unpleasant animal could see into the future and thus always attach itself to a master whose fortunes were on the upturn. Having on the death of its first owner, Thomas Holland, earl of Kent, 'found its way by its own instinct to King Richard, whom it had never before seen and who was then in distant parts', it had become his constant, rather sinister companion. 'Whithersoever the king went and wheresoever he stood or lay down it was ever by his side with grim and lion-like face, until the same king ... fled at midnight by stealth ... from his army.' Apparently disgusted by such cowardice, it had thereupon deserted him and found its way unaided across country to Henry, who was lodging at the time with his army in the monastery of Shrewsbury. There, Adam tells us, he saw a wonderful sight. 'As I looked on, it crouched before him, whom it had never before seen, with a submissive but bright and pleased aspect.' A greyhound being already one of the superstitious Henry's badges, he took this as a good omen and, 'hearing of its qualities, believing that thereby his good fortune was foretold, welcomed the hound right willingly and with joy and let it sleep upon his bed'.

On seeing its former royal master again the two-faced creature ignored him. 'When it was brought to him it cared not to regard him at all other than as a private man whom it knew not'; a piece of disloyalty which, Adam tells us, not surprisingly the 'king took sorely to heart'.

In its entirety the story is too improbable to accept, but that it had some foundation in fact seems likely from its appearance also in Froissart. It seems that Henry took advantage of the incident by having made collars of linked greyhounds and distributing them to his friends as his livery along with the SS collars.

Not only the king's former pet defected from the losing side. Richard had to endure the sight of his own ministers wearing the Lancastrian livery in place of the white hart which they had been proud enough to display on their doublets a fortnight before. In the short time that elapsed between Richard's capture and arrival in London the white hart badge was nervously shed by everyone except an esquire called Janico d'Artas, a Gascon, Créton tells us. Even our chronicler and his knight had hastened to bend the knee to the conqueror on his arrival at Flint, terrified for their lives. They had persuaded Lancaster herald to plead to Henry on their behalf as he entered the castle, and they had been overjoyed when the duke stopped and listened to their frightened greeting, then addressed them kindly in their own language, 'My children, fear not, neither be dismayed at anything that you behold and keep close to me and I will answer for your lives!' It left them in no mind openly to show their preference for Richard.

The one sensational new recruit to the royal cause was forced to abandon it by Richard himself. Henry's twelve-year-old son and namesake, the future Henry V, whom Richard had taken to Ireland as a hostage and there knighted, had formed a deep affection for the unlucky king. So much so that on the lad's return to England (he had been sent for by Henry whom he joined at Chester) he chose to spend his time in Richard's company, regarding his father as a traitor. Henry's threats were of no avail until Richard himself gently persuaded the boy to leave his side.

Another desolating feature of the journey was the failure of a number of rescue attempts. Loyal Welshmen, who repeatedly raided the marching army, succeeded only in burning a few houses and carrying off some plunder before being forced to flee back into the mountains, their attacks eventually discouraged after some of them, caught by Henry's soldiers, were tied to their own horses' tails, drawn over the cobbles and so killed. A plot to rescue Richard during the night at Lichfield likewise came to nothing. In desperation he had climbed down knotted sheets from his room in a tower into the garden, but was caught at once 'and most villainously thrust back into the tower'.

Instead of benefiting the king, these escape attempts resulted in his being watched day and night by ten or twelve armed guards whose presence, Créton writes indignantly, prevented him sleeping. But how else could Henry keep his royal captive secure on the march through hostile territory?

Perhaps most dispiriting of all for Richard was the arrival at Chester, right at the start of the journey, of a deputation of London aldermen demanding that he be executed forthwith, for this deputation showed that his subjects were beginning to turn against him personally; it was no longer simply his government they opposed. Henry's reaction to this bloodthirsty request was firm and certainly crucial to our assessment of his character. Instead of agreeing to Richard's murder or execution and afterwards denying responsibility, as he could have done with ease and to his own advantage at this stage of his progress to the throne - since a dead Richard would have saved Henry a lot of trouble - he expressed horror at the Londoners' suggestion. Politely, of course, because Londoners were too important to offend, but unequivocally. Even the hostile Créton admits that he refused the request, 'as prudently as he could, saying, "Fair Sirs, it would be a very great disgrace to us for ever, if we should thus put him to death; but we will bring him to London, and there he shall be judged by the parliament."'

Henry thus showed himself to be no mere opportunist but a man of principle. And his words clearly impressed the city dignitaries, because when they again met him with his royal captive on their arrival outside London, no further suggestion of violence was made. Henry handed Richard into their custody with the words, '"Fair sirs, behold your king. Consider what you will do with him." And they made answer with a loud voice. "We will have him taken to Westminster", then they took him through back ways to the palace.'

The parallel that Créton draws here between Henry handing over Richard to the aldermen and Pontius Pilate delivering Jesus to the rabble is absurd, since the dignitaries were responsible for law and order in London and the measures they now took were for Richard's own safety at a time when the mob was yelling for his blood. Only a little while before, they had descended on Westminster, forced their way through the palace gates and rampaged through the royal apartments, demanding the king. On failing to find him, they had seized the dean of the King's Chapel, John Slake; a king's knight, called Sir John Selby; and a number of the monks and thrust them into Newgate prison. In these circumstances, if Richard was to be lodged without harm at the palace, it was essential that he be taken there as secretly as possible.

Assessment of Henry's treatment of Richard demands examination not only of what the chronicles say, but also of what they omit. In even the most partisan account of the journey to London there is no claim that the king was chained or surrounded by placards and criers proclaiming his ill deeds to people lining the route. So while we may doubt the pro-Lancastrian Walsingham's description of Henry riding beside him and treating him with special honours, we may also question the Dieulacres chronicle's comparison of his treatment on the journey to that of a captive servant. While Henry had every reason to hate the cousin who had tried to ruin him, there are few signs that he treated him cruelly.

With his entry into London the worst of Henry's own problems were over. Having delivered the king into safe hands, Henry himself rode on to a hero's tumultuous welcome from the city. Entering through the Aldgate, he was greeted by the loud playing of bands of minstrels, mingled with the pealing of church and monastery bells, in such a jubilantly noisy reception that, the hostile author of the *Traison et Mort* observed, 'you could not even hear God thundering'.

The hero's own feelings at his triumph were more mixed, judging from his demeanour on entering the capital. He rode to St. Paul's, first to give thanks to God for the victory, then to gaze at his father's tomb, where he was seen to weep. Tears of guilt, as well as grief perhaps, as, faced with Gaunt's stern effigy, he was reminded that, had the great duke of Lancaster been alive still, he never would have approved of this rebellion against the Lord's anointed.

Henry rested that night at the bishop's palace at St. Paul's, and the following morning Richard was taken from Westminster to the Tower by water, this palace cum prison being the only possible place nearby for a captive of his importance. Here, probably in the White Tower, whose rooms were both strong enough to prevent him escaping and comfortable enough to accommodate him in some luxury, he was to spend the next few weeks, while his fate was decided.

The *Traison et Mort* describes a last interview between the cousins. Henry's behaviour is depicted as courteous and kind with an undercurrent of cunning, Richard's as outraged and defiant. According to this story, Henry arrived at the Tower with the duke of York and his son, Aumerle, and sent a message by the young earl of Arundel asking Richard to come to him, a message to which the king retorted proudly, 'Go tell Henry of Lancaster that if he wishes to speak to me he must come to me'.

Courteously, Henry obeyed, as though still bound to do so, and in Richard's presence he alone of the three visitors respectfully doffed his hat.

Thus confronted, Richard began by denouncing the man who had pretended to be his close friend. Aumerle, he said, had 'foully betrayed' and given him 'false counsel' to put Gloucester to death. Richard cursed the hour in which York's son had been born. Aumerle then defiantly flung down his bonnet at Richard's feet, provoking a royal outburst reminiscent of the uncontrolled tantrums of his youth. The king kicked the bonnet 'two or three paces from him, and said to him, "Traitor! I am king and thy lord, and will still continue king; and will be a greater lord than I ever was, in spite of all my enemies; and you are not fit to speak to me!"'

At this point Henry appeared to come to Richard's aid; he forbade Aumerle to retort. And when Richard demanded of him, 'Why do you keep me so closely guarded by your men-at-arms? I wish to know if you acknowledge me as your lord and king, or what you mean to do with me?' Henry replied coolly, 'It is true you are my king and lord, but the council of the realm have ordered that you should be kept in confinement until the day of the meeting of parliament'.

Richard then rounded on Henry accusing him with York and Aumerle of being a 'false traitor' and offered to prove it 'against any four of the best of you with my body like a loyal knight as I am', and in his turn threw down his bonnet.

Whereupon, instead of retorting hotly himself, Henry 'fell on his knees and besought him to be quiet till the meeting of parliament', where he promised, 'everyone would bring forward his reason'.

Henry even appeared to be moved by Richard's plight, for when the king pathetically begged him, 'At least ... for God's sake let me be brought to trial, that I may give an account of my conduct and that I may answer to all they would say against me', Henry reassured him, 'My lord, be not afraid, nothing unreasonable shall be done to you'.

But if Richard's suffering on this occasion briefly aroused Henry's pity, the quandary he now found himself in left little room for indulging such an emotion. His problem was: how to depose a king? What authority was high enough to deprive such an exalted being of his crown? A solution had been found when in 1327 Edward II, first deposed by parliament, had then abdicated. He had not wanted to abdicate - he had wept during the ceremony - but had been forced to do so under the threat that, if he refused, his son would be disinherited. No such threat could be held over Richard who did not even consider it possible for a king to abdicate. He was prepared to concede that he could hand over the power of government, as he had done during his minority, but not that he could ever cease to be king. At his coronation, he believed mystical characters had been imprinted by divine grace on his soul, making him more than man, and nothing could alter that. It quickly became apparent to Henry that this awkward conviction was at the root of Richard's whole being. His was indeed a dilemma.

After a few days spent in the bishop's palace at St. Paul's, Henry moved to his father's favourite castle at Hertford to consider with his advisers other solutions. The simplest answer to his problem would be to prove that Richard had never had any right to the throne at all, that there was truth in the legend that Henry's direct ancestor, Edmund Crouchback, had in reality been the elder of King Henry III's two sons, made to appear the younger because he was deformed in mind and body. Then Henry of Lancaster would be the rightful king anyway, and deposition and abdication both mercifully become unnecessary.

Soon messengers were riding to all the major abbeys in England, demanding - ironically, in Richard's name - copies of their chronicles, while there converged on the stone and timber buildings of Westminster Palace a commission to consider their findings. Among the black-gowned canon lawyers on humble ponies and lordly bishops with large and brilliant escorts, came our chronicler, Adam of Usk. For days these learned men pored over the hand-written manuscripts, and then came to what was for Henry a maddening, most inconvenient conclusion: there were absolutely no grounds to dispute the generally accepted evidence that Crouchback had been the younger of the brothers. The legend was no more than a legend. They were not time servers and it was a conclusion from which Henry could not shift them.

So Henry's quandary remained; and to make a solution all the more urgent, law and order in the country began to break down. Already since the invasion there had been a 'great number of manslaughters, robberies, larcenies, mayhems, extortions, oppressions, regratings (lamentings), excesses of labourers and craftsmen and other mischiefs ... to the terror of the people', for England had virtually no legal government. Henry had done his best to fill the gap with proclamations issued 'by advice of Thomas, archbishop of Canterbury, Henry, duke of Lancaster, and of Henry, earl of Northumberland, Ralph, earl of Westmorland, and other great men, princes and lords of the realm', under which authority writs were sent to sheriffs all over England, ordering them 'to busy themselves in keeping of the peace and their justiceship'. They were informed that the disorders were 'contrary to the duke's intent', and for good measure that the king 'will in nowise endure the same'.

These writs were stamped with the royal seal. In the king's name also Henry had appointed a new treasurer, replacing Lescrope, beheaded at Bristol, with his own constant, trusted companion, John Norbury, who had gone into exile with him in Paris.

But the floods of anarchy threatened soon to break through this temporary expedient. Henry and his friends urgently needed some firmer, more convincing basis of authority.

From Henry's personal point of view also there was another reason for speed: at the moment he rode the crest of a wave of popularity which would not last for ever. He must somehow establish himself on the throne before that wave broke. So, since none of the hitherto considered methods of deposing the king was in itself satisfactory, he decided to use all three. First, some kind of abdication would have to be forced out of Richard, if not in public, then in private, and to this end spies kept watch on him to report any sign that he had become more malleable. One of these spies on 21 September was Adam of Usk, who looked on while the king dined and found him, 'musing on his ancient and wonted glory and on the fickle fortune of the world'.

Adam informs us that: 'The king discoursed sorrowfully in these words: "My God! A wonderful land is this and a fickle, which hath exiled, slain, destroyed or ruined so many kings, rulers and great men and is ever tainted and toileth with strife and variance and envy". And then he recounted the histories and names of sufferers from the earliest habitation of the kingdom'. Another scene that found its way into Shakespeare's *King Richard II*.

Our chronicler left the Tower 'much moved at heart' but full of good tidings for his master. In such a low state of mind surely something could be forced out of Richard. A form of abdication was therefore prepared for him to sign.

Armed with this document at nine o'clock on 29 September, a special commission, consisting of some fourteen people, led by Northumberland and Westmorland, and representing the three estates of England, the Lords spiritual and temporal and the Commons, went to see Richard in the Tower. For a description of this interview we have only the official record in the parliament roll, but ignoring what we know to be untrue and reading between the lines, we can gain a general idea of what happened.

In the report the commission asks Richard to fulfil his promise to abdicate made at Conway when he was 'at his luste and liberte'. (Untrue since we know that promise was never made.) Richard agrees but says that first, he requires a copy of the document to study and an interview with Henry, duke of Lancaster and Thomas, archbishop of Canterbury, his cousins. His use of the word 'consanguineis' at this juncture has emotional overtones suggesting that he is about to try and drive a bargain with them, perhaps to plead for his life in return for signing the document. (Threats against his life had probably been used to make him co-operate either before or during the interview.) This assumption is given weight when the roll goes on to describe Richard as, 'desiryng much and abydyng longe the komyng off the duke off Lancastre', his anxiety being quite out of place since in fact he has a very short time to wait. In the official report Henry and Arundel arrive to see Richard that very afternoon. The roll goes on to say that after Richard has talked to them 'apart' he agrees to sign and becomes very cheerful. He reads the abdication document aloud, signs it 'with a gladde chere', draws the gold signet ring from his finger and places it on Henry's as a sign that he wishes him to be his successor. These are indications that a bargain has been struck and a weight taken off his mind.

But if Henry thought he had won the day he had reckoned without Richard's cunning. It is clear that, either just before or just after signing the statement of abdication, Richard had qualified it by a formal protestation in which he declared that, 'he did not wish nor was it his intention to renounce those signs or characters impressed upon his soul by the sacramental unction', in other words, that he had abdicated from government but not from kingship. Omitted of course from the report in the parliament rolls, the story comes to us from too many independent sources to be doubted; it appears in the *Annales* and the *Monk of Evesham* as well as an early fifteenth century unprinted manuscript. For Henry it was a serious development, for should the protestation become general knowledge the abdication document would be discredited. He had to act at once.

On 30 September, the day after Richard had signed the abdication, there took place in Westminster Hall the decisive event. Packed around the room, beneath Richard's marvellous new hammer beam roof, decorated with gilded angels and white harts, were all those who had come to London for the parliament, the lords spiritual and temporal seated in their usual places on either side of the throne, and the shire knights who represented the commons, as well as justices, doctors of law, notaries and a multitude of others who had not been called to parliament, but were there to represent the people.

But over this gathering no king or royal deputy presided on the dais beneath the canopy of estate. The great chair of estate gleaming with cloth of gold was unoccupied.

The reason for the vacant throne was at once made plain by Richard's proctors, the archbishop of York and the bishop of Hereford. To the assembly they announced that the king had abdicated, then in the first person, as though Richard himself were speaking, the archbishop of York read aloud the abject document that Richard had signed the previous day, first in the original Latin then in English as it is reproduced here:

In the name of God, Amen! I Richard by the grace of God kyng off England and off ffraunce and lorde off Ireland, quyte and assoyle (absolve) Erchebysshopes, Byshopes ... Dukes, Marquys, Erles, Barons, Lordes and alle my other Liege me(n) both Spyrituell and Seculer ... ffrom her othe of ffeute and homage ... I Resigne all my Kyngly Mageste, Dignyte and Crovne ... And also I renounce to the name, Worship and Regaly and kyngly hynes ... And with dede and worde I leve off and Resigne hem and goo ffro hem ffor euermore ... ffor I wete, knowleche, and ... deme my sylff to be and have bene Insuffisant, vnable, and vnprofitable, and ffor myn ... Desertes not vnworthely to be putt down. And I swere on the holy Euaungelies (gospels), by me bodely touched, that I shall neuer contrarye ... to this resignacion ... So God me helpe and thes holy Euaungelies! I Richard, kyng aforseyd, with myn owne hande have wretyn me vnderneth here.

Nobody mentioned that the king had already contradicted that oath made 'on the holy Euaungelies'. Instead, immediately after it had been read, his abdication was put to the assembly and accepted by most, if not all, of the Lords and Commons, as the official record maintains.

The assembly then decided that, since Richard was no longer king, his style henceforth would be that of a simple knight, 'Sir Richard of Bordeaux'. In order, as it was said, to avoid 'mys-conceytes and evyll suspecions', there followed an explanation of why Richard's abdication had been sought, a long list of his alleged crimes. Thirty-two specific charges had been drawn up relating particularly to the events of 1387 and 1397. Although they dealt with the government of the country as a whole the charges harped repeatedly on the wrongs suffered by Henry, the duke of Gloucester, the earl of Warwick and the Arundels, a selection being read aloud.

It was stated that Richard: had given away the crown's possessions to unworthy favourites; at Shrewsbury in 1387 he had threatened the justices into making a new definition of treason aimed against the appellants; he had encouraged Robert de Vere to raise the royal banner 'opynly ayens his pees'; he had first attempted to destroy Gloucester, Arundel and Warwick in 1387, then pretended to forgive them and finally arrested them ten years later; he had proclaimed that they were to be tried only for new extortions and 'not for no gaderynges, confederacyes ne rydynges', yet he had had them tried and condemned for those very things; he had had the duke of Gloucester murdered; he had broken oaths made to Thomas Arundel and Henry of Lancaster, exiling the latter 'ayens all manere rihtnysnesse and lawes and usages off the Rewme (realm) and ayens alle lawe off armes and knyhthode'; he had 'with grete vygour ordeyned upon grete peynes that ther shulde no manere man speke ne pray to hym ffor no maner grace ne mercy ffor Herry Duk off Lancastre ... ayens all bondis of charitie ...'

He was accused of breaking faith. The Clerk, reading out the charges, declared that, 'the same Kyng is wont ... to be so variable and ffeyning in his wordes and writynges and also contrarie to himsylff ... that almost ther was no levying man myht ... trust in hym ... he was holde so vntrewe and vnstable'. He was also accused of illegal extortion and tyranny. He had illegally extracted loans, fines and blank charters from his subjects and impoverished them. He had declared openly that 'his lawes weren in his mouthe and other while in his breste. And that he allone myht chaunge the Lawes off his Rewme and make newe'. And most serious charge of all, since it involved the fundamental bond between king and people, he was accused of having broken his coronation oath to 'do evyn and rihtfull Justice and Rihtwysnesse in mercy and Trouthe by all his power and myht'.

Accusation followed accusation - stepping stones to the next carefully planned stage of Richard's downfall - until finally they came to their destined end, and it was put to the assembly that Richard was unworthy to be king and should be deposed. At this point a hitch occurred in the hitherto perfectly smooth proceedings. Thomas Merks, bishop of Carlisle, who had been with Richard when he was captured near Conway, rose to protest, boldly pointing out that it was illegal to sentence the king in his absence, that even the lowest criminal was entitled to hear the crimes with which he was charged before being condemned. But the mood of the gathering was against this brave and loyal bishop. Merks was hastily silenced while the irregular proceedings resumed their predetermined course, with a committee supposed to represent the people formally declaring:

> We pronounce, discerne and declare the same Kyng Richard ... to have be and yitt to be vnprofitable, vnable, vnsufficient and vnworthy to the Reule and gouernance off the fforseyd Rewmes and lordshippes ... we pryve hym off alle kyngly dignyte, and worship, yiff eny kyngly worship leffte in hym ... we depose hym ... fforbedyng expressly to alle ... subgetes and his lieges ... that noon off hem ffrom this tyme fforth to the fforseyd Richard, as kyng and lorde off the fforseyd kyngdomes and Rewmes, neyther obeye, ne in no manere wyse be entendaunt.

After this - when Richard himself had abdicated and an assembly of parliament and people had then deposed him - it might be presumed that he had been thoroughly and completely unkinged. But Henry and Arundel thought of yet another measure that could be taken, further to loosen that tiresomely strong bond between monarch and people. In the abdication document Richard had already renounced his subjects' fealty and homage. The people must themselves also voluntarily withdraw these things from him, it was decided by the assembly, and for this purpose and to apprise him of his deposition, a committee should visit Richard of Bordeaux in the Tower the following day.

Having thus finally disposed of the former king, it was time to consider the naming of his successor.

All this time the proceedings had been dominated by that empty chair of estate, gleaming with cloth of gold and symbolising the throne of England. Now that it had formally been pronounced void it was time to decide who should occupy it. This was the moment for Henry to rise from his seat among the peers and prove his right. No easy task, when everyone present knew that, by virtue of descent from Gaunt's elder brother, the duke of Clarence, the strongest claim after Richard's belonged to someone else, the eight-year-old earl of March.

Henry rose to his feet, 'merkyng hym mekely with the signe off the crosse in his ffor heede, and in his breste, nempnyng the name of Crist', and dealt with the situation as vigorously as if he were about to ride against an opponent in a joust. He spoke in plain English so that everyone could understand.

> In the name of Fadir, Son, and Holy Gost, I Henry of Lancastre chalenge this rewme of Yngland and the corone with all the membres and the appurtenances als I that am disendit be right lyne of the blode comyng fro the gude lorde Kyng Henry therde, and thorgh that ryght that God of his grace hath sent me with helpe of my kyn and of my frendes to recover it, the whiche rewme was in poynt to be undone for defaut of governance and undoyng of the gode lawes.

In reality it was a terrible ragbag of claims: his royal blood, the discredited Crouchback legend,the suggestion that God had chosen him through victory. There was only one sound argument among them; that he was the man for the moment, the one who could put right what was wrong with the country, and this by itself had never before been a valid qualification for kingship in England. But after Richard's misrule of the past two years, the country craved just such a man; and as in the abdication and deposition, the flaws in logic were ignored by the assembly, ruled by the guiding maxim of the times, 'Necessitas non habet legem'. Asked if they would accept Henry as their king, they consented loudly. In a dramatically telling gesture, worthy of the absent Richard, Henry then held up his hand wearing the royal ring, declaring that Richard himself had placed it there the day before. Thus, he was Richard's choice, as well as theirs.

It was now the turn of the Church to set its venerable seal on the proceedings. Thomas Arundel, acting again in the capacity of archbishop of Canterbury, led Henry by the right hand to the unoccupied royal throne, where the archbishop of York joined them. Henry knelt praying for a few moments at its foot, after which the archbishops, holding his arms, helped to seat him upon the gleaming chair of estate.

Arundel then preached a sermon to expel any lingering doubts about the young earl of March's claim to the throne. It was based on the text, 'Vir dominabitur in populo', a man shall rule among the people. God had been good to them, Arundel said, He had not given them a child as their ruler, as He had threatened to do once to the Israelites, and he quoted lengthy and impressive biblical passages describing the characteristics that made children unfit to rule. He concluded: 'Whanne a childe regnyth, thanne selff wille and luste regnyth; and Reson is outlawyd, wher that wille only regnyth and Reson goth his way; And stedfastnesse is chased; And so it ys lyke grete perylle to ffalle. But off this perylle we ben delyuered. Quia vir dominabitur in populo.' The usurpation was complete.

By 'indirect crook'd ways', Shakespeare's graphic phrase, Henry had arrived at the throne, which he now occupied as king on the basis of seizure disguised as legality. The last chapter now opened for Richard.

XVIII   DEATH OF A KING

'For God's sake let us sit upon the ground,
'And tell sad stories of the deaths of kings.'
William Shakespeare, *Richard II*

It was an extraordinary achievement. Setting out from France with only a handful of men, in twelve weeks Henry had invaded England, deposed her king and placed himself on the throne. From being a landless exile he had both recovered his rich Lancastrian inheritance and acquired the crown's possessions, vast estates, great palaces and priceless jewels, not to mention a kingdom of subjects. From being non-existent, his prospects were suddenly brilliant. Nevertheless, they were not without attendant shadows, among them the fear that, once the euphoria of revolution was over, these same subjects might begin to regard him as the usurper he was.

By every possible means he tried to improve his image, choosing for the date of his coronation 13 October, the feast of the translation of St. Edward, Richard's patron saint, portrayed in statuary as founder of the line of English kings. And during his preliminary two day stay in the Tower, when it was customary for the monarch to bestow the accolade on a number of knights, he created a new military order, the Order of the Bath.

Purified by the ritual of bathing - for a usurper needs all the symbols of purity he can muster - clad in blue and green check mantles and hoods lined with miniver, his Knights of the Bath included his own three younger sons, Thomas, John and Humphrey. With their twelve-year-old brother, already knighted by Richard in Ireland, these little boys in their priestlike garb rode the following day before King Henry in the procession through the city. The usurper himself, with his red-brown hair capless in the falling rain, rode in a 'shorte cote of clothe of gold after the maner of Almayne ... mounted on a whyte courser ... the garter on his left legge', defiantly oblivious of the fact that he had broken his oath of loyalty to the order's sovereign, at present imprisoned in the Tower at his command. Visibly giving support to the new king, London's mayor and aldermen rode with him, gowned in scarlet, their hoods also lined with miniver, while, echoing the colours of the royal livery, the city's conduits gushed red or white wine, instead of water. Inside his prison, tormented by what feelings of frustration and anger we can imagine as he heard his rival cheered, the deposed king was hidden from view.

Henry had made several changes in the coronation ceremonies. To present the usurpation as a romantic adventure, he had introduced a new symbol into the procession from Westminster Palace to the abbey the next morning. As he advanced shoeless on the striped carpet beneath the purple canopy - which tinkled with silver bells and was supported on silver staves by Knights of the Cinque Ports - he was preceded, not just by three swords, but by four. Taking pride of place in its black and gold sheath was the sword of Lancaster, the weapon Henry had worn when he landed at Ravenspur. It was followed by the two swords 'wrapped in red and bound round with golden bands to represent twofold mercy' and the Curtana borne naked and without a point to symbolize 'justice without rancour'.

But the most important innovation of all was in the unction itself. Henry was anointed with an especially holy oil, said to have been discovered during his exile in France by Thomas Becket, one of the most venerated of English saints, and it was poured for the first time in the history of English coronations from a golden ampulla in the shape of an eagle.

With the introduction of this miraculous oil Henry had done all he could to whitewash his usurpation, and the ceremony in the abbey proceeded remarkably smoothly. 'Robed finely in red and scarlet and ermine', there bent the knee to do him homage and fealty all the peers of the realm, including Richard's brother and nephew, John and Thomas Holland, suspect but nonetheless welcome recruits to Henry's cause. And at the banquet in Westminster Hall that followed the coronation, they stood among the other lords in an impressive row before the new king while he dined.

Nevertheless Henry could not help but feel anxiety, especially at the entrance of his champion. It was a sensitive moment when, wearing Henry's armour and carrying his sword, Sir Thomas Dymock rode into the room and reined his horse to a halt between the laden tables, while a herald proclaimed first in French then in English the traditional challenge:

> Iff ther be eny man hyh or lowe, off what astate or condicion he be, that wole say that Herry kyng off Englond that here is, and was this day corovnyd, that he is not rihtfull kyng ne rihtfully corovnyd, anoon riht now or allys at what day oure lorde the kyng wole assigne, I wille darrayne (settle the matter by) bataylle with my body and preve that he lieth ffalsly.

Before anyone else could seize this perfect opportunity to contest the usurper's right, 'Herry kyng off Englond' himself spoke. 'If need be, Sir

Thomas I will in mine own person ease thee of this office.' It was a threat from the foremost jouster in England that no one cared to face. So under Richard's magnificent painted roof, carved with his white hart badge of loyal service, the champion's challenge went unanswered and the usurper's coronation banquet finished without incident. Afterwards Henry took up residence in the palace.

However, he could still not feel wholly secure. Aware of the need to continue every possible form of propaganda, he had widely spread abroad the fable of the miraculous origin of the holy oil with which he had been anointed. Coming into full flower in a fifteenth century manuscript, it shows the extraordinary lengths to which he and his advisers felt it necessary to go to bolster up Henry's claim to the throne; it is a gauge of their anxiety.

The story of the oil's discovery tells how one night, while Thomas Becket was praying in the church of St. Colombe in the town of Sens, the Virgin had appeared to him, 'having on her breast a drop of water shining more brightly than fine gold', and holding in her hand a little stone ampulla in an eagle of gold. And after she had taken this drop of water and put it in the ampulla, she said:

> This is the unction by which the kings of England should be anointed, not those who reign now but those who shall reign. For those at present reigning are evil and their successors will be also ... and for their sins will lose many things, but other kings of England will come who will be anointed with this unction and will be good and obedient to the Church. The first of these will recover in peace and without violence the lands of Normandy and Aquitaine which his predecessors will have lost. This king will be very great among kings and it is he who will build many churches in the Holy Land and chase out the pagans ...

The legend has an interesting history, for Henry and his advisers had not invented it, they were too cunning for that. According to the *Annales* an allegedly miraculous ampulla was among the treasure carried by Richard to Ireland and taken from him at Chester by the archbishop of Canterbury. The story of its origin first appears in a letter from the pope to King Edward II, which declared that a phial of oil for the unction of English kings, presented by the Virgin to Thomas Becket, had been discovered in France, accompanied by a written prophecy.

Only a few details in the story had been changed, but these were crucial. The Lancastrian version said that the ampulla had been discovered, not in the reign of Edward II, but in that of Edward III, and

212

that the written prophecy that accompanied it made no specific mention of which king was first to be consecrated with the oil, whereas in the pope's letter the fifth king after Henry II was specified, namely Edward II.

In an age that believed in a God who actively concerned himself in human affairs, this story convinced many people. And it went some way to counter the belief that the deposition of a ruler was a sin visited by signs of divine displeasure. The tempest dropping fire at the beginning of Shakespeare's *Julius Caesar* illustrates a centuries old English superstition; and Richard's downfall was preceded by signs scarcely less alarming than those that accompanied the Roman general's murder, according to Adam of Usk who, although he served Henry, was sympathetic to Richard. Monsters were born: in Usk, a calf which had two tails, two heads, four eyes and four ears; in the parish of Llanbatock, a boy with a single cyclops eye in his forehead; while in London two royal servants had an upsetting surprise at dinner. Served with eggs, they found in five of them 'the distinct face of a man, exact in every respect, and having the white in place of hair standing clear of the face above the forehead and coming down the cheeks to the chin'.

Even Henry himself was not immune to the belief that he had sinned in deposing Richard. Most unfortunately for his peace of mind he was a usurper with a sense of guilt. Having deposed Richard and seized his throne, he wished to hurt him no further. But in the months that succeeded his coronation be was repeatedly urged to put another burden on his conscience, that of Richard's death. Councillors, members of parliament, deputations of Londoners repeatedly told him the unwelcome truth, that neither he nor his realm would be secure while his predecessor lived. Henry refused to listen. He had harmed his cousin enough. Besides, as we have seen, he had probably promised Richard his life and had gained his trust. The commission that visited the Tower on the day after Richard's deposition had reported him as saying that, 'after all this he hoped' that his 'cosyn wolde be goode lord to hym', a humble plea from the once proud king that must have touched Henry's heart. Henry was to do his best to be a 'goode lord' against considerable opposition. When nagged on the subject, yet again by his council, Froissart tells us: 'the kyng gave none aunswere, but departed fro them ... and lefte his counsayle communyng togyder, and the kynge wente and toke a faucon on his hande, and passed over that matter'.

However, the matter refused to be passed over for long, because if he was not to be killed, what was to be done with Richard? Some decision would have to be made. He could not be left for ever in the Tower, where he could easily become the subject of a rescue attempt which, if it were successful, might plunge the country into civil war; the Peasants' Revolt had shown how vulnerable that fortress could be. The former king's future was one of the questions upon which Henry's first parliament was asked to pronounce.

On 23 October it was asked to decide 'for the security of the king and all the estates of the realm' what should be done with Richard of Bordeaux, 'formerly king ... saving his life which the king wished should be saved in all ways'. On 27 October, in Westminster Hall, Henry in person announced the decision: he was to be imprisoned in perpetuity in a safe and secret place. In view of Richard's protestation that he was still the rightful king, it was the kindest sentence that was possible, unwisely so in the opinion of most of Henry's advisers.

Because the sentence was difficult to implement, it being almost impossible to keep secret the whereabouts of such an important prisoner, the chronicles abound with rumours. According to the *Traison et Mort* it was first arranged to move the deposed king from the Tower disguised as a forester, but he found the commoner's black spurs the ultimate humiliation and refused to wear them, complaining, 'I am a loyal knight ... I never forfeited my knighthood'. The chronicler tells us that, on hearing this, Henry relented and sent him a pair of gilt spurs instead, at the risk of thus betraying the royal identity. And so attired, the king finally left London, according to Adam of Usk, being 'carried away on the Thames in the silence of dark midnight, weeping and loudly lamenting that he had ever been born'. Other chroniclers report that he left on 28 October for Gravesend in Kent, whence he was moved to Leeds Castle and then up north to Pontefract in West Yorkshire.

No more safe and secret place could have been found than this family castle with its great tri-lobal keep and towers bristling with turrets, a place so strong that it would resist Oliver Cromwell's guns for twelve months in the seventeenth century, and so loyal to the House of Lancaster that Henry had used it as an early staging post in his invasion. To make it even more secure, its custodian was Henry's step-brother and favourite companion in arms, Thomas Swynford. Here Richard was indeed isolated among enemies.

In Pontefract Castle we lose sight of him for several months, so completely that we cannot even be sure in what part of this fortress he was kept. Visitors to the castle in 1634 were shown what was reputed to be his room at the top of the highest tower, while nineteenth century antiquaries decided, on the contrary, that his cell was 'a very narrow wretched chamber formed in the thickness of the wall' with 'two very small, narrow windows next the court'. Perhaps both rooms were used, one at the easy beginning of Richard's captivity, one at its harsh end. However this may be, in these discouraging surroundings in Yorkshire the deposed king languished while Henry, having as he hoped solved the problem of Richard, dealt with other aspects of his own and the new regime's security.

One of the first essentials was to make sure of the support of the lords. Upon this, a medieval king depended, and it was partly because he had offended so many of his barons and bishops that Richard had lost his throne. Now Henry set himself the difficult task of trying to win over Richard's friends and relations, the dukes of Exeter and Surrey, the earls of Salisbury and Gloucester, and perhaps most dangerous of all, the strangely incalculable duke of Aumerle, who though he had almost certainly betrayed Richard to Henry in Ireland, might well turn coat again. It was from these nobles, Henry knew, that rebellion and an attempt to restore Richard to the throne would be most likely to come.

To try and win their loyalty Henry had offered a steel hand in a velvet glove, clemency backed by threat. First the five lords who had appealed the 'indivisible trio', Gloucester, Arundel and Warwick, of treason in the autumn of 1397 were themselves put on trial before Henry's first parliament which gathered in the White Hall on 6 October. With the assistance of William Bagot, brought over from Ireland to be a prosecution witness, all were accused of contributing to the duke of Gloucester's downfall, while Aumerle was alleged personally to have despatched to Calais the two yeomen who murdered the duke, smothering him with pillows.

As these charges were read, gages and hoods rained pellmell on to the floor, symbols of approval reminiscent of Brembre's trial in the Merciless Parliament of 1388, although its cruelty was not to be repeated. Henry wanted friends, not enemies. Having thus given the accused lords a small taste of the bitter medicine they had meted out to their victims in 1397, his parliament let them off lightly. Briefly imprisoned pending the trial, they were merely deprived of the titles and lands with which Richard had rewarded them for their activities against the duke of Gloucester and the earls of Arundel and Warwick. The duke of Aumerle, against whom the accusations had been loudest, reverted to the title of earl of Rutland, the duke of Exeter to earl of Huntingdon, the duke of Surrey to earl of Kent, and the earl of Gloucester to Lord Despenser, while the earl of Salisbury suffered no demotion at all. (John Beaufort also lost his title, marquis of Dorset, reverting to earl of Somerset, although to make up for this loss, Henry promptly appointed his half-brother chamberlain of England.)

In delivering this decision, Justice Sir William Thirning accepted their plea that they had acted 'by cohercion and constreyning off the last kyng'.

He contended that anything done with the consent of parliament could not be accounted treason, and that if they were punished for their action in the 1397 parliament, 'meny of the Kynges lieges sholde be in the same case'. Therefore it had been decided to treat them mercifully. But after this mild statement, he added a grim warning that such leniency would not be repeated. Addressing them directly, he ordered, 'that ye be nat privily consellyng ne helpyng to Kyng Richard in ne thing off the worlde; that yff ye do ye shull be helde as traytours to the kyng'.

Richard's friends had been wholly forgiven but for this time only, should they offend again they would be treated with the full severity of the law. They had thus received a powerful incentive to serve the new king, but it remained to be seen whether it would be strong enough to destroy all loyalty to the old one.

Henry's first parliament was to repeal all the acts of Richard's parliament of 1397-98, but this was not enough to satisfy most of his former subjects. The people had looked on the duke of Gloucester as their shield against the tyrant and a scapegoat for his downfall was needed.

In view of the fact that Surrey, Exeter, Gloucester, Salisbury and Aumerle had been joined in the appeal against the duke, they had got off easily indeed. As a scapegoat for his murder, Henry was obliged to make use of a comparatively innocent underling. Since the yeomen alleged to have smothered him had wisely fled the country or hidden, the choice fell on the person who had kept the door while the murder was committed. John Hall, who had probably done no more than obey the orders of his superiors, was publicly butchered at Tyburn and his head sent to be publicly displayed in Calais, the scene of the crime. It was an ugly incident untypical of the new reign. For apart from the deaths of Hall, Bushy, Green and Lescrope, the revolution had been mercifully almost bloodless.

The new reign had also begun almost without disruption of the machinery of government. Practically all those who had served Richard continued to serve Henry, apart from a very few chief officers and servants whom he replaced. And as his most recent biographer, J.L. Kirby, remarks 'the whole administration ... continued as usual apparently unmoved by the change of king' - like the royal seal, which remained unchanged except that the name 'Henricus' was substituted for 'Ricardus'.

Strangest of all, the chroniclers do not relate a single public demonstration in Richard's favour. His friends appeared to have forgotten him. And as this momentous year drew to an end, it began to look as though Henry's advisers had worried him unnecessarily by urging him to put Richard to death; that the deposed king had ceased to be a danger and merely imprisoning him for the rest of his life would prove safeguard enough. This was Henry's own view, at least until Christmas. He spent this festival at Windsor where a disturbing incident occurred. After a banquet he and the Prince of Wales fell ill, and suspecting poison, he had second thoughts.

In his fright, he was heard to exclaim that he wished Richard were dead, an exclamation that filled his counsellors with hope that he had at last seen sense. The *Traison et Mort* tells us that a deputation of eleven, including the archbishop of Canterbury, the duke of York and the earls of Arundel, Northumberland, Westmorland and Warwick, came to him the following day and begged him on their knees to clothe his words in deeds. But by now Henry had recovered both his health and his nerve and was shocked by their request. He reminded them: 'King Richard has been our sovereign lord a long time and was sentenced and condemned in open parliament to perpetual imprisonment ... So God help me, I will by no means act in opposition to the open parliament'. The only sop he would give their anxiety was the promise, 'if there shall be any rising in the country in his favour he shall be the first to die for it'.

It was the best they could get out of him, and they trooped disappointed out of his presence, perhaps reflecting that things had been suspiciously quiet for too long. If so, their fears were about to be realised. On New Year's day, after the customary exchange of presents, most of the lords and courtiers rode away from the castle, the younger members to London to prepare their gear for the tournament at Windsor on Twelfth Night; until which time Henry and his family could relax in comparative privacy. The competitors in the tournaments usually spent this interval in the festivities supervising the embellishment of their armour, with gilt and azure enamel and curious engraving, choosing the colour of their plumes and selecting the badges and mottoes to be painted or embroidered on their shields and horse trappings. For the tournament that marked the end of the Christmas season was always a marvellous and spectacular entertainment.

But Richard's friends in the year 1400 had other plans for Twelfth Night. Their minds that January week were engaged on a far grimmer business than their appearance in the lists. During the coming tournament they planned to murder Henry and all four of his sons, utterly to stamp out the usurper and his brood, and to this end the winter days were spent secretly gathering their forces.

The plotters included those very lords to whom Henry had been so merciful. With John and Thomas Holland, Salisbury and Despenser, were joined Thomas Merks, bishop of Carlisle, who alone had dared to protest at Richard's deposition in Westminster Hall, Roger Walden, Richard's archbishop of Canterbury, now supplanted by Thomas Arundel, and more strangely, the abbot of Westminster who had played a major part in Henry's coronation. Among the many lesser men who followed their lead were Sir Thomas Blount; Sir Thomas Shelley, master of the household to the earl of Huntingdon; Sir Bernard Brocas, a Gascon knight; and two priests, William Feriby and the graceful, auburn-haired Richard Maudelyn, who was the former king's double, his chaplain and special favourite, accompanying him to Ireland and afterwards to Conway Castle.

The plan was for rebel soldiers to be hidden in the wagons that would lumber through the castle gates, apparently crammed with nothing more alarming that equipment for the tournament. Once safely inside the walls, these hidden men would spring out and murder the king and his sons. Afterwards, dressed in luxurious robes and riding from town to town to raise the country, Maudelyn would impersonate his master until the former king himself could be released from Pontefract Castle to lead the rebellion.

How Henry learned of the plot is uncertain, the French chronicles claiming it was through the turncoat Rutland, who having joined the rebels, then thought better of it and confessed first to his horrified father, the duke of York, and then to the king. But the *Eulogium* has a more appealing version, it states that the conspiracy was discovered through a tender-hearted prostitute sharing her favours between a rebel and a member of Henry's household and taking pity on the latter. However this may be, Henry was warned just in time to gather up his four young sons and ride furiously with them for London, whose walled haven he reached none too soon.

For that same evening at twilight the Hollands, Salisbury, Despenser and some four hundred archers and men-at-arms rode up to the gates of Windsor Castle to find their birds flown. The Hollands had never shown much sense and they now ran true to form. Dismayed and confused at this unexpected turn of events, they wasted precious hours. Instead of at once pursuing and attempting to kill the king before he could himself raise an army, a course which would have offered them at least a chance of success, they spent that night in Windsor Castle; and the next morning rode to the now vanished palace at Sonning where the child queen was then living. There they vowed their loyalty to her, and young Holland tore Henry's collars and badges off the arms and necks of her servants, then collecting them and Isabel's courtiers all in one room, boastfully addressed them with a flamboyant disregard for the truth, according to Walsingham's *Annales*.

Benedicite! What has happened that the lord Henry of Lancaster so flees from my face, who was so extolling his own strength and warlike spirit? Lords and friends, be it known to you all that Lord Henry of Lancaster has fled to the Tower of London with his sons and friends, with me in pursuit, and it is my intention to go to King Richard who was and is your true king and has now escaped from prison and is lying at Radcot Bridge with a hundred thousand men, and so ye who love King Richard and the queen ... arm yourselves as swiftly as you can, and follow me as soon as you are ready on the road to Wallingford and Abingdon, bringing with you from your home whatever you can.

It was an exploit more gallant than politic.

Leaving Sonning at last, they rode first to Wallingford and then to Abingdon where, making a similar proclamation, they attempted with small success to rally the townsfolk to their cause.

Meanwhile Henry had used his time more effectively. The Londoners in large numbers had rallied to his standard. And when news of the size of his army reached the rebels they panicked. After a skirmish at Maidenhead Bridge they fled, their forces dividing. John Holland, earl of Huntingdon, made for Essex; while stopping on the way at Wantage and Farringdon to make their proclamations in favour of Richard, the earls of Kent and Salisbury and Lord Despenser made for Chester, intending to gather a new army in the royal palatinate. But they were not even to reach it, prevented by the people in this part of the country who equated Richard with financial exaction, forced loans, blank charters, and lack of respect for Englishmen's traditional liberties.

When Kent (Thomas Holland) and Salisbury stopped for the night at Cirencester and rashly proclaimed that Richard was king again, the horrified townsfolk rose against them. The earls were first arrested by the bailiffs, then roughly seized and beheaded by the mob. Despenser, who had escaped from his inn over the roof, reached the Bristol Channel where he got as far as embarking in a boat. But he was recognized and arrested by the boat's captain and taken to Bristol, where he, too, was beheaded by a mob at the market cross. Henry's propaganda had certainly won the hearts of the commons.

Fleeing into Essex, John Holland, earl of Huntingdon, fared no better. He had the misfortune to fall into the hands of Henry's mother-in-law, countess of Hereford, who had no pity for the man who had helped to procure the deaths of two close relatives, her brother, the earl of Arundel, and her son-in-law, the duke of Gloucester, whose widow, the countess's daughter Eleanor, had died that October. The fact that her captive was married to Henry's sister, the flighty Elizabeth, made no difference to the embittered dowager. She delivered him into the hands of her servants, 'clowns and workmen' who, paying no more heed to the law than the people of Cirencester and Bristol, hustled him to Pleshy Castle, dragged him to the spot where the duke of Gloucester had surrendered to Richard, and there beheaded him.

By one means or another, most of the other leaders of the rebellion were also seized and slaughtered. Of those who survived the vengeance of the mob to face formal trial, Richard's double, Maudelyn, Sir Bernard Brocas and William Feriby were brought to London, taken to Tyburn and hanged, then beheaded.

Sir Thomas Blount and twenty-five others, captured at Cirencester then marched all the way to Oxford, painfully on foot, were butchered in the Green Ditch at Oxford Castle, their gory heads being sent thence to decorate London Bridge. Meanwhile their bodies, 'quartered after the manner of beasts taken in the chase', were carried to London 'partly in sacks and partly slung on poles between men's shoulders ... and afterwards salted' to be suspended above the city's gateways.

Lesser men were reprieved from such a noisome and unpleasant fate. Of the rebels adjudged to death before Henry at Oxford, twenty-two were pardoned within a month, while a further fifteen condemned to outlawry were pardoned in the same period, and John Ferrour, he who had saved Henry as a boy in 1381 from the vengeance of the peasants, was immediately given a free pardon.

Leniently treated as usual by virtue of its cloth, the Church got off almost scot-free. Of the three eminent clerics who had been party to the plot, Roger Walden and the abbot of Westminster were imprisoned very briefly in the Tower, and even Thomas Merks, bishop of Carlisle, remained there for only six months.

The rebellion had been crushed, but it had destroyed Henry's fragile sense of security. He and his sons had survived by pure luck. He knew now that Richard still had friends in high places, including the Church. So it was in a black mood that he rode to London to give thanks for his victory at St. Paul's. When the prelates advanced from the cathedral in procession to meet him, reverently singing *Te Deum Laudamus* and sprinkling him with holy water, he rounded on them with fierce words:

> By St. George! 'twere a fine sight to see us all here assembled, provided we were all true and faithful one towards another, for certainly there are some traitors amongst us; but I vow to God that I will gather up the weeds and will clear my garden of them and will sow good plants, until my garden shall be clean within my ditches and walls, unless some of you repent.

The rebellion had made Henry see things at last in their true colours and they made unpleasant viewing. He was at last forced to recognize the depressing truth: Richard living, however safe and secret his prison, was and would always remain an inspiration to revolt. His death was now politically necessary, and Henry was not the only one to realize it. Henceforward the royal prisoner's end was daily expected.

By what means he died will never be known for certain. The French author of the *Traison et Mort* favours an axe blow on the head by the assassin, Sir Peter Exton, the version later made famous by Shakespeare. But this theory was disproved when, on examining Richard's skeleton towards the end of the last century, no sign of any wound in his skull was found. So the cause of death given by most English chroniclers is now preferred: that Richard died of starvation; although of this theory also there are two versions. The more favourable to the House of Lancaster insisted that Richard's starvation was voluntary, that after hearing of the deaths of his friends, he lost heart and refused food for four days, then on trying to eat again found that 'the conduits of his body were contracted' and so died. Adam of Usk, on the other hand, stated that the starvation was imposed and that Sir Thomas Swynford tormented the king 'with starving fare'.

To help us decide between these accounts, we are lucky enough to have four extraordinary pieces of documentary evidence: a council minute dated 8 February 1400; and three items in the issue roll of the exchequer, which were written in the same hand under 20 March 1400, signifying that the incidents referred to took place before that date.

The council minute follows a memorandum of proposed business to be put before the king. It recommended that, 'if Richard formerly king should still be living as was supposed, it should be ordered that he should be securely guarded for the safety of the king's estate and of his kingdom'. The minute replying to the memorandum goes one significant and suspicious step further; it states, '… the king should be advised, if Richard be living, that he should be placed in such safe keeping as the lords decreed and that, if he be dead, he should be shown openly to the people so that they could have knowledge of the fact'.

The murderous nature of this minute became even more apparent when Edward Maunde Thompson (editor and translator of Adam of Usk's *Chronicon Angliae*) discovered, on examining the official document, that this was a censored version, it had supplanted an original minute that had been cut away, presumably because too incriminating. That it was a specific order to kill the king seems very likely in view of the exchequer payments that follow, each progressively more sinister:

> To William Loveney, clerk of the Great Wardrobe, sent to Pontefract Castle on secret business, by order of the king, 66s. 8d.
> To a valet of Sir Thomas Swynford, coming from Pontefract to London, to certify to the king's council of certain matters which

concern the king's advantage, including the hire of one horse for speed, 26s. 8d.

To another valet, sent from London on behalf of the council to Pontefract Castle, to the guards and keepers of the body of Richard, late King of England, 6s. 8d.

In the light of these items we must conclude that Richard was murdered.

There was in the funeral arrangements no vengeful touch. On the contrary, Henry seems to have wished to do the dead king as much honour as was consistent with political wisdom. While Richard could not be buried as regally as instructed in his will - his body robed in white velvet or satin with a gilded crown and sceptre and a ring with a precious stone on his finger - his obsequies were still conducted with splendour and care. He was elaborately embalmed, wrapped in fine linen and enclosed in a lead coffin, his face from the bottom of the forehead to the throat left bare so that his former subjects should know him. The horse-drawn carriage, covered with a black cloth on which his coffin rested, was adorned by the four banners that he himself might have chosen, two bearing the arms of St. George and two those of his patron saint, Edward the Confessor. A hundred torch-bearers in black surrounded the carriage as it travelled slowly south from Pontefract to London, stopping for the night at various prominent places, and, on reaching the capital, the cortege was met by thirty torch-bearers in white who escorted it to St. Paul's, where the body lay for two days. This was a matter of expediency, it being important for the security of the realm that the former king should be seen to be dead by as many people as possible. Nevertheless, during this time his body was reverently treated. Religious services were held, attended on the first day by King Henry himself, who paid for a thousand masses to be said for Richard's soul.

No dishonour was intended when on the second night the body was taken away secretly for burial. In an age ever searching for new saints and miracles such discretion was essential if he was not to be regarded as a cult figure, like King Edward II, Thomas, earl of Lancaster and the recently executed earl of Arundel, whose graves had become the focus of pilgrimage. With the abbot of St. Albans officiating, he was buried in the Dominican priory of King's Langley in Hertfordshire, which was by no means an unkindly chosen place. Divided from the priory only by a wicket, the little country palace here was one Richard had been especially fond of as a young man; where he had often come with his first queen and his favourite courtiers and where presumably he had been happy. There was another reason also for choosing King's Langley; it was the burial place of his elder brother, Edward of Angoulême who had died at the age of seven.

Just over thirteen years later, the usurper Henry was to follow his cousin to the grave.

They were years full of troubles, one disaster following another, the rebellions of the Percys, popular anger at his execution of the archbishop of York, worst of all the terrible debilitating illness that made him bald and hideous and unable even to ride. Ironically, like Richard, he was to be forced into perpetual battle to defend the royal prerogative against parliament's encroachments; he was to be haunted by rumours that the former king was alive, and the end of his reign was to be darkened by a power struggle with his own eldest son.

Throughout, he never ceased to feel guilt for Richard's fate. We see him trying to assuage it by studying questions of morality in the library he had built for himself at Eltham Palace, with carved bosses of angels and archangels on the wooden ceiling, and seven windows of glass painted with holy figures. Here, Capgrave tells us, he liked nothing better than 'to spend great part of the day in solving and unravelling hard questions', for he 'was a studious investigator in all doubtful points of morals, and that as far as his hours of rest from the administration of his government permitted ... he was always eager in the prosecution of such pursuits'.

That these pursuits still failed to ease his conscience we can deduce from his frequently repeated desire to revisit Jerusalem, a pilgrimage that implied special remission for sins. And, also, from the extraordinarily abject nature of the will he made ten years after the usurpation. In it he referred to himself as a 'sinful wretch' and spoke of his life as 'misspendyd', humble phrases echoed in the will of Archbishop Arundel, who shared the responsibility for the perjuries that had led to Richard's capture. As the historian, K.B. McFarlane pointed out, 'at this date there is nothing like their two wills outside those of some repentant heretics'. Revealingly this humility extended to Henry's own funeral arrangements, too. His body, he instructed, was not to be buried at Westminster Abbey, traditional last resting place of English kings, but at Canterbury. For his tomb's design, contrary to custom, he gave no instructions at all, refusing to concern himself with such earthly immortality. On his death he wished to leave no image of his greatness, showing an extraordinary desire for self-effacement.

Racked by his disease, Henry was also haunted by the fear that the struggle between himself and Richard would be repeated between his own two elder sons, Henry and Thomas. And when, while residing at Eltham Palace in December 1412, he fell gravely ill, he called the Prince of Wales to him and said:

My sonn, I feare me sore after my departure from this life, some discorde shall sourd and arise betwixt thee and Thomas, thie brother, the duke of Clarence, whereby the realme may be brought to distruction and misserie, for I knowe you both to be of so great stomake (pride) and courage; wherefore I feare that he thoroughe his high mynde will make some enterprise against thee intendinge to vsurpe vppon the, wch I knowe thie stomake (pride) may not abide easelye. And for dread hereof, as oft as it is in my remembraunce, I sore repent me that euer I charged myselfe wth the crowne of this realme.

Although this melancholy speech was to appear in written form for the first time nearly a century later, its substance is generally believed to be authentic, handed down to posterity by the king's second son, Thomas, duke of Clarence.

From that illness the forty-six-year-old king partially recovered, only to fall fainting in Westminster Abbey three months later, appropriately enough as he made an offering before the shrine of Richard's patron saint, Edward the Confessor. He was carried into the Jerusalem Chamber in the adjoining abbot's house and placed on a straw pallet beside the fire.

Capgrave tells us that his confessor, John Tille, was called and it was suggested by the lords who stood around waiting for the end, that the king should be induced to repent for three things: the death of King Richard, the execution of Archbishop Scrope, and the usurpation of the crown. Henry replied: 'For the to first poyntis I wrote onto the Pope the veri treuth of my consciens. And he sent me a bulle with absolucion and penauns assigned, whech I have fulfilled. And as for the third poynt, it is hard to sette remedy, for my children will not suffir that the regalie (royal power) go oute of oure lynage.'

Capgrave would have heard this report from his patron, Henry's youngest son, Humphrey of Gloucester, one of the lords who waited in the chamber with the dying king.

His troubled conscience is also reflected in the famous account by Monstrelet who relates that, as the king's end finally approached, the crown was placed, as was the English custom, on the bed beside him, so that his successor could take it the moment life departed. When Henry appeared no longer to be breathing his attendants covered his face, and the Prince of Wales took the crown and left the room. Shortly afterwards the king recovered full consciousness, the cloth fell from his face and he asked what had happened to the crown. On being told, he sent for his son and demanded an explanation. And when the prince said he had taken it believing his father was dead, the king replied, sighing, 'Good son, what right could you have to the crown, when I had none? And this you know well.' 'My lord,' responded the prince, 'as you have held and kept it with the sword, so will I keep it as long as I live.'

Three stories of this kind are too many to disregard. There are no similar stories of death-bed guilt and repentance told of King Henry VII who less than a century later was to usurp the throne from King Richard III.

Henry IV died on 20 March 1413 still without having made any arrangements for his tomb. The splendid monument in Canterbury Cathedral is due to his second wife, Joan of Navarre, who commissioned it from Richard's architect and mason, Henry Yevele. It was she who ordered the alabaster effigy and suspended above it a canopy where, carved all round the edge in gold, was Henry's motto 'souveraigne', repeated again and again, like a spell set in stone to convince those critical spirits who might not agree to his right to the title of monarch.

Among those who appear to have questioned this right, was his own eldest son and successor.

Ironically the very same banners and guidons of arms that had decorated Henry IV's funeral procession to Canterbury were to fly a year later over the procession that bore the body of King Richard from his first modest grave at King's Langley to Westminster Abbey. There, at last, as instructed by King Henry V, who had never ceased to love him more than his own father, Richard joined his queen, Anne of Bohemia, in the great bronze tomb adorned with the insignia of kingship and the triumphant epitaph he had chosen for himself. It has been translated as follows:

> Perfect and prudent,
> Richard by right the second,
> Vanquish'd by fortune,
> Lies here now graven in stone,
> True of his word,
> And thereto well refound:
> Seemly in person
> And like to Homer, as one
> In worldly prudence.
> And ever the Church in one
> Upheld and favoured;
> And casting the proud to ground
> And all that would
> His royal state confound.

The victorious epitaph was not so inappropriate after all.

Bibliography

Anglo-Norman Letters and Petitions, ed. M.D. Legge, Anglo-Norman Text Society (Oxford, 1941)
(Annales) Annales Ricardi II et Henrici IV in Chronica Monasterii S.
Albani, Johannis de Trokelowe, ed. H.T. Riley, Rolls series (London, 1865)
The Anonimalle Chronicle, 1333-1381, ed. V.H. Galbraith (Manchester, 1927). See also Oman
Armitage-Smith, S., *John of Gaunt* (London, 1904)
Aston, M.E., *Thomas Arundel* (Oxford, 1967)
Archaeologia VI, XVI, XX, XXIX, Society of Antiquaries

Baldwin, J.F., *The King's Council in England during the Middle Ages* (Oxford, 1913)
Barron, Caroline M., 'The Tyranny of Richard II', B*IHR* XL (1968)
Bean, J.M.W., 'Henry IV and the Percies', *History* XLIV (1959)
Bellamy, J.G., 'The Northern Rebellions in the Later Years of Richard II', *BJRL* XLVII (1965)
Beltz, G.F., *Memorials of the Most Noble Order of the Garter* (London, 1841)
The Brut or the Chronicle of England, ed. F.W.D. Brie. Early English Text Society, orig. series, 136
(BIHR) Bulletin of the Institute of Historical Research
(BJRL) Bulletin of the John Rylands Library

(Cal. Close Rolls) Calendar of Close Rolls (London, 1900-)
Calendar of Letter Books of the City of London, ed. R.R. Sharpe (London, 1901-7)
(Cal. Pat. Rolls) Calendar of Patent Rolls (London, 1901-)
Calendar of State Papers in Venice (London, 1864-)
Capgrave, John, *The Chronicle of England*, ed. F.C. Hingeston, Rolls series (1858)
　　　　”　　　　”　　*Liber de Illustribus Henricus*, ed. F.C. Hingeston, Rolls series (1858)
Chaucer, Geoffrey, *The Poetical Works*, ed. F.N. Robinson (Cambridge, Massachusetts, 1933)
Chandos Herald, *The Black Prince*, ed. H.O. Coxe, Roxburghe Club, 1842
Chrimes, S.B., *An Introduction to the Administrative History of Medieval England* (Oxford, 1959)
Chronicon Angliae, ed. Edward Maunde Thompson, Rolls series (1874)
Chronique de St. Denys - See Monk of St. Denys
Clarke, M.V., *Fourteenth Century Studies*, ed. L.S. Sutherland and M. McKisack (Oxford, 1937)

Cokayne, G.E., *The Complete Peerage*, ed. V. Gibbs, etc. (London, 1910-59)

Collis, Maurice, *The Hurling Time* (London, 1958)

Cooper, W.M., 'The Meeting Places of Parliament in the Ancient Palace of Westminster', *Journal of British Archaeological Association*, 3rd series III (1938)

Créton, Jean, *Histoire du Roy d'Angleterre Richard*, ed. and trans. John Webb, *Archaeolgia*, Society of Antiquaries (1824)

Curtis, E., *Richard II in Ireland* (Oxford, 1927)

Davies, J.D.G., *King Henry IV* (London, 1935)

(Davies Chron.) *An English Chronicle of the reigns of Richard II, Henry IV . . .* , ed. J.S. Davies, Camden orig. series 64 (1856)

De Regimine Principum by Egidio Colonna, trans. Henri de Gauchi, ed. T. Wright, Roxburghe Club (1860)

Devon, F. (editor), *Issues of the Exchequer from King Henry III to King Henry VI* (London, 1837)

The Dieulacres Chronicle, ed. M.V. Clarke and V.H. Galbraith, 'The Deposition of Richard II', *BJRL* XIV (1930)

(DNB) Dictionary of National Biography

The Diplomatic Correspondence of Richard II, ed. E. Perroy. Camden 3rd Series XLVIII (1933)

Douet d'Arcq, L., *Choix de Pièces Inédites Relatives au Règne de Charles VI*, Societe de l'histoire de France (1863-4)

du Boulay, F.R.H. and Barron, Caroline (editors), *The Reign of Richard II: Essays in Honour of May McKisack* (London, 1971)

Duls, Louisa, *Richard II in the Early Chronicles* (The Hague, 1975)

Earle, Peter, *The Black Prince* (London, 1972)

(EHR) English Historical Review

Emerson, Barbara, *The Black Prince* (London, 1976)

Edwards, J.G., 'The Parliamentary Committee of 1398' *EHR* XL (1925)

Eulogium Historiarum sive Temporis, ed. F.S. Haydon, vol. III, Rolls series (1863)

Evans, Joan, *English Art 1307-1461* (Oxford, 1949)

Favent, Thomas, *Historia sive Narracio de Modo et Forma Mirabilis Parliamenti*, ed. May McKisack, Camden 3rd series 37 (1926)

The First English Life of Henry the Fifth written in 1513, ed. C.L. Kingsford (Oxford, 1911)

The Forme of Cury, ed. Samuel Pegge and printed by J. Nichols, Society of Antiquaries (1780)

Foster, J., *Some Feudal Coats of Arms* (London, 1902)

Fortescue, Sir John, *The Governance of England*, ed. Charles Plummer (Oxford, 1885)

Froissart, Jean, *Chroniques*, ed. K. de Lettenhove, 25 vols. (Brussels, 1867-77). Also trans. John Bourchier Lord Berners, ed. W.P. Ker, 6 vols. (London, 1901-3), Globe edition, 1 vol. (London, 1895); and by Thomas Johnes, 2 vols. (London, 1839)

Forde-Johnston, James, *Great Medieval Castles of Britain* (London, 1979)

Furnivall, F.J., *Early English Poems and Treatises on Manners and Meals in Olden Time* (London, 1868)

Galway, Margaret, 'Froissart in England', *University of Birmingham Historical Journal*, vol. VII, pp. 18-35 (1959)

Galbraith, V.H., 'A New Life of Richard II', *History* (1947)

" " *The St. Albans Chronicle 1406-1420* (Oxford, 1937)

John of Gaunt's Register 1372-6, ed. S. Armitage-Smith, 2 vols. Camden 3rd series 20, 21 (1911); 1379-83, ed. E.C. Lodge and R. Somerville, 2 vols. Camden 3rd series 56, 57 (1937)

Goodman, Anthony, *The Loyal Conspiracy, the Lords Appellant under Richard II* (London, 1971)

The Great Chronicle of London, ed. A.H. Thomas and I.D. Thornley (London, 1938)

Gough, R., *The History and Antiquities of Pleshy* (London, 1803)

" " *Sepulchral Monuments of Great Britain*, 6 vols. (London, 1786)

Gower, John, 'The Tripartite Chronicle', *The Major Latin Works of John Gower*, trans. E.W. Stockton (Seattle, 1962)

Hall, Edward, *Hall's Chronicle, containing the History of England during the Reign of Henry IV, etc.*, ed. Sir Henry Ellis, 6 vols. (London, 1809)

(Hardyng Chron.) Chronicle of John Hardyng, ed. Henry Ellis (London, 1812)

Harvey, John, *The Plantagenets* (London, 1948)

" " *Gothic England 1300-1550* (London, 1948)

" " *The Black Prince and his age* (London, 1976)

Historia Anglicana by Thomas Walsingham, ed. H.T. Riley, 2 vols. *Chronica Monasterii S. Albani*, Rolls series (1863-4)

Holmes, G.A., *The Estates of the Higher Nobility in Fourteenth Century England* (Cambridge, 1957)

Hope, W. St. John, 'On the Funeral Effigies of the Kings and Queens of England, *Archaeologia* LX (London, 1897)

(Household Ordinances) *A Collection of Ordinances and Regulations for the Government of the Royal Household*, Society of Antiquaries (London, 1790)

Hutchinson, Harold F., *The Hollow Crown* (London, 1961)

'Inventory of the Goods and Chattels belonging to Thomas Duke of Gloucester . . . 1387' ed. Viscount Dillon, *Archaeological Journal*, p. 275, 2nd series, 54 (1897)

Jacob, E.F., *The Fifteenth Century, 1399-1485* (Oxford, 1961)

Johnson, Paul, *The Life and Times of Edward III* (London, 1973)

Jones, R.H., *The Royal Policy of Richard II* (Oxford, 1968)

Jusserand, J.J., *English Wayfaring Life in the Middle Ages*, trans. L. Toulmin Smith (London, 1950)

Kantorowicz, E.H., *The King's Two Bodies, Studies in Medieval Political Theology* (Princeton, N.J., 1957)

Kenilworth Chronicle, see Clarke, p. 98

Kingsford, C.L. *English Historical Literature in the Fifteenth Century 1399-1485* (Oxford, 1961)

Kingsford, C.L. (editor), *Chronicles of London* (Oxford, 1905)

(Kings' Works), Brown, R.A., Colvin, H.M. and Taylor, A.J., *The History of the King's Works*, vols. I and II (London, 1963)

Kirby, J.L., *Henry IV of England* (London, 1970)

The Kirkstall Chronicle 1355-1400, ed. M.V. Clarke and N. Denholm-Young, *BJRL* XV (1931)

(Knighton Chron.) *Chronicon Henrici Knighton*, ed. J.R. Lumby, 2 vols., Rolls series (1895)

Langland, William, *The Vision of Piers Plowman*, ed. W.W. Skeat (Oxford, 1886)

Lapsley, G., 'The Parliamentary Title of Henry IV', *EHR* XLIX (1934)

"   "   'Richard II's "Last Parliament"', *EHR* LIII (1938)

Lewis, N.B., 'Simon Burley and Baldwin of Raddington', *EHR* LII (1937)

"   "   'The "Continual Council" in the early years of Richard II', *EHR* XLI (1926)

Liber Benefactorum of St. Alban's Abbey, Cotton MS, Nero VII

Lingard, John, *History of England* III (London, 1823)

Lydon, J.P., 'Richard II's Expeditions to Ireland', *Journal of the Royal Society of Antiquaries of Ireland* XCIII (1963)

Mathew, Gervase, *The Court of Richard II* (London, 1968)

McFarlane, K.B., *Lancastrian Kings and Lollard Knights* (Oxford, 1972)

"   " *John Wycliffe and the Beginnings of English Nonconformity* (London, (1952)

McKisack, May, *The Fourteenth Century* (Oxford, 1959)

Moberly, G.H., *The Life of William Wykeham* (London, 1867)

(Monk of Evesham), *Historia Vitae et Regni Ricardi Secundi, Angliae Regis*, ed. Thomas Hearne (Oxford, 1729)

Monk of St. Denys, *Chronique du Religieux de Saint-Denys 1380-1422*, trans. M.L. Bellaquet, 2 vols., *Documents Inedits sur l'Histoire de France* (Paris, 1839-40)

(Monk of Westminster), *Polychronicon Ranulphi Higden*, vol. IX, ed. J.R. Lumby, Rolls series (1886)

Myres, J.N.L., 'The Campaign of Radcot Bridge in December 1387', *EHR* XLII (1927)

Monstrelet, Enguerrand de, *La Chronique*, ed. L. Douet d'Arcq, Societe de l'histoire de France (1857-62)

Mum and the Sothsegger ed. Mabel Day and Robert Steel, Early English Text Society, Orig. series, CXCIX (1936)

Nicolas, Sir N.H., *The Scrope and Grosvenor Controversy*, 2 vols. (London, 1832)

(Nicolas Chronicle), *A Chronicle of London*, ed. Sir N.H. Nicolas (London, 1827)

Nichols, J.G., 'Observations on the Heraldic Devices discovered on the Effigies of Richard II and his Queen', *Archaeologia* XXIX

Norris, H., *Costume and Fashion*, vol. II (London, 1927)

Oman, Charles, *The Great Revolt of 1381* containing a translation of part of the *Anonimalle Chronicle* (Oxford, 1906)

'The Ordenaunce and Fourme of Fightyng within Listes', *The Black Book of the Admiralty*, ed. Sir Travers Twiss, Rolls series (1871)

Palmer, J.J.N., 'The Anglo-French Peace Negotiations, 1390-96', *TRHS* 5th series XVI (1966)

"   "   *England, France and Christendom 1377-99* (London, 1971)

"   "   'Articles for a Final Peace between England and France, 16 June 1393', *BIHR* XXXIX (1966)

Palmer, J.J.N., 'English Foreign Policy 1388-99', *du Boulay and Barron*

Passingham, W.J., *A History of the Coronation* (London, 1937)

Planche, J.R., *A Cyclopaedia of Costume*, 2 vols. (London, 1876-9)

Polychronicon Ranulphi Higden contains *John of Malvern's Chronicle*, trans. Trevisa VIII, ed. J.R. Lumby, Rolls series (1882)

Proceedings and Ordinances of the Privy Council of England, ed. N.H. Nicolas (London, 1834)

Political Poems and Songs, ed. T. Wright, Rolls series, 2 vols. (1859-61)

Ramsay, Sir James H., *Genesis of Lancaster*, 2 vols. (Oxford, 1913)

Rosenthal, Joel T., *Nobles and the Noble Life 1295-1500* (London, 1976)

Riley, H.T., *Memorials of London* (London, 1868)

Rotuli Parliamentorum, vol. III (London, 1783)

(Royal Wills) *Collection of the Wills of the Kings and Queens of England*, ed. J. Nichols (London, 1780)

Rymer, *Foedera Conventiones Litterae*, ed. G. Holmes, 20 vols. (London, 1704-35)

Sandford, F., *A Genealogical History of the Kings and Queens of England and Monarchs of Great Britain*, ed. S. Stebbing (London, 1707)

Select Documents of English Constitutional History 1307-1485, ed. and trans. S.B. Chrimes and A.L. Brown (London, 1961)

Shakespeare, William, *King Richard II*

        ”   ”   *King Henry IV, Parts I and II*

Sisam, Kenneth (editor), *Fourteenth Century Verse and Prose* (Oxford, 1950)

(Smith, Expeditions), *Expeditions to Prussia and the Holy Land made by Henry, Earl of Derby . . . accounts kept by his treasurer*, ed. Lucy Toulmin Smith. Camden new series, LII (1894)

Somerville, Sir Robert, *History of the Duchy of Lancaster*, vol. I (Duchy of Lancaster, 1953)

Stamp, A.E., 'Richard II and the Death of the Duke of Gloucester', *EHR* XXXVIII (1923)

Stanley, Dean, *Historical Memorials of Canterbury* (London, 1854)

     ”   ”   *Memorials of Westminster Abbey* (London, 1868)

Steel, Anthony, *Richard II* (Cambridge, 1941)

Stow, John, *Annales or a general chronicle of England* (London, 1631)

     ”   ”   *The Survey of London* (Everyman edition)

Stretton, Grace, 'Some Aspects of Medieval Travel', *TRHS* 4th series VII (1924)

Stubbs, W., *The Constitutional History of England*, vol. II (Oxford, 1887)

Suggett, Helen, 'The Use of French in England in the Late Middle Ages', *TRHS* 4th series, XXVIII (1946)

Tait, J., 'Did Richard II Murder the Duke of Gloucester?', *Owen's College Historical Essays*, ed. T.F. Tout and J. Tait (Manchester, 1907)

Tout, T.F., *Chapters in the Administrative History of Medieval England*, 6 vols. (Manchester, 1923-35)

(Traison et Mort) *Chronique de la traison et mort de Richart Deux Roy Dengleterre*, ed. with English translation by Benjamin Williams, English Historical Society (1846)

(TRHS) Transactions of the Royal Historical Society

Tuck, Antony, *Richard II and the English Nobility* (London, 1973)

Tyler, J.E., *Henry V* (London, 1838)

Usk, Adam of, *Chronicon Adae de Usk*, ed. and trans. Edward Maunde Thompson (London, 1904)

'A Wardrobe Account of 16-17 Richard II, 1393-4', ed. W. Paley Baildon, *Archaeologia* (1911)

Weever, J., *Ancient Funerall Monuments* (London, 1631)

Wey, William, *Itineraries of William Wey*, Roxburghe Club (1857)

Whalley Abbey Chronicle - see Clarke, M.V.

Wright, H.G., 'The Protestation of Richard II in the Tower in September 1399', *BJRL* XXIII (1939)

Wright, H.G., 'Richard II and the Duke of Gloucester', *EHR* XLVII (1932)

Wylie, J.H., *History of England under Henry the Fourth*, 4 vols. (London, 1884-98)

Ypodigma Neustriae, ed. H.T. Riley, Rolls series (1876)

Notes & Sources

chapter 1

The Black Prince's wall hangings are described in his will, Brewer pp. 96-7. 'A great and grievous sickness', *Grafton, Chronicle*, p. 48. Alice Perrers bewitched the king, see *Chronicon Angliae*, p. xlviii, and for her portrayal of the Lady of the Sun, *Nicolas, Chronicle*, p. 70. Richard's appointment as regent on the ship Grace de Dieu is described in *Historia Anglicana* vol. I, p. 315. For whereabouts of Gaunt's children after Blanche's death, see Kirby, p. 14, *Gaunt's Register 1372-6*, nos. 299, 524, 525, 940, 965 etc. For Constance's reception in London, see *Anonimalle Chronicle*, ed. Galbraith, p. 69. For presents to his children, see *Gaunt's Register 1372-6*, nos. 1342-3. For cost of their apartments and Henry's establishment, see Kirby, p. 94, Beltz, p. 237. Edward III presented Constance with a crown according to *Gaunt's Register 1372-6* no. 1133. For Tutbury Castle preparations see *Gaunt's Register 1372-6*, no. 1236. Gaunt rode with his hand on Katharine Swynford's bridle, *Chronicon Angliae*, p. 196. For John Beaufort's birth, see Armitage-Smith, pp. 462-3. For Gaunt's illegitimate daughter Blanche, see Armitage-Smith, pp. 460-l. Katharine Swynford announces the birth of Constance's daughter and performs other tasks for the duchess, Tyler, p. 6 from Pell Rolls, *Gaunt's Register 1372-6* nos. 409-10. For the duke's kindness to Aimée of Melbourne and Elyot, 'the wise woman', see his *Register*, nos. 706, 983. For his damoiselles and their tasks, see ibid. nos. 473, 608, 728, 1123, 1127, 1133, 1145, 1174, 1661. For Richard's new barge and other changes in his household on becoming Prince of Wales, see Tout, vol. III, p. 312, vol. IV, pp. 189-92.

chapter 2

For first record of Henry in Richard's retinue, see Beltz, pp. 237. For King Edward III's concern for Richard see *Froissart, Johnes*, p. 509. King Edward's illness and recovery diet is described in Tout, vol. III, p. 308, *Anonimalle Chronicle*, ed. Galbraith, p. 95. The royal family's farewell to the Black Prince at Berkhamstead is described by *Froissart, Johnes*, p.709. For decorations on Edward's tower, La Rose, at Windsor Castle, see Mathew, p. 13, and for Richard's and Henry's creation as Knights of the Garter there, Beltz, p. 11. King Edward's death is described in *Historia Anglicana*, vol. I, pp. 326-7 and *Chronicon Angliae*, pp. 142-46. Instead of walking, Richard was carried to his coronation in Westminster Abbey, according to *Anonimalle Chronicle* ed. Galbraith, p. 109, *Historia Anglicana*, vol. I, p. 377 and *Chronicon Angliae*, p. 161. Afterwards, Sir Simon Burley carried him to Westminster Hall,,according to *Monk of Westminster*, p. 223. For the meaning of the ceremony to Richard, see Wright, 'The Protestation of Richard II', particularly p. 162. Burley's manual for princes and its significance is discussed in Clarke, p. 120 and Jones, pp. 154-5. In describing the significance of alterations in Richard II's coronation ceremony I have followed McKisack, p. 399. Curtana was 'naked and without a point', according to Adam of Usk, p. 187. The visit to the Abbey of St. Albans by King Richard, Henry and Robert de Vere is recorded in *Liber Benefactorum*, folio 129 d, Goodman, p. 153. For Gaunt's confrontation with Courtenay in St. Paul's see *Anonimalle Chronicle* ed. Galbraith, pp. 103-4 and *Chronicon Angliae*, pp. 118-20. 'None of his ancestors had ever been a traitor . . .' Armitage-Smith, p. 193 from *Rotuli Parliamentorum*, vol. III, p. 5. For Gaunt's room in the palace see Mathew, p. 32. Details of Henry's marriage to Mary de Bohun are in *Gaunt's Register 1379-83*, vol. I, pp. 179-80. The birth of their first son is recorded in Henry's own accounts printed in Wylie, vol. IV, pp. 166-7.

chapter 3

Richard was at Windsor when the Peasants' Revolt began, according to *Anonimalle Chronicle* ed. Galbraith, p. 138. For 'the wages of a carter, ploughman or shepherd . . .' see Ramsay, vol. II, p. 140. The riots at Brentwood are described in the *Anonimalle Chronicle* trans. Oman, pp. 187-8, and Richard's first messages to the rebels in ibid, p. 191. For their 'wache worde', see *Anonimalle Chronicle* ed. Galbraith, p. 139, and for public detestation of Gaunt, *Chronicon Angliae*, p. 196. 'Oohan pe Mullere ha ygrounde smal, smal, smal,', is printed in Sisam, p. 161. For Henry's presence in the Tower, see *Knighton Chronicle*, vol. II, p. 132. For Richard's feeling for the regality at this date, see *Anonimalle Chronicle*, Oman, p. 201, and for the peasants' message 'that they had risen to deliver him' ibid, p. 191. The destruction of Haselden's property is described in ibid, pp. 124, 190, and Constance's flight to Knaresburgh Castle in Armitage Smith, p. 249. John Ball's sermon is in *Chronicon Angliae*, p. 321. For date of Richard's abortive interview with the rebels at Blackheath, see Galbraith, *Anonimalle Chronicle*, ed. Galbraith, p. 194. 'They began to shout . . . as though all the devils of hell . . .', comes from *Froissart, Johnes*, vol. I, p. 1658. The peasants' bloodthirsty petition is described in *Anonimalle Chronicle*, Oman, p. 192. 'They took all the torches they could find . . ', ibid, p. 195. Further destruction at the Savoy is described in *Chronicon Angliae*, p. 289. For Richard's proclamations from the Tower and the rebels' response, see *Anonimalle Chronicle*, Oman, pp. 196-7. King Richard told them that 'they might go through all the realm of England . . .', ibid, p. 198. The City Corporation's account of Richard's betrayal is in Collis, p. 274, quoting *Calendar of Letter Books of the City of London*. 'A wicked woman raised a cry . . .', according to *Anonimalle Chronicle*, Oman, p. 197. The archbishop of Canterbury 'heard two masses or three', ibid, p. 198. For Henry's remarkable last minute rescue from death by John Ferrour see Tyler, p. 7. 'You do not wish to shoot your king . . .' Duls, p. 16, trans. from *Historia Anglicana*, vol. I, p. 465. Richard ordered 'two knights to conduct' the rebels home, *Anonimalle Chronicle*, Oman, p. 203.

chapter 4

Richard's charters to the rebels were proclaimed 'lately issued in haste', Steele, p. 89. 'You have been and are villeins', the king pronounced, Duls, p. 16, from *Historia Anglicana*, vo. II, p. 18. Henry and Elizabeth of Lancaster escorted Queen Anne of Bohemia into London, according to his accounts in Wylie, vol. IV, p. 166, *Gaunt's Register 1379-83*, vol. I, nos. 714-15. For Henry's attire at Richard's wedding, see Wylie, vol. IV, p. 166. For Henry's life style see Kirby, pp. 20, 21, McFarlane, *Lancastrian Kings and Lollard Knights*, pp. 19, 21 and *Gaunt's Register 1379-83*, no. 206. Henry washes the feet of fifteen poor men see Cokayne, vol. VI, p. 417, Beltz, p. 237. Hugh Waterton pleads the cause of Henry's tenants, see his accounts in Wylie, vol. IV, p. 167. For trial of 'the hermit', see McFarlane, p. 223. Henry was a regular member of his father's retinue, according to *Gaunt's Register 1379-83*, vol. I, pp. 6, 10. For truce negotiations with France in 1383-4, see Rymer, *Foedera*, vol. VII, pp. 412-3, *Chronique de St. Denys*, vol. I, p. 299, and for expedition to Scotland, Armitage-Smith, pp. 276-8, Tuck, p. 91. Henry claims his wife's revenues, Cokayne, vol. VI, p. 477. For Henry's and Mary de Bohun's life together see his accounts in Wylie, vol. IV, p. 324. Their households joined by Gaunt's mistress and illegitimate daughter, see Wylie, vol. III, p. 258, vol. IV, p. 159. Burley 'in some sense' Princess Joan's 'lover', Mathew, p. 18. For Richard's books see Harrison, p. 8, Devon, *Issues*, p. 213. For Burley's appearance etc. see Duls, p. 51, Rymer, *Foedera*, vol. VII, p. 310, Wallon, vol. I, pp. 485-6 and for his clothes, Clarke, p. 120. For parliament's attempt to reorganise Richard's household after the Peasants' Revolt, see Tuck, pp. 54-7. For Richard's improvements to his palaces and new abode on the island of La Neyt see *Kings Works*, vol. II, p. 998, Mathew, pp. 32-4, 'More knights of Venus than of Bellona', *Historia Anglicana*, vol. II, p. 156. For courtiers' fashions see *Political Poems*, vol. I, pp. 275-6 and for Richard's handkerchiefs Clarke, p. 117. For Gaunt's oath to the Black Prince, see Chandos Herald, p. 331. For friar's accusation of treason against Gaunt, see *Monk of Westminster*, pp. 33-59, Tout, vol. III, pp. 392-3, Armitage-Smith, p. 285, and for King Richard's attitude to the plot to kill Gaunt the following year see *Monk of Westminster*, pp. 55-59. For argument between Richard and Gaunt in Scotland see *Monk of Westminster*, p. 65 and *Historia Anglicana*, vol. II, pp. 131-2. Gaunt and Constance presented with crowns of gold, Knighton, vol. II, p. 207. Henry becomes Gaunt's deputy in the duke's absence, Armitage-Smith, p. 310.

chapter 5

Thomas of Woodstock was 'full of corage' and Edmund of Langley 'full of gentylnesse' according to *Hardyng Chronicle*, p. 329. A 'portrait' of the former is in *Liber Benefactorum*, folio 110. For his tapestries, books and character see Goodman, pp. 79-81 and for his financial problems, Tuck, p. 102. For the earl of Arundel's temperament and wealth see Goodman, pp. 82, 109, and for the earl of Warwick's possessions, ibid, p. 141. For treatment of Richard's favourites that offended the barons see Tuck, pp. 74, 76, 84. De Vere commanded 'with a glad countenance to sit in a higher place . . .' Rosenthal, p. 33 from *Rotuli Parliamentorum*, vol. III, p. 210. For retinues of Henry and Arundel brought to London see Goodman, p. 128 and for the abbot of Westminster's intention to defend the coast, see D.N.B. For aftermath of French threat see McKisack, p. 442. King Richard would not at parliament's request dismiss even the meanest of his scullions, *Knighton Chronicle*, vol. II, p. 215. For the royal dukes' sense of outrage at de Vere's repudiation of their niece, see *Historia Anglicana*, vol. II, p. 160, *Monk of Westminster*, p. 95. 'If the king . . . should alienate himself from his people . . .' Stubbs, vol. II, p. 497, *Knighton Chronicle*, vol. II, pp. 217-9. The Commons begged him 'most humbly . . .' *Select Documents*, pp. 136-7. 'Anything done in this parliament . . .' ibid, p. 137. For de Vere's residence in Cheshire, see Clarke, p. 118. For King Richard's barefoot procession from Charing Cross Mews to Westminster Abbey, see *Monk of Westminster*, p. 104, and for appellants' badges, Gower, p. 292. The prophecy 'Let the fox . . .' appears in *Annales*, p. 206, trans. Duls, p. 75. The escape of Richard's favourites is recounted in *Knighton Chronicle*, pp. 250-1. 'The citizens . . . would not be willing to fight . . .' from *Monk of Westminster*, pp. 108-9. For de Vere's pursuit and defeat by the appellants see Myers, particularly pp. 23, 24. 'carts packed with gold and silver . . .' Duls p. 46 from *Knighton Chronicle*, p. 253. The victorious ride of the five rebel lords through Oxford is described in Usk, pp. 6, 145.

chapter 6

'They spoke severely to the king . . .', *Monk of Westminster*, pp. 114-5. The indivisible trio are described as 'continuing their malicious, false and treacherous purposes . . .' in *Rotuli Parliamentorum*, vol. III, p. 376. For Richard's temporary deposition in the Tower and Henry's part in re-instating him, see ibid, p. 431, *Select Documents*, p. 145, and Clarke, pp. 91-5, which includes an excerpt from the *Whalley Abbey Chronicle*. The correspondence between Henry and his father is recorded in McFarlane's transcripts of the earl of Derby's accounts in Magdalen College, Oxford. Henry dined in the Tower with Richard as a token of the king's love, according to *Historia Anglicana*, vol. II, p. 172; *Knighton Chronicle*, p. 256 states that not only Henry but also Thomas Mowbray, earl of Nottingham, supped with the king and spent the night in his apartments. For arrests and expulsions of royal officials and courtiers and portents of divine displeasure that followed, see *Monk of Westminster*, pp. 115-7, Tout, vol. III, pp. 428-30, *Historia Anglicana*, vol. II, pp. 172-3, *Knighton Chronicle*, pp. 256-7. For matching shining robes given by Henry to his fellow appellants for the parliament see McFarlane transcripts and Beltz, p. 238. For the appeal of Treason against the five lords see *Rotuli Parliamentorum*, vol. III, pp. 229-45, *Select Documents*, pp. 146-9 and *Monk of Westminster*, pp. 122-35. 'In such high crimes' which 'touched the person of the king . . .', *Select Documents*, p. 148. "An honourable and profitable judgement . . .' Ramsay, vol. II, p. 253. Three hundred and fifty gages were tossed at the king's feet, according to the *Monk of Westminster*, p. 149. For Tresilian's capture and execution see *Knighton Chronicle*, vol. II, pp. 292-3, *Monk of Westminster*, p. 178. For attempts to save Sir Simon Burley from execution see *Monk of Westminster*, pp. 176-7; Henry's attempt is described in *Historia Anglicana*, vol. II, p. 174. Richard pleads for Burley's life in the Bath House, *Rotuli Parliamentorum*, vol. III, p. 376. For the oaths and the act of pardon intended to protect the appellants see ibid, pp. 229-45, *Select Documents*, p. 149, *Monk of Westminster*, pp. 153, 159, 160, 162-3, and for he lords' renewal of coronation oaths see Favent, p. 24.

chapter 7

The Scottish invasion of England is described by the *Monk of Westminster*, pp. 177-8 and the Commons demands in the Cambridge parliament by ibid, p. 190. For the storming of a manor house by Sir John Pelham see du Boulay and Barron, pp. 134-5. Richard 'ejected from his household about four hundred persons', see the comment of Steele, p. 180. Richard Medford was 'released from prison in June . . .', Tuck, p. 136. 'Hit was answerede he hade xxti yere in age . . .' *Polychronicon* vol. VIII, p. 489. 'Desirous of the good and prosperous rule of his kingdom . . .' *Select Documents*, pp. 151-2. 'To your peril be it if any evil arise from this', *Privy Council Proceedings* p. 12, Tuck, pp. 139-40. For the earl of Northumberland's petition that Gloucester and Arundel be restored to royal favour, see *Privy Council Proceedings*, p. 12. Gaunt's welcome by the king and the London dignitaries after his return to England is described in *Monk of Westminster*, p. 219. For stories of Gaunt's advice to Richard to put Henry to death, see *Traison et Mort*, pp. 203-4. For the 'great bed of red and white check camaca' left in Gaunt's will to Henry, see Armitage-Smith, p. 427. Henry's part in the Jousts of St. Ingelvert is admiringly described in the *Chronique de St. Denys*, vol. I, p. 681. Henry's preparations to go on crusade are detailed in *Smith, Expeditions* which contains his relevant accounts, an invaluable source of information on his activities at this period. Children begging outside their cottages for bread are mentioned in *Knighton Chronicle*, p. 314. For the meaning of 'reysen' see du Boulay and Barron, p. 156.

chapter 8

For Richard's jousts at Smithfield where his new white hart badge was first used see *Monk of Westminster*, p. 241, Beltz, p. 253, *Monk of Evesham*, p. 122, Clarke, p. 277 and *Froissart, K. de Lettenhove*, vol. XIV, pp. 260-4. For Richard's attempts to abolish private armies of retainers see Tuck, pp. 146-8. King Richard, Gloucester and the Arundel brothers all took part together in Gaunt's hunting party, according to *Knighton Chronicle*, vol. II, p. 313. Lords were reappointed to commissions of the peace, Tuck, pp. 147-8. For Richard's plan to have King Edward II canonised see Devon, *Issues*, pp. 247-8, 259, Du Boulay and Barron, p. 203, McKisack, p. 467. Men as well as women at Richard's court painted their cheeks and lips, Brewer, p. 114, Mathew, p. 25. Hoccleve's description of Gaunt's clothes is quoted in Mathew, p. 28. For poetry specially composed to read aloud to the court see frontispiece of *Troilus and Criseyde* in MS No. 61, Corpus Christi College, Cambridge and Brewer, pp. 150, 196. '. . . but if the slevis slide on the erthe . . .' *Mum and the Sothsegger*, pp. 16-17. Gloucester's shipwreck is described in *Monk of Westminster*, p. 262, and Henry's campaign in Prussia and Lithuania in *Smith, Expeditions* and du Boulay and Barron, pp. 153-72. For Lithuanian boys brought back to Prussia by Henry see ibid, pp. xxxi, 52, 90, 91, du Boulay and Barron, p. 170. Henry arrived back in England looking 'hale and hearty' according to *Monk of Westminster*, p. 247.

chapter 9

The story that Gaunt tried to have Henry recognised as heir to the throne appears in *Eulogium*, vol. III, pp. 361, 369, 370, and *Hardyng Chronicle Archaeologia*, vol. XVI, pp. 139- . It is disproved in Armitage-Smith, pp. 359-62. Henry's expenses from March to December 1391 are detailed in his accounts in Wylie, vol. IV, pp. 159-63, McFarlane, *Lancastrian Kings and Lollard Knights*, p. 23. For Henry's part in diplomatic negotiations in France see *Froissart, K. de Lettenhove*, vol. XIV, p. 377 and for background, Palmer, 'Anglo French Peace Negotiations'. For the French desire for peace and most Englishmen's dislike of it, see *Froissart, K. de Lettenhove*, vol. XV, p. 79. The entertainment of the English embassy in Amiens is colourfully described in the *Chronique de St. Denys*, vol. I, pp. 735-43. For Gaunt's subsidies to Henry for a second crusade see Kirby, p. 35, Smith, *Expeditions*, p. xlviii. His full and revealing accounts for the second journey to Prussia and from there to the Holy Land are in Smith, *Expeditions*. For Henry's meeting with the future pope and Lucia Visconti see Wylie, vol. IV, p. 128. For Henry's continence see Kirby, pp. 195-6 and especially Wylie, IV, p. 134 which seems to me utterly to disprove the theory that Henry died of venereal disease. The 'pokkes' from which according to his accounts he twice suffered in 1387 may have been measles or smallpox. At a time when great men made little attempt to keep secret their extra marital relations it is highly unlikely that any philandering on Henry's part could have gone unreported by all the chroniclers. For other theories on the nature of the disease that afflicted Henry as king see Wylie, vol. IV, p. 153-5, Davies, pp. 279-81. For Richard's vastly increased expenditure on the great wardrobe see du Boulay and Barron, p. 197, Tuck, p. 150, Tout, Vol. VI, p. 108. For Richard's quarrel with London see chapter IX in Du Boulay and Barron and for the incident that sparked it off, *The Brut*, p. 345. For the ceremony of reconciliation and London's final reception of the king and queen see also *Monk of Westminster*, p. 278, Green, p. 608. '. . . until the king shall otherwise ordain', du Boulay and Barron, p. 191, and 'a dromedary with a boy seated on its back . . .', ibid, p. 195 from *Monk of Westminster*, p. 278. For statues of king and queen erected on London Bridge see du Boulay and Barron, p. 196.

chapter 10

For the duke of Gloucester's attitude to peace see *Froissart, K. de Lettenhove*, vol. XIV, p. 314, and for the embassy to France in 1395 see *Annales*, p. 157. The king walked arm-in-arm with Gloucester, *Rotuli Parliamentorum*, vol. III, p. 313, Gower, p. 306. Richard presents the earl of Arundel with a diamond, Devon, *Issues*, p. 253. For the appellants' careers and possessions in the 1390s see Goodman, and for the Northern rebellions, see Bellamy, *Annales*, p. 159, Tout, vol. III, p. 483, Tuck, p. 166, Armitage-Smith, p. 351. 'The necessity of ruling in cooperation with the great nobles . . .' Galbraith, p. 230. For Richard's lenient treatment of the rebel leader, Talbot, see Tout, vol. III, p. 484. 'felonies, murders' etc. *Cal. Pat. Rolls*, 1396-9, p. 109. Henry examines rebel prisoners, Bellamy, p. 266. The quarrel between Gaunt and Arundel is described in *Annales* 162, 166 and Armitage-Smith, pp. 355-6, *Rotuli Parliamentorum*, vol. III, pp. 313-14. 'I dare to call God to witness . . .' Galbraith, p. 232. For new pardon demanded and received by Arundel see Bellamy, p. 269. Disputes between the appellants are described in Tout, vol. III, p. 484. Presents exchanged between the duke of Milan and Henry are listed in his accounts in Wylie, vol. IV, p. 165. The king of France sends his jester, Wylie, vol. IV, p. 165. 'On his head a chaplet like a coronet of four roses . . .' Mathew, p. 74 from Stow, p. 363. Henry gave Chaucer a scarlet gown, Kirby, p. 22. Henry's New Year jousting attire is described in his accounts in Wylie, vol. IV, p. 164. Katherine Swynford issued with robes of the garter, Beltz, p. 250. For Constance's death see Gaunt's accounts printed in Armitage-Smith, p. 449. For Anne of Bohemia's funeral see Green, p. 611, and for burning of Sheen, Usk, p. 8. For Mary de Bohun's death, see *Monk of Westminster*, p. 283, *Historia Anglicana*, vol. II, p. 214, *Annales*, p. 168, Devon, p. 231. For break up of Henry's home, see Green, pp. 308, 310, Wylie, vol. IV, p. 171.

chapter 11

The Black Prince reigned here 'seven years in joy . . .', and entertained 'every day at his table . . . more than eighty knights and four times as many esquires', Chandos Herald, p. 127. For the French and English kings' desire for a permanent peace so that they could pit their joint might against the Turk, see Palmer, *England, France and Christendom*, pp. 180 et seq. *Froissart, Johnes* vol. II, p. 538. Objections in parliament to the terms of the peace treaty are reported by the *Monk of Westminster*, p. 282. For Gloucester's bullying personality see *Froissart, Johnes*, vol. II, p. 576. My account of the unsuccessful English attempts to foist Gaunt as hereditary duke on Aquitaine is based on Palmer, *England, France and Christendom*. For the proclamation in Bordeaux Cathedral, for Richard's threat to put an end to 'debates and dissensions' and the Gascons' retort, see ibid, pp. 158, 160. Richard with his fleet leaves for

Ireland still 'clad with his train in weeds of mourning', Usk, p. 151, with ironbound chests of gold and silver, Devon, *Issues*, p. 258. For his retinue see Goodman, p. 62, Tuck, p. 173, Hutchinson, p. 148. How the Irish 'kings' were taught 'civilised' English manners is vividly described in *Froissart, Johnes*, vol. II, pp. 580-1. The appearance and alleged habits of the Lollards are described in *Polychronicon*, vol. VIII, p. 444 and Capgrave, *Chronicle of England*, pp. 244-5. Richard threatened the Lollards and their protectors with death 'unless they recovered their senses', *Annales*, p. 183. For description of Froissart's collection of love poems presented to Richard see *Johnes*, vol. II, p. 577. After the council meeting at Eltham Palace that destroyed Henry's hopes of becoming duke of Aquitaine, he and Gloucester 'issued out of the chamber . . . and came into the hall . . .' *Froissart, Berners*, Globe edition, p. 429. Gaunt married Katherine Swynford 'to the amazement of all', *Annales*, p. 188. For *Whalley Abbey Chronicle* see Clarke, p. 91. For account of ceremonies in which Richard received from King Charles his future queen, eight-year-old Isabel from her father, King Charles of France see *Annales*, p. 188 et seq. For presents made to little Queen Isabel see *Traison et Mort*, pp. 108-17.

chapter 12

For Richard's references to his friends 'living in parts across the sea', see McKisack, pp. 466-7, *Monk of Westminster*, pp. 238, 239, 264. For the macabre scene at Colne Priory see *Annales*, p. 185. For England's prosperity see *Polychronicon*, vol. VIII, p. 520, Jones, p. 68. Richard's protest at the Haxey bill and the obsequious speeches of the Commons, Lords and bishops are printed in *Rotuli Parliamentorum* III, pp. 338, 339, 341 and *Select Documents*, pp. 165-6. For banquet confrontation between the king and the duke of Gloucester see *Traison et Mort*, pp. 118-21, and for political background Palmer, *England, France and Christendom*, pp. 7, 116, 117, 172. For different versions of the Arundel Castle dinner conversation see *Traison et Mort*, pp. 121-7 and *The Brut*, pp. 588-9. I discount the former chronicle's story of a plot since charges to this effect were not made in the September 1397 trials of the lords, also no action was taken against those clerics also alleged to be a party to the conspiracy. My account of the arrests follows *Annales*, pp. 203-6 since this chronicle was written at the Abbey of St. Albans whose abbot was Gloucester's godfather. For proclamations that the arrests of the lords were 'for the peace of the people . . .' see *Cal. Close Rolls* 1396-9, p. 197; 'for great number of extortions, oppressions, grievances, etc. . . .' ibid, pp. 197, 208. The manner of Gloucester's death is discussed in Tait. For atmosphere of threat surrounding the surviving lords, see Usk, p. 191. Details of Henry's banquet and newly furbished state barge are in his accounts, Wylie, vol. IV, pp. 174, 183, 184. For proceedings of September 1397 parliament see *Rotuli Parliamentorum*, vol. III, p. 347, *Select Documents*, p. 167 et seq., Usk, p. 152 et seq., and for Henry's and Mowbray's exoneration, *Rotuli Parliamentorum*, vol. III, p. 156. Sir John Bushy addressed the king 'devising adulatory and unusual words incongruous to mortal men . . .' see *Annales*, p. 210. Released from terror of their lives, the lords shed tears, Usk, p. 156. Henry and Mowbray declared 'innocent of malice' and the king bears witness to their 'loyalty and good fame', *Rotuli Parliamentorum*, vol. III, pp. 353, 376. Arundel's trial is described in Usk, pp. 157-8. For Gloucester's confession, see Tait, p. 207. For Henry's new surcoat and seal see accounts in Wylie, vol. IV, pp. 173-4.

chapter 13

Richard's 'dignyte, Regalye and honourable estate', Kingsford, *Chronicles*, p. 52. 'With admirable and long-lasting patience . . .' *Kirkstall Chronicle*, p. 131, translated in Duls, p. 94. For fines and blank charters exacted in 1397-98 see Barron, 'The Tyranny of Richard II', particularly pp. 7-8. For attempt to censor mail going in and out of the country see *Cal. Close Rolls, 1396-9*, p. 288, Tuck, p. 199. Richard was haunted by dreams of the executed earl of Arundel and ordered his body disinterred and reburied in the middle of the night, according to *Annales*, p. 219. For Cheshire Archers, see Usk, pp. 169-70, *Political Poems*, vol. I, p. 381, *Annales*, p. 237, Tuck, p. 187, du Boulay and Barron, p. 269, 'Dycun, slep sicury quile we wake, and dreed nouzt quile we lyve sestow', *Kenilworth Chronicle* in Clarke, p. 98. 'Aftir this, the kyng in solenne dies and grete festis . . .' *Davies' Chronicle*, p. 12. 'For tho that had hertis on hie on her brestis . . .' *Mum and the Sothsegger*, p. 8. For prophecy that a toad would destroy Richard see *The Brut*, p. 590. Richard's claim that Gaunt had advised him to put Henry to death is in *Traison et Mort*, pp. 203-4. For suspicious recogniz- ance by Bagot see *Cal. Close Rolls 1396-9*, pp. 291-2. 'He shulde rather whan he herde the wordes fyrste . . .' *Froissart, Berners*, vol. VI, pp. 310-l. Henry's account of Mowbray's words on the road from Brentford to London is recorded in *Rotuli Parliamentorum*, vol. III, pp. 360, 382. The confrontation between Henry and Mowbray at Oswestry is described in *Traison et Mort*, p. 142 and the hearing of their case before the Court of Chivalry, in ibid, pp. 144-9. 'He that is convicte and discomfite . . . shalbe hedid or hanged . . .', 'The Orden- aunce and Fourme of Fightyng within Listes', p. 325.

chapter 14

Henry sends to Count of Virtues for jousting armour, according to *Froissart, Berners*, pp. 309-10. For doubt about divine intervention in the duel see *Monk of Westminster*, p. 247 and for Mowbray's joust with the earl of Mar, *The Brut*, p. 348. 'One day he said to the king in jest . . .', *Chronique de St. Denys*, vol. II, p. 673. For Henry's sojourn at Kenilworth see Wylie, vol. IV, p. 176, and for Richard's at Baginton Castle, Hutchinson, p. 195. The scene of the duel is described in *Traison et Mort*, pp. 149-58. For meaning of taking the quarrel into his own hand, a law of the duel, see 'The Ordenaunce and Fourme of Fightyng within Listes'. Henry's sentence was generally believed to be unjust, according to *Annales*, pp. 225- 6. 'We might as well have gone to the great parliament . . .', *Traison et Mort*, p. 158. The royal promise that Henry should receive his inheritance even while still in exile is recorded in *Cal. Pat. Rolls 1396-9*, p. 425. 'The kynge humyled hym greatly . . .', *Froissart, Berners*, vol. VI, pp. 318-9. 'My lord of Derby can go and play . . .', Froissart quoted in *Traison et Mort*, p. 157. Henry to be allowed a household of two hundred people, etc. see *Rotuli Parliament- orum*, vol. III, p. 383. For Henry's sensational departure from London see *Froissart, Berners*, vol. VI, p. 319.

chapter 15

For the exiled Henry's warm welcome in France see *Froissart, Berners*, vol. VI, pp. 321, 339, 340, and for the earl of Salisbury's snub, ibid. pp. 342-3, Creton, p. 148. Sir John Dymock's visit to England is described in *Froissart, Berners*, vol. VI, pp. 335-6. Gaunt's bequests to Richard are in the duke's will printed in Armitage-Smith, p. 426. He succumbed to 'a great weakness', *Eulogium*, p. 381 quoted in Armitage-Smith, p. 407. Richard was at Gaunt's funeral according to *Annales*, p. 232. How the parliamentary committee was used to ruin Henry is described by Edwards. For Henry's disinheritance, see *Rotuli Parliamentorum*, vol. III, p. 372. The dismemberment of his estates is described and discussed in Somerville, pp. 134-5 and Jones, p. 99. The coronation oath from *Liber Regalis*, is in Passingham, pp. 113-4. Archbishop Arundel's adventures in exile are described in Créton, p. 49 and his arrival in Paris as a humble priest, by *Froissart, Berners*, vol. VI, p. 355. 'It was considered shameful and degrading for free men to live under a tyrant', Barron, 'Tyranny of Richard II', p. 1. For pardons offered and withheld by Richard in 1397-9 see ibid pp. 7, 17 and *Cal. Close Rolls 1396-9*, p. 438. Young Thomas Arundel's escape is described in *Traison et Mort*, p. 161. *Prophetia Aquilae*, the prophecy of the eagle, is printed in Usk, p. 172. For Richard's censorship of letters see *Cal. Close Rolls 1396-9*, pp. 288, 488, 489 and Barron, 'Tyranny of Richard II', pp. 15-16. Richard's reply when asked why he was sighing is in *Annales*, p. 238 translated in Hutchinson, p. 208. The mayor of London swears 'not only to uphold the acts of the Westminster and Shrewsbury parliaments . . .', Barron, 'Tyranny of Richard II', p. 15. For summons to Milford Haven see *Cal. Close Rolls*, p. 489. For Richard's seizure of horses, bread, cows, ships, etc. before his campaign in Ireland see Créton, p. 21. The treaty of friendship between Henry and the duke of Orleans is printed in Douet d'Arcq, vol. I, pp 157-60 and is also summarised in *Chronique de St. Denys*, vol. II, p. 701. For the duke of Berry's advice to visit the royal abbey see ibid, p. 707. That this duke supported Henry's designs on the English crown is further suggested by the fact that, with Orleans, he attended Henry's coronation. For Henry's promise to the abbot relating to Derehurst Priory see *Chronique de St. Denys*, p. 707 and *Traison et Mort*, p. xxxiii.

chapter 16

Estimates of the number of men in Henry's invasion force vary. I have accepted Adam of Usk's 'scarce three hundred', p. 174, which is not far from the *Annales*, p. 242 estimate. For the duke of York's wholly erroneous information on the quantity and destination of Henry's force see *Cal. Pat. Rolls, 1396-9*, p. 596 and for his first attempt to muster an army, *Cal. Close Rolls, 1396-9*, p. 518. For Henry's crooked course at sea, 'appearing as though about to land, now in one part of the kingdom, now in another', see *Annales*, p. 242 and for John Pelham's capture of Pevensey Castle, *Cal. Pat. Rolls, 1396-9*, p. 596. For Latin poem 'On the Expected Arrival of the Duke of Lancaster' see *Political Poems*, vol. I, pp. 366-8. Henry 'sent a small boat ashore - with some people who planted his banner on the land . . .', *Traison et Mort*, p. 179. Henry is met by Robert Waterton, etc., Usk, p. 25, Somerville, p. 137. For Henry's itinerary after landing see *Kirkstall Chronicle*, p. 132. Men regarded the idea that they should fight against the duke of Lancaster 'almost as a joke', *Annales*, p. 244. There came to Henry at Pontefract 'a great multitude of gentlemen', *Kirkstall Chronicle*, p. 132 translated in Tuck, p. 215. For the earl of Westmorland's effigy see Foster, p. 147. Henry's letters of propaganda are printed in *Traison et Mort*, pp. 180-2. For his oath at Doncaster see *Hardyng Chronicle*, pp. 350, 352. The earl of Northumberland's early knowledge of Henry's perjury was revealed by Bean, pp. 219-20. The maxim 'Necessitas non habet legem', necessity has no law, was used by Henry, Kirby, p. 161; see also Créton, p. 143. For the duke of York's writ of 16 July regarding a force to be stationed on the coast of Kent to repel invaders see *Cal. Pat. Rolls 1396-9*, p. 592. Kenilworth Castle had been already recaptured by his own retainers for Henry, see Tuck, p. 214. 'A eron is up and toke his flyt . . .', *Political Poems*, vol. I, p. 365. No one in York's army was willing to shoot a single arrow against the duke of Lancaster, *Monk of Evesham*, p. 152. He 'pulled out a letter from his pouch of blue velvet . . .', *Traison et Mort*, p. 186. In their rush to escape Henry's wrath the citizens of Bristol scramble through doors and windows and down ropes according to the *Kirkstall Chronicle*, p. 36, Clarke, p. 101. Richard slips away from his own army in the grey habit of a Minorite friar, Créton, p. 77 and illuminations. Créton p. 167 indicates that these are meant to be faithful representations of actual events. Aumerle and Percy cause the army to disband and soldiers loot Richard's treasures, Créton, pp. 99-104. For Henry's itinerary from Bristol to Chester see Usk, pp. 174-5. His envoys to Richard included Thomas Arundel according to *Rotuli Parliamentorum*, vol. III, although he is not mentioned by Créton. For account of events in Conway Castle see Créton, pp. 135-40.

chapter 17

For importance of Dieulacres Chronicle see Clarke, pp. 53-89, Henry's arrival at Flint Castle and confrontation with Richard is described in Créton, pp. 155-71. Unlike his report of the negotiations and betrayal at Conway the French squire's account of the dramatic events at Flint is considered to be first hand, Créton having ridden here in the retinue of the earl of Salisbury while Richard was still in his seaside castle. Marching through Cheshire, Henry's troops were offered poisoned wine and ale, according to Usk, p. 176. For Richard's desertion by his uncanny greyhound, Math, see ibid, p. 196, *Froissart, Johnes*, vol. II, p. 693 and *Berners*, vol. VI, p. 369. 'My children, fear not, neither be dismayed . . .', Créton, p. 373. For Henry's reply to the London aldermen who wanted Richard instantly executed see Créton, p. 177, Usk, p. 179. How the vengeful London mob sought Richard in Westminster Palace is described in Kingsford, p. 19 and *Great Chronicle of London*, p. 51. Richard was taken from Westminster to the Tower by water according to *Annales*, p. 251; in view of the Londoners' hostility this is a more likely route than the one through the City described in *Traison et Mort*. A description of a last interview between the cousins is in ibid, pp. 216-8. For Richard's conviction that he could not abdicate see Wright, pp. 157, 162. For attempts to prove the truth of the Crouchback legend see *Annales*, p. 252, Usk, pp. 182-3. England was suffering from a 'great number of manslaughters, robberies, larcenies, mayhems . . .' according to *Cal. Close Rolls 1396-9*, p. 512. 'My God! A wonderful land is this and a fickle . . .', Usk, p. 182. The official account of King Richard's abdication and deposition is in *Rotuli Parliamentorum*, vol. III, pp. 415-24, *Select Documents*, pp. 184-91. Closely following this account but in English are *The Great Chronicle of London*, pp. 51-7 and the Julius B II MS. printed in Kingsford, *Chronicles*, pp. 19-47. 'Desiryng much and abyding longe . . .', ibid, p. 21. The translation of Richard's abdication is from ibid, p. 21. For protest of the bishop of Carlisle see *Traison et Mort*, pp. 221-2. 'Merkyng hym mekely . . .', Kingsford, *Chronicles*, p. 43. 'I Henry of Lancastre chalenge this rewme of Yngland . . .', *Rotuli Parliamentorum*, vol. III, pp. 422-3, *Select Documents*, p. 191. For Archbishop Arundel's sermon on the text 'Vir dominabitur in populo' see Kingsford, *Chronicles*, p. 45.

chapter 18

For the little princes' robes in the coronation procession see *Traison et Mort*, pp. 225, 231, and for Henry's, *Froissart, Berners*, vol. VI, p. 380. The sword of Lancaster's first appearance at a coronation is described in Usk, p. 187. 'Robed finely in red and scarlet and ermine', ibid, p. 187. For the king's champion's challenge see Kingsford, *Chronicles*, pp. 49-50; and for Henry's declaration that 'if needs be' he would take his champion's place, Usk, p. 188.

For the legend of the miraculous oil see *Archaeologia*, vol. XX, pp. 266-7, Wright, p. 161, *Annales*, pp. 297-300, *Eulogium*, vol. III, p. 380, *Historia Anglicana*, vol. II, pp. 239-40, Capgrave, *Chronicle of England*, pp. 273-4, Duls, pp. 118-19. Omens following Richard's deposition are reported in Usk, pp. 191, 197. Stories of Henry's reluctance to murder Richard, although repeatedly urged to do so, appear in *Froissart, Johnes*, vol. II, pp. 707-8, *Froissart, Berners*, vol. VI, p. 397, *Traison et Mort*, pp. 230, 235, *Chronique de St. Denys*, vol. II, pp. 738, 740, Duls, pp. 177-8. For sentence of perpetual imprisonment on Richard, see *Select Documents*, p. 198. On leaving the Tower Richard was to be disguised as a forester according to the *Traison et Mort*, pp. 227-8, but he was 'carried away on the Thames' according to Usk, p. 191. His prison is described in *Traison et Mort*, p. 249 and *Archaeologia*, vol. VI, p. 311. For his hope that his 'cosyn wolde be goode lord to hym' see *Select Documents*, p. 193. Twelfth Night tournament preparations were described by Edward Hall, quoted in *Traison et Mort*, p. 231. Henry gathers an army of Londoners overnight, *Traison et Mort*, p. 234. Young Thomas Holland's speech at Sonning is in *Annales*, p. 324, and there is a description of his and the earl of Salisbury's arrest at Cirencester in *Anglo-Norman Letters*, p. 116. For the executions of the rebels, see *Traison et Mort*, pp. 240-7, *Historia Anglicana* vol. II, pp. 244-5, Usk, pp. 197-8. For John Ferrour's pardon see Tyler, p. 7. Henry's symbolic threat to gather up the 'weeds' and clear his 'garden' is in *Traison et Mort*, p. 93. For rumours and reports of Richard's death see *Froissart, Johnes*, pp. 701, 702, 709, *Traison et Mort*, p. 248, *Chronique de St. Denys*, vol. II, pp. 738-40, *The Brut*, pp. 590-1, *Hardyng Chronicle*, p. 357, Duls, pp. 169-78. For the council minute of 8 February, 1399, which appears to recommend his murder see Usk, pp. 201-2, Ramsay, vol. II, p. 369 and for the other sinister exchequer payments that follow, Wylie, vol. I, pp. 114-5. Richard's instructions regarding his own funeral are in *Royal Wills*. For Richard's funeral see *Traison et Mort*, p. 261, *Annales*, p. 331. King Henry's fear that after his death his second son, Thomas, might try to usurp the throne from the Prince of Wales is recorded in *The First Life of Henry V*, p. 14. The famous death bed scenes are in Capgrave, *Chronicle of England*, pp. 302-3 and Monstrelet, vol. II, p. 238. The same flags that adorned Henry's funeral procession were also used for Richard's final journey from King's Langley to Westminster Abbey, see Hope, p. 534. The translation of Richard's epitaph comes from Sandford.

INDEX

Angle, Sir Guichard d', 4, 19

Angoulême, Edward of, 2, 222

Anne of Bohemia (1366-94), 25-26, 32, 41-42, 48, 71, 73; begs for Burley's life, 79; 81, 95, 109, 113-114, 124; death, 125-126, 131; 134, 222, 225

Appleton, William, 39

Aquitaine, duchy of, 1-2, 6, 8, 15, 106-107, 115-117, 120-122, 127-131, 134. 141

Arnold of Bearn, Sir Peter, 129

Artas, Janico d', 199

Arundel, Richard, Earl of (1346-97), 47, 49, 55-61, 64-66; Admiral of England, 82-87, 96, 106, 116, 119-121, 125, 128, 131, 144, 148-149; beheaded, 150, 152, 154; 158, 168, 206, 215, 222

Arundel, Thomas, Earl of (1381-1415), 176, 201, 217

Arundel, Thomas (1353-1414), Bishop of Ely, 62, 75, 86; Archbishop of York, 96; Archbishop of Canterbury, 140, 144, 148, 175-176, 183, 187-188, 192, 194, 196, 203-204, 206-208

Arundel Castle, fateful dinner at, 143, 158

Audley, Sir James, 16

Aumerle, see Rutland, Earl of,

Austria, Albert of Hapsburg, Duke of, 109

Bagot, Sir William, 153, 158, 165, 183, 186, 189-191, 215

Ball, John, 30-31, 34

Bampton, Thomas, 29

Barentyn, Dru, 179

Beauchamp, Sir John, 56, 62, 74, 78, 80

Beauchamp, Thomas, see Warwick, Earl of

Beauchamp, Sir William, 116

Beaufort, Henry, Cardinal (d. 1447), 10, 124

Beaufort, John, Earl of Somerset, 10, 90-91, 124, 139, 145; Marquess of Dorset, 151, 160, 178, 186, 191; reverts to Earl of Somerset, 215

Beaufort, Joan, 10, 45

Beaumont, Henry, Lord, 74

Beaumont, Sir John, 131

Becket, Thomas, 211-212

Beckwith, William, 117-118

Belknap, Robert, 29

Berners, Sir James, 74, 78, 80, 148

Berry, Duke of, 58, 107, 127, 171, 180-181, 197

Blount, Sir Thomas, 74, 84, 218, 220

Bohun, Eleanor de, wife of Thomas of Woodstock, 24, 219

Bohun, Humphrey de, Earl of Hereford (d. 1373), 24, 44-45

Bohun, Mary de, 1st wife of Henry of Bolingbroke, 24, 92, 104, 108, 124; death, 126; 188

Bolingbroke, Henry of (1366-1413) background comparisons with Richard, 1; childhood, 4-16; Earl of Derby, 13; at Richard's coronation, 19, 22; married life, 24-25, 44-45, 107-108, 124, 165; and Peasants' Revolt, 27-40; at court and as Gaunt's heir, 41-44, 46-48, 51-53, 54-58, 62, 66-67, 116-118, 139; defeats de Vere at Radcot Bridge, 68-68; political acumen, 72-74, 78-81, 83, 88; 2 years in Europe, 89-94, 99-104; appearance and character, 104-105, 110; embassy to France, 105-107; further travels, 108-110, 114-115; situations pertaining to attempt on the crown, 118-119, 134, 136, 156-161, 174-175; and father's quarrel with Arundel, 120-122; friendship with Duke of Milan, 123; widowed, 125-126; as inheritor of Aquitaine, 127-129, 133; out of national affairs, 130-131; and Lollards, 132, 135, 143; submits to King's will, 146-147, 149-151; Duke of Hereford, 151; trial by combat, 161-168; banishment, 168-170; in France, 171; plans to invade, 176-179, 181; invasion and usurpation, 182-216; plot to murder Henry, 216-221; and Richard's death, 221-225; death, 225

Bourbon, Duke of, 107

Brembre, Sir Nicholas, 63, 65-66, 74-75, 77

Bridlington, John of, 104, 177, 183

Brittany, Duke of: Brest restored to, 141, 167

Brocas, Bernard, 218, 220

Burgundy, Philip, Duke of, 58, 95, 106, 127, 173

Burley, Sir Simon, 4, 17, 19, 22, 29, 32, life style, 46-49; arraignment, 74; death, 78-80, 82, 148, 150

Burnel, Lord, 74

Burton, Thomas de, 11

Bushy, Sir John, 129, 138-139, 147-149, 153, 162, 167-168, 183, 186, 191

Camoys, Lord, 74

Castile, Constance of, 2nd wife of John of Gaunt, 5-7, 9-11, 23, 42, 52-53, 87; death, 125

Castile, Henry of Trastamare, King of, 5, 7-8, 32

Castile, Henry III, King of, m. Catherine of Lancaster prior to his accession, 72, 82

Castile, Juan I, King of, 52

Castile, Pedro 'the Cruel', King of, 5

Chandos, Sir John, 16

Charlton of Powis, Lord, 116

Chaucer, Geoffrey, 5, 11, 23, 48, 73, 99, 123

Chaucer, Philippa, 11

Cheshire Archers, the 96, 138, 145, 151, 155

Cheshire revolt, the 117-120, 131

Clanvowe, Sir John, 50, 74, 84

Clarence, Lionel of Antwerp, Duke of (d. 1386), son of Edward III, 15, 25, 72, 116, 134, 207

Clarence, Thomas, Duke of, brother of Henry IV, 11, 224

Cobham, Lord, 77, 79

Coucy, Philippa de, Countess of Oxford, 61

Courtenay, Sir Peter, 191

Courtenay, William, Bishop of London (1342-96), 20-22; Archbishop of Canterbury, 50-51, 70, 78, 81

Coventry duel, the, 161-168

Créton, Jean, 192, 194, 196-200

Crouchback, Edmund, son of Henry III, 202

Dagworth, Nicholas, 74, 84

Dalyngbridge, Sir Edward, 112

Desmond, Earl of, 179

Despenser, Thomas, Lord, 139; Earl of Gloucester (1397), 215; reverts to Lord Despenser, 215, 218-129

Devereux, Sir John, 51, 74, 84

Devereux, Sir Nicholas, 74

Dublin, Archbishop of, 64

Durant, Sir John, 79

Dymock, Sir John 172

Dymock, Sir Thomas, 211

Edward I (1239-1307), 32

Edward II (1284-1327), 15, 71, 97; attempted canonisation of, 97, 104; 202, 212, 222

Edward III (1312-77), 1-9, 12-16; death, 17, 22; 27-28, 53-54, 56, 59, 61, 73, 83, 97, 110-111, 130, 172

Edward, Prince of Wales, 'the Black Prince' (1330-76), 1-6; death, 4; 8, 12, 15, 49, 79, 110, 127

Edward V, 71

Elmham, William, 74

Elyot, 'the Wise Woman', 11

Exton, Nicholas, 66

Exton, Sir Peter, 221

Farringdon, Thomas, 37

Ferrers, Robert Lord, 186

Feriby, William, 195, 218, 220

Ferrour, John, 39, 220

Fishmongers' Gild, 77

Fordham, John, Bishop of Durham, 60, 74

France, Charles V, King of, 2

France, Charles VI, King of, attempt to invade England, 57-58, 76, 95, 106-107, 123, 127, 135, 171-172, 174-175

Gascons, their obstinacy, 129-130, 133

Gerberg, Alyne, 12

Gilbert, John, Bishop of Hereford, 86, 205

Gloucester, Duke of *see* Woodstock, Thomas of

Gloucester, Earl of *see* Despenser

Golafre, Sir John, 74, 84

Gower, John, 123

Grace de Dieu, flagship, 4, 8

Green, Sir Henry, 153, 183, 186, 191, 216

Hales, Sir Robert, 29-30, 32, 36-37, 39

Haseldon, Thomas, 33

Haxey, Thomas, his bill, 139-141, 143

Hende, John, 112

Henry II, 15, 106, 131

Henry III, 202

Henry V, 45, 199, 210, 216-217, 222-223, 225

Henry VII, 96, 177, 225

Hereford, Bishop of, in 1399, John Trevenant, 205

Heretics Statute (1401), 20

Herle, Hugh, 23, 91

Holland, John, half-brother of Richard II, Earl of Huntingdon, 37-38, 50, 53, 90, 106, 117-118, 139, 145, 150; Duke of Exeter, 151, 160, 173, 176, 192, 211, 215; reverts to Earl of Huntingdon, 218-219

Holland, Sir Thomas, 1st husband of Joan of Kent, 4

Holland, Thomas, Earl of Kent (d. early 1397), half-brother of Richard II, 37-38, 198

Holland, Sir Thomas (1374-1400), son of the above, nephew of Richard II, 131, 139, 144-145, 150; Duke of Surrey, 151, 157, 160-161, 166, 173, 179, 192, 211, 215; reverts to Earl of Kent, 215,217-219

Hungary, Sigismund, King of, 109

Isabel of France (1390-1408), 2nd wife of Richard II, 134-136, 141, 171, 219

Isabella of France (1292-1358), queen of Edward II, 14, 15

Jacquerie, the (1358), 34

Jagiello, King of Poland and Lithuania, 100-101

Joan of Kent, Princess of Wales (d. 1385), 3-4, 19, 22, 79, 94

Joan of Navarre, 2nd wife of Henry IV, 225

Jousts of St. Inglevert, 90, 94, 165

Kingeston, Richard, Archdeacon of Hereford, 91, 108

Lancaster, Blanche of, 1st wife of John of Gaunt, 5, 10, 172-173

Lancaster, Catherine of, m. Henry III of Castile, 10, 23-24, 53, 72, 82, 169, 181

Lancaster, Elizabeth of, m. John Holland, 5-6, 11, 23-24, 41, 53, 219

Lancaster, John of Gaunt, Duke of (1340-99), 2, 5, 55-56; 2nd marriage, 6-10; relations with Katherine Swynford, 10-11, 14-15; at variance with King, 19-23, 49-52; 24, 26; and Peasants' Revolt, 30-32, 35-37, 43-46; contends Castilian throne, 52-54, 57-58, 72-73; in King's favour, 86-89, 96, 139; receives duchy of Lancaster in perpetuity, 89; 96, 104; embassy to France, 107-109; 113, 115-116, 117, 120, 127; hostility to Arundel, 120-122; 128; and claim to Aquitaine, 36-39, 133-134; preaches absolutism to King, 137, 149, 156-160, 165; death, 172-173, 178, 200, 207

Lancaster, Philippa of, m. King John of Portugal, 5-8, 11, 23, 53, 72, 82, 169

Lancaster, Thomas of, 157, 160

Lancekrona, Agnes, 61, 63

Langley, Edmund, Earl of Cambridge (1341-1402), 15, 24, 32, 52, 54, 56; Duke of York, 56, 61, 79, 106; Regent, 131, 148, 161; 2nd regency, 178, 182, 201-202, 217-218

Latimer, Lord, 9

Lescrope, Sir William (1399), 131, 145, 153; as Earl of Wiltshire, 157, 183, 191, 195, 203

Leventhorpe, John, 185

Littlington, Nicholas, 18

Lollards revolt, the, 132

Lovel, Lord, 74

Lovell, Sir John, 84

Lyon, Richard, 9

MacMurrough, Art, King of Leinster, 131, 179, 186

Maidstone, Richard, 113

Mar, Earl of, 165

March, Earls of, see Mortimer

Mare, Peter de la, 9, 21-22

Martyn, Geoffrey, 75

Maudelyn, Richard, 218, 220

Mawfield, Gilbert, 123

Medford, Richard, Bishop of Chichester, 84

Melbourne, Aimée of, 12

Merks, Thomas, Bishop of Carlisle, 207, 217

Milan, Gian Galeazzo Visconti, Duke of, 110, 123, 164

Mohun, Lady, 74

Molyneux, Lady, 74

Montague, John see Salisbury, Earl of

Montendre, William, 23

Morieux, Sir Thomas, husband of Gaunt's bastard daughter, Blanche, 53

Mortimer, Roger, 1st Earl of March (1287-1330), 14

Mortimer, Roger, 4th Earl of March (d. 1398), 131, 134, 179

Mowbray, Thomas, Earl of Nottingham (1405), 47, 49, 67-68, 72, 86, 90, 116, 122-123, 126, 131, 139, 143-144, 146, 149; Duke of Norfolk, 151; warns Henry of plot against them, 157-161; trial by combat, 161-163; banishment, 168-170.

Navarre, King of: regains Cherbourg (1394), 141

Neville, Alexander, Archbishop of York, 65-66, 75-76, 78, 80, 96, 137, 148

Neville, Ralph, Earl of Westmoreland, 187-188, 191, 203, 217

Norbury, John, 203

Northampton, John of, 137

Norwich, Bishop of, 186

Orleans, Charles, Duke of, m. Richard II's
  widow, 33, 71, 107, 180
Ormond, Earl of, 179
Ostrevant, Count of, 94-95

Parliaments: the Good (1377), 8-9; the
  Salisbury (1384), 49, 62; the Wonderful
  (1386), 59-60, 64, 66, 74, 78; the Cambridge (1388), 83, 95; the Merciless
  (1388), 74-81, 86, 119, 124, 138, 145,
  147-148, 159, 174, 179, 215; the
  Shrewsbury (1398), 159, 168, 173, 176,
  179
Peasants' Revolt, the (1381), 26, 27-40, 41,
  46-47, 56, 63, 74, 77-78, 213
Pelham, Sir John, 83, 183
Percy, Henry, 1st Earl of Northumberland
  (1408), 19, 21, 65, 86, 106, 178, 187-188,
  191, 203-204, 217, 223
Percy, Henry, 'Hotspur' (1364-1403) com-
  mands fleet against French, 58; taken
  prisoner by Scots, 90, 187, 196, 223
Percy, Sir Thomas, 106, 144, 192
Perrers, Alice (d. 1400), 3, 9, 17
Philippa of Hainault, queen of Edward III,
  10, 15
Plantagenet, Edward see Rutland, Earl of
Pleasance, le, 154
Pleasington, Robert, 75
Pole, Michael de la, 47-48, Earl of Suffolk,
  56-61, 64-66, 75-76, 80, 137
Portugal, King John of, 52, 72, 82, 87
Poynings, Lady, 74

Rabe, Marshal, 102
Raddington, Sir Baldwin, 78
Richard II (1367-1400) childhood, 1-5, 8-
  13, 14-17; coronation, 17-20; 22-24;
  marriage, 26, 41; and Peasants' Revolt,
27-40, 42-43; autocracy, 45, 49-50, 127,
  147-150, 152-154, lack of judgement,
  56-65; 'cunning and resolution' 66-69;
  prisoner in the Tower, 70-73; and
  Merciless Parliament, 74-81, 89;
  'tolerant rule', 84-89, 92-93; and Smithfield tournament, 94-95; his court, 97-
  100, 102-103, 105-106, 108, 110-111;
  quarrel with City of London, 111-115;
  and the Cheshire rebellion, 117-118;
  outcome, 118-122, 123; death of queen,
  124-125; fatal French policy, 127-130,
  133-134; remarries, 134-136; and de
  Vere's death, 137-138; public quarrel
  with Gloucester, 141-144, 146; rewards
  supporters with respendent titles, 151;
  neurotic symptoms, 154-157; and
  Mowbray/Henry fracas, 158-162; and
  Coventry duel, 162-163, 165-169, 171;
  and Henry's inheritance, 173-179; fatal
  expedition to Ireland, 182-190; return
  and dethronement, 191-215; murder
  plot ensures Richard's doom, 216-220;
  death and burial, 221-222
Roet, Sir Payne, 10
Rushook, Thomas, Bishop of Chichester,
  74, 78
Rutland, Edward, Earl of, son of Edmund,
  Duke of York, 131, 139, 143, 145; Duke
  of Aumerle, 151, 160-161, 166, 174, 178,
  190, 196, 201-202, 215; reverts to Earl of
  Rutland, 215, 218

St. Pol, Count of, 94, 106-107
St. Pol, Countess of, 107
Salesbury, John, 74, 78, 80
Salisbury, Bishop of, and affray in Fleet
  Street, 112
Salisbury, John Montague, Earl of (d. 1400),
  139, 145, 157, 160, 171, 190, 195, 197-
  198, 216, 218-219
Saxe Teschen, Duke of, 26

Selby, Sir John, 200
Shelley, Sir Thomas, 218
Sigismund, King of Hungary, 109
Skirlaw, Walter, Bishop of Durham, 106
Slake, John, 200
Smithfield Tournament, the, 94-95
Stafford, Edward, Bishop of Exeter, 146
Stanley, Sir John, 118
Statute of Labourers (1351), 28-29
Stury, Sir John, 132-133
Sudbury, Simon, Archbishop of Canterbury, 20, 29, 30-32, 38-39, 56
Suffolk, Earl of see Pole, Michael de la
Surrey, Duke of, see Holland, Thomas
Swinderby, William, 43
Swynford, Katherine, 10-11, 23, 45, 139
Swynford, Sir Thomas, 10, 23, 45, 90-91, 214, 221

Talbot, Sir Thomas, 118-119, 131
Teutonic Knights, the, 91, 101, 108
Thirning, Sir William, 215
Tille, John, 224
Tresilian, Robert, 41, 63, 65, 75-77
Trivet, Sir Thomas, 51, 74
Turkey, Bayezid, Sultan of, 128
Tyler, Wat, 31, 35, 39

Ufford, Thomas, Earl of Suffolk, 57
Uske, Thomas of, 78, 99

Venour, William, 113
Vere, Aubrey de, 20, 37, 51, 74
Vere, Robert de, Earl of Oxford (1362-92), 13, 16, 20, 23, 32, 34, 37, 47-51; Duke of Ireland, 60; marriage scandal, 61-66; defeat at Radcot Bridge, 68-69; 75-76,

80; death, 138-139, 174
Visconti, Bernabo, Duke of Milan, 25
Visconti, Gian Galeazzo see Milan, Duke of
Visconti, Katherine, 25
Visconti, Lucia, 110

Walden, Roger, Archbishop of Canterbury, 189, 217, 220
Walworth, William, 35, 39
Waterton, Hugh, 42, 45, 101, 172
Warwick, Thomas Beauchamp, Earl of (d. 1401), 56-57, 65-66, 87, 116, 122, 143-144, 149, 151-152, 206, 215, 217

Wenzel, King of Bohemia, Holy Roman Emperor, 25, 109
Westminster, Abbot of, 220
Westmoreland, Earl of see Neville, Ralph
Wiltshire, Earl of see Lescrope, William
Woodstock, Thomas of, Duke of Gloucester (1355-97), 24, 44, 51; character, 15, 54-56, 71, 141-142; Duke of Gloucester, 57, 96, 100, 106, 115-118, 122, 127-129, 131, 133, 141-144, 148, 150, 152, 157-158, 161-162, 201, 206, 215-216, 219
Wyclif, John, 20, 43; death, 132
Wykeham, William of, 28, 148, 178

Yevele, Henry, 225
York, Archbishop of, in 1399: Richard Scrope, 205, 208, 224
York, Edmund, Duke of see Langley
York, Richard, Duke of, 71
Ypres, Sir John, 21

Zouche, Lord de la, 74